BWB39909931

THE ETERNAL LIGHT

TWENTY-SIX RADIO PLAYS FROM
THE ETERNAL LIGHT PROGRAM

THE ETERNAL LIGHT

BY

MORTON WISHENGRAD

With a Foreword by Louis Finkelstein,
President, The Jewish Theological Seminary of America

CROWN PUBLISHERS   NEW YORK

COPYRIGHT, 1947, BY MORTON WISHENGRAD

All plays copyright, 1944, 1945, 1946, by The Jewish Theological Seminary of America, except *A Second Exodus*, copyright, 1944, by the National Broadcasting Company; and *The Battle of the Warsaw Ghetto*, copyright, 1943, by Morton Wishengrad.

The plays in this volume are fully protected by copyright. No performance of them, public or private, whether for gain or for charity, may be made without the written permission of the author's agent, Milton E. Krents, 386 Fourth Avenue, New York 16, New York, to whom application for use should be made. This book may not be reproduced either in whole or in part for any purpose whatsoever, except for review, without the permission of the author's agent.

PRINTED IN THE UNITED STATES OF AMERICA

FOR ROSE

FOREWORD

By Louis Finkelstein,
President, The Jewish Theological Seminary of America

The interpretation of Judaism to the present age is an especially arduous task. The Prophetic concept of man, as ideally a "Suffering Servant" who must accept misfortune as part of the Divine process and yet must make continual battle against human misery as part of his duty to God, is complex and profound. It is not easily translated into the simplicity of words and apparently is at variance with the culture of an age which makes human happiness in the narrow sense the standard of value.

The problem of the interpretation of Judaism, as of other religions, is complicated by the general confusion of our culture. Judaism, like Christianity and Islam, seems curiously foreign to a world which has failed to organize its data into any integrated system of thought and which must therefore approach any order of value judgments with doubt and suspicion.

In its Biblical and Rabbinic phases, Judaism utilized symbolic action to express its ideas. In the modern world, one of the major difficulties which Judaism encounters is the fact that efforts to interpret it are limited to exposition and exhortation. Modern art, music, drama or pageantry rarely portray the ideas of Judaism so that "he who runneth may read," while he who pauses will fully comprehend. The painter, the sculptor, the musician and the man of letters who desire to interpret the ancient traditions through their special skills, suffer from lack of adequate basic material and from lack of understanding of the place of their arts in the exposition of Judaism to the modern world.

As in other complexities of life, a clear appreciation of the problem is a major step toward its solution. But the understanding of the problem of the relation of art to scholarship in the modern world itself requires scholars who have a share in esthetic creation, and artists who have a taste for scholarship. Given co-operation among such men who have overcome the modern tendency toward increasing specialization, we may be able to lay the basis for the more complete interplay of thought between the creative artist and the technical scholar. There may emerge from co-operation and mutual understanding between the discoverer of truths and the creator of works of beauty a new phenomenon in civilization, the team of scholar-artist.

The Eternal Light Radio Program, to which Morton Wishengrad has rendered so notable a contribution through the scripts collected in this book, constitutes an effort to interpret Judaism from this point of view in at least one form of art. The author's literary grace and charm and his scholarly ability have been combined in preparation of the scripts with the rare mastery of Biblical and Rabbinic lore available to the author through his association with the Jewish Theological Seminary of America. In a way, The Eternal Light Radio Program suggests how an artist and a group of scholars can co-operate to translate ancient, abstract ideas into effective modern dramatics.

The selflessness and true piety necessary for any co-operative human enterprise must be summoned in an especially high degree in such an undertaking as *The Eternal Light*. The author of this volume and Dr. Moshe Davis, who collaborated with him more frequently and more continuously than any other member of the Seminary Faculty, have risen to high levels of devotion in their determination that the educational enterprise which united them should succeed.

These scripts must be considered from this point of view, an initial effort to solve through collaboration a difficult problem, which transcends any individual's gifts. Aside, therefore, from their great intrinsic merit and their educational value, the scripts may point the way to a new phase in the interpretation of the Jewish tradition. Perhaps the author of the future "Guide for the Perplexed" will not be an individual, but a society, a society in which each person will co-operate with the others as do the members of an orchestra. The effort reflected in this work and similar undertakings in other fields of thought and art may be the first signs of a new trend in our age, a trend toward synthesis rather than analysis. The time may have come when the age of specialization in scholarship, art and thought is giving way to a new age of integration.

The Eternal Light Radio Program, valuable as it is, appears to be particularly important when thus considered as part of a wider tendency toward co-operation among men of diverse skills, toward the common goal of understanding such difficult and complex ideas as religion. For Judaism, the synthesis between the skills of the artist and the scholar, may open new paths to creativeness and understanding. There may yet emerge a new type of Jewish Academy, in which scholars, artists, interpreters and thinkers will collaborate, as self-effacingly as did the ancient teachers of Jerusalem whose names have in many instances been forgotten, but whose combined labors created those great monuments of Jewish tradition as inspiring today as they were in their own time.

Each Sunday millions of listeners are informed that *"The Eternal Light* is presented by the National Broadcasting Company and its affiliated independent stations in co-operation with the Jewish Theological Seminary of America." We wish to acknowledge here a deep and continuing debt to NBC. From the inception of the program the company has made available its time and facilities with unstinting generosity. Above all, the Seminary is grateful to Mr. David Sarnoff and to Mr. Niles Trammel for their continuous assistance.

It has been a rewarding experience to be associated with such men as Dr. James Rowland Angell, public service counsellor of the National Broadcasting Company, and Dr. Max Jordan, who, before his return to Europe as NBC foreign correspondent in Switzerland, was director of religious programs for the company.

Milton E. Krents, without whose guidance *The Eternal Light* could not have come into being, has served as producer of *The Eternal Light* for the Seminary since the program's inception. When he discussed the program with the NBC authorities, it was Dr. Jordan who gave it his immediate approval and who eagerly undertook the arduous task of carrying it through. There were broadcasting experts who regarded a dramatic series as an unwelcome innovation in religious programming; nevertheless, the National Broadcasting Company, always a pioneer in the field of public service, embarked on the new project with enthusiasm. That enthusiasm has been maintained by Mr. Dwight Herrick, manager of the NBC public service department, and his assistant, Mrs. Doris Corwith.

Grateful acknowledgment should also be made to *The Eternal Light* radio committee of the Jewish Theological Seminary under the chairmanship of Judge Edgar J. Nathan, Jr., and to Miss Edith Blackmer, supervisor of *The Eternal Light* for the Jewish Theological Seminary.

CONTENTS

Foreword by Louis Finkelstein	vii
Radio as a Medium of Drama	xiii
The Tender Grass	1
Moses Mendelssohn	15
The Battle of the Warsaw Ghetto	31
The Parable of Reb Yisroel	47
Thomas Kennedy	63
A Pity for the Living	79
A Sound of Music	93
A Rhode Island Refuge	109
Schechter	123
The Black Death	139
The Microscope and the Prayer Shawl	153
How They Knocked the Devil Out of Uncle Ezra	169
Hunger	187
A Chassidic Tale	199
A Second Exodus	213
The Death of Akiba	229
The Day of the Shadow	245
The Broken Sabbath of Rabbi Asher	259
Brandeis	275
My Father's Talis	291
The Ransom of Rabbi Meir	305
My Cousin Avigdor	321
Rabbi Israel Salanter	335
My Favorite Assassin	351
For a Suit of New Clothes	367
The Lantern in the Inferno (*Facsimile Script*)	381
Glossary of Radio Terms	411

RADIO AS A MEDIUM OF DRAMA

*"All music is what awakens from you
when you are reminded by the instruments."*
                                    WALT WHITMAN

I.

Until Lee De Forest invented the audion tube, the drama was confined to a stage and a silver screen and bound to a chair in a theatre. The audion tube changed that. It broke down the walls of the theatre and made drama as free as the air and just as ubiquitous. It also debased the drama, at least so the critics say. The critics say a good deal more. They say it out loud and quite often and sometimes through a microphone. One of their more fashionable phrases is, "The degeneracy of radio."

Now this is quite unfair. For what the critics mean to attack is not radio but drama, and not even drama but the cultural climate it portrays. For radio does not create a culture; it expresses it. Radio drama is a medium of culture. It is a tool.

An automobile does not manufacture bank-robbers; it transports them. It also transports clergymen. It is neither blameworthy because it does the first nor is it an instrument of piety because it does the latter. It is merely an automobile, a tool.

If there are manifestations of culture in the American scene that are adolescent or provincial or banal, the camera will photograph them, the printing presses will publish them, and radio will transmit them. And if the schoolmasters say therefore that radio is degenerate, they will be guilty of an irrelevancy. If they allege that radio is an instrument of a debased culture, then it will be relevant to inquire who originated that culture, nourished it, fostered it, and debased it.

The critics are on firmer ground when they point to radio drama's three main divisions and suggest that things could be improved.

With a few saving exceptions the creatures of the daytime serial inhabit an intellectual slum, a world of the "organ bridge" and the dramatic pause, where trouble is attenuated and the paragon is generally "John." The technique of the soap opera has been stamped out by the newspaper comic strip and prefabricated by the true-confession pulp magazine.

Radio's night time drama is better but it is equally derivative. It is more sophisticated than the daytime serial to the same degree that the slick-paper magazine is more sophisticated than the pulp product. But with a few outstanding exceptions it springs almost entirely from the crime thriller, or some diluted Hollywood opus, or the Sunday supplements, resembling each of its examples but less satisfying than each, and somehow meaner.

The last of these rather broad divisions is radio's good intention and its unhappy nuisance: the sustaining, non-commercial, network-sponsored drama.

Sustainers are of two kinds, the network showcase for a drama program which it hopes a sponsor will buy, and a second and more nondescript species which is cursed by adjectives like "educational," "religious," "historical," "public-service" and other audience-deterrents. To the network this latter species of sustaining program represents a double loss of revenue. First, it is presented on time that could be profitably sold. Second, it usually entails a network outlay for talent. To the public the sustainer is a test of stamina, doggedness, and the spirit of adventure. For it is hidden away or actually buried in time-slots accessible only to insomniacs, people who never eat lunch or dinner, reluctant students under compulsion of their teachers, and other marginal listeners.

Now all this would seem to confirm the charge that radio has debased the drama. If a house is to be judged mainly by the roaches in the cellar, this is true. But tools, like nations and races and institutions, are entitled to be judged in terms of their best capabilities and not their worst. And at its best, and there have been sustaining programs to prove this each year, radio is a medium of drama that is versatile, economical, and good.

But how can it be good, ask the critics? It is an inhibiting medium. It reduces an actor to a voice, it consists solely of sound, it limits the theatre to one dimension. The answer is that radio's greatest limitation is radio's greatest asset. It is because radio drama has a single dimension that it is more versatile than the stage; it is because radio drama is reduced to sound that it is more poetic than the screen.

This is not paradox. One hundred and thirty years ago, Goethe wrote: *"In der Beschrankung zeigt sich erst der Meister*—It is working within limits that the craftsman reveals himself."

Within the limits of sound—and radio is either the sound of a word or the sound of music or the sound of a special effect, as a door shutting—a good craftsman of drama can create all the dramatic illusions of comedy or tragedy. Because his audience is denied sight, the radio writer is spared the necessity of involving the producer in the high cost of stage sets, special lighting effects, and costuming. Sound-effect is a carpenter, music is an electrician, the inflection of an actor's voice is the costumer.

Only a writer who has written a play in recent years knows how great an advantage this is. The playwright is no longer greeted with, "Is it good?" The first question is, "How many sets does it require, how large a cast?" The stage producer cannot afford to consider a script that calls for more than two sets and eight characters. Costs are too prohibitive. A multiplicity of sets and a large cast would make it impossible for a play to return its "nut" or initial producer's investment in less than a year or more of continuous performance before packed houses. And so playwrights now warp and distort their themes in order to squeeze their action into a single set. The radio medium is a good deal more flexible than the theatre. It is also more poetic. Radio is all illusion, all poetry and fantasy. A sound-effects technician in a Radio City studio crumples a scrap of cellophane while a voice says, "fire," and in Akron, Ohio, a housewife will think she smells smoke in the kitchen. Out of the sound of a voice and the prejudices of his own imagination, a listener will create the attributes and measurements of a full-dimensioned human being. Whatever leads to this process of imaginative construction is poetry.

The most uninspired pedestrian, the most helplessly earthbound listener does something like this every day when he switches on his radio. Accuse him of imagination and he will retreat in embarrassment. But he is still one of the radio audience that translates the symbols of every music bridge into significant and rewarding meaning, every sound effect, every dramatic pause in which silence holds the center of the stage. This listener has never heard of ellipsis but he will never stop supplying for himself the images he will conceive from the words which a radio writer has deliberately omitted. This listener is found every day in an Iowa farmhouse or a Delaware barbershop or an Oregon garage. He is creating dimension out of sound and character out of dimension—making poetry and not knowing it.

If there is one thing that radio can do better than the stage or the screen, it is fantasy. Consider Charlie McCarthy and Mortimer Snerd. To the theatre audience they are a ventriloquist's trick. To the radio audience they are old and cherished members of a Sunday evening circle. The fantasy is the greater because it has stopped being fantasy and become real. Edgar Bergen will sometimes "fluff" a line; not Charlie. Charlie makes no mistakes. See fantasy in the theatre and you know that the actors are only playing. But hear fantasy on the air and it is more earnest than life, and surely, anything more earnest than life is pure fantasy.

These are not arguments that radio drama is better than theatre drama. That would be tantamount to arguing the superiority of watercolors over oils. Each is superior and each is inferior. It depends on the subject and what you are trying to do with it. It depends on the craftsman's respect for his medium and his ability to make it accomplish his ends.

Of course the critics are right and radio can be improved. But radio drama's greatest lack is not good microphones but good writing. The shoddy writing that now disfigures most of daytime programming is not an organic attribute of the medium, it is a functional disorder of the industry.

For the past fifteen years a portion of the industry has argued that no one compels the listener to tune in. This is like a manufacturer advertising that the best thing about his radio is that you can turn it off.

Several of the networks and many of the agencies argue further that the public is getting what it wants. Which public told them? When has the public been given an opportunity to express a preference? And because there are no true yardsticks of public opinion, programming is congealed and frozen into old, tried, and tired themes. There are few real improvements only limitations, because the tradition is always to be against the next step.

If the industry had greater imagination it would offer large inducements, as Hollywood does, to writers established in other fields to come to radio drama and invigorate it. Every serious writer now in radio would welcome such competition. For every serious writer in radio, and that means the writer who respects the medium and has something to give it, is the victim of a literary inferiority-complex.

There is room for good writing everywhere across the radio board, and most particularly in the daytime serial. Abused as the soap opera may be, this is, or it could be, an ideal format for characterization. Forget for a moment the stereotypes which run a formularized gamut between *Life Can Be Beautiful* to the *Road to Life* to *Portia Faces Life*. The quarter-hour daytime serial need not forever be what it substantially is now—a world where the sentimental formula substitutes for the idea, where slogans replace characterization, where manly men and womenly women rear poster-children who carefully over-enunciate platitudes in an environment of endless tribulation and unmitigated woe. At least if there would be some wit to the woe—or even tragedy!

Think what Dickens would have been able to do with the format? Or Balzac or Trollope or Mark Twain? Here is the format and the technique to make Mr. Pickwick and the two Wellers come alive again and inhabit the airwaves for several years, which should be long enough for any daytime serial. Here are quarter-hour segments in the lives of people which could transfigure a part of each day with dramatic truth and an intimation of humanity instead of presenting as they now do a lolly-pop on the instalment plan.

Here is the opportunity long sought by the dramatist anxious for leisurely characterization or the novelist who wishes to remain with his characters and see them grow. Men like Dickens and Trollope and Galsworthy would not have spurned a medium offering a daily audience numbered in the tens of millions.

In other words, there is nothing wrong with the technique of the quarter-hour show. All it needs is new content.

The half-hour program has developed remarkably imaginative uses for sound and music. It has experimented, and nearly always on sustaining programs first, with montage effects through sound or music; it has been able to achieve motion through shifting voice perspective; it has rediscovered the dramatic possibilities of the story-teller's use of narration and given it many forms and variations. If radio has not yet produced its literary classic it has certainly produced literary craftsmen whose contribution to drama is now visible in the increasing use of narration in the legitimate theatre and the motion picture.

If these things are true, why don't writers established in other fields turn to radio?

A writer, because he is a writer, must deal necessarily in his own ego. He can tolerate the enforced loneliness of creation, he can withstand critical onslaughts, he can abide and overcome the misunderstanding of his editors, but he cannot stand anonymity. It is not a matter of publicity. It is a matter of recognition.

Novelist and poet write for financial reward but also in the faith that perhaps in a paragraph or a line of verse they are erecting a verbal monument to themselves, that they are creating something good which will give pleasure for many years. They have the satisfaction of the printed page and the bound volume, the substance of a line of type spelling out an author's name. This is an emolument of writing which compensates for sacrifice and is as important as the financial return.

Against this the radio writer opposes the twist of a dial, a puff of air, a momentary place in space and then—total evaporation. The book once laid down can be picked up; the play seen once can be seen again. But the radio program completed is lost forever. This galloping mortality of the radio script breeds dissatisfaction and soreness and festers into a writer's grudge against the medium.

A fine writer whose recent success on the Broadway stage followed years of anonymity in radio announced himself through with the medium and added with asperity, "Writing for radio is like writing in a dark closet."

The industry has done very little to mitigate this condition. On the contrary, it has almost gone out of its way to emphasize the impermanence of a radio script by discouraging the idea of a repetition of a broadcast. This is a prejudice of long-standing, which, as much as any other factor, drives good writers from the medium. For it sets up a criterion of novelty. It establishes the mischievous principle that good writing is less preferable than new writing. It reduces the radio writer to a hack who must inevitably exhaust the material congenial to himself and who must exhaust himself in meeting an imperious daily or weekly deadline.

Deadlines can be wonderful things. Without them very little would ever be written; for the writer who claims that he enjoys writing is probably a liar or a psychotic. And so deadlines insure composition. But radio overdoes a good thing. There are three hundred and sixty-five days in the year, twenty-four hours to the day, sixty minutes to the hour. And radio fills a majority of those hours every day and every week in every month of the year. Each of those hours and quarter-hours are deadlines for some writer.

Those are exhausting deadlines. For a half-hour script can require as little as six to eight hours for composition and as much as ten days. If the author is painstaking, if he will taste and weigh and balance a phrase before he lets it stand; if he is given to rewriting and to polishing, a weekly half-hour script can be arduous labor. What the recurrent, inexorable deadline accomplishes is to place an unwholesome stress on facility and "dependability." The dependable writer is not the writer whose words are judged in terms of quality, but in terms of whether they were brought in on time. One result is that glibness becomes a virtue. Besides, what people will forget so easily need hardly be composed with too much pain.

The wonder is not that there is so much mediocre writing on the air but that there is so much fine writing. There are radio writers who create each month the equivalent of one full-length play. On the Broadway stage a successful play will run for a year or more. On the air that play or its radio equivalent dies after its first performance and its epitaph is, "When will the next script be ready?"

To continue the parallel, the playwright may build a play around the idiosyncrasies of a star actor, but apart from the benevolent meddling of the producer and the criticism of the director, he is on his own. The radio writer who labors in the commercial vineyards must satisfy not only an advertising agency editor but also an agency account representative, a sponsor, a sponsor's wife, and a network censor. He may be compelled to eliminate a phrase or even a scene which offends no one and which is admittedly well-handled because the sponsor has conceived a visceral dislike to it. A large corporation will submit its advertising matter to a magazine without asking that a phrase be deleted from a feature article; but it can and will set itself up as an arbiter of taste over radio programs which it sponsors.

These are handicaps that face the writer engaged in radio drama. There is another which is equally serious. There are many radio reviewers but few critics. Reviewing is sometimes characterized by log-rolling or venality, sometimes by ignorance or vulgarity. When the reviewer is well-disposed toward the medium, which is not often the case, or possesses an insight into the problems of the medium, which is even less often the case, he is swamped by a continuous tide of new and old programs clamoring for citation. He is nagged and badgered by press agents. He is penalized by inadequate space-allotments and intimidated by his readers who expect him to be an authoritative drama critic, music reviewer, forum analyst, and reporter on technical trade developments. There are conscientious reviewers who are breaking their hearts by trying to do all these things and do them with honesty. But there are many more reviewers who are badly trained for their task and who are demonstrably incompetent.

It comes finally to this: The radio medium cannot rise above the culture of which it is essentially an expression and an instrument; but it can, at least, try to express the occasional peaks of that culture and not merely its mediocrities. It will do this better if writers now employed by the medium are encouraged not to abandon it; it will do this better if writers established in outside fields are offered inducements to come to it and provide fresh content for increasingly stale forms. The refinements of method and the preoccupation with technique are more sterilizing than advantageous. The medium needs writers who have something to say about the culture.

Never in history has there been an agency of dramatic communication more intimate than radio or more democratic. But democracy is no license for mediocrity, and intimacy is no invitation to vulgarity. When radio offends, it offends twice, because the offence is committed in the home.

This intimacy of radio is the bane of every ministerial voice in a frock coat. You do not enter the home of a friend with a horatory strut. You do not make stump speeches to your brother.

Good radio drama is always modest.

At this moment there are book publishers fumbling for the key to reach the thirty or fifty thousand readers who constitute the pattern-makers of our culture. Radio can also reach them. For every potential reader-audience for the good book numbered in the thousands, radio opposes a potential listener-audience numbered in the millions. Those millions deserve to be well served.

II.

What of the medium itself and its mannerisms?

A movie is projected against a screen; a play is produced

within the boundaries of a stage and a theatre; radio drama is book-ended by time. The time is binding. What distinguish radio drama are its speed, tightness, compression, the quick-beginning, the climax and conclusion on the calculated split-second.

Restaurateurs will confide that many a mediocre dinner is saved by a good cup of coffee. No radio drama has ever been saved by a good last scene. For, if the beginning does not hold attention, no listeners are around for the climax. And so radio pitches hard for the opening scene or the opening block of narration. This must be arresting. This must capture the listener, hold him, and promise good things to come.

For this reason seasoned writers will labor long over an opening. They will, for example, devote hours to an opening narration which may consist of only a few lines. But, if the opening finally satisfies, two important things will have happened. First, the listener-attention that is so necessary will be obtained. Second, the opening will be a target and a horizon for the balance of the script. Every succeeding line must measure up to it. The line or the scene that doesn't will have to be rewritten. It is the best kind of challenge to the writer because it is self-imposed. It will bring self-imposed travail but it will end in a good script.

A device employed to obtain this quick start is known as a "teaser." This is radio parlance for the attention-getter we have discussed.

In the halcyon days of the silent films and the Pearl White serials each installment would end with the heroine in desperate straits. Before the final fade-out Pearl White would be strapped by the villains to the ties of a railroad track or else she would be left to dangle from a cliff, supported only by three fingers and a head of hair. The function of the cliff-hanging was to bring the audience back the following week half-dead with suspense. The radio teaser is the cliffhanger technique stood on its head. The note of excitement and suspense, sometimes stated without explanation, opens the drama. The opening of *The Death of Akiba* in this volume is such a device. It is a species of dramatic loss-leader, the "special" that is put in the window at marked-down prices to induce the shopper to come in and buy a few other things that are marked up.

The teaser is found in all writing. It is the introductory jest of the after-dinner speaker, the minister's prefatory parable, the light anecdote that begins the serious magazine article, the action-packed opening of the short-story and the novel.

Within the tight half-hour format it would seem that a writer would have to make a choice of either plot or characterization but not both. However, this need not be so. If the plot is carefully outlined before the first line is written and if the characters are equally planned in advance, there will be a meshing.

The radio writer should know how each scene will end, where it will lead, how long it will take to go there. The short story writer or the novelist can begin with an incident, feed it words, give it motion, and follow wherever it will lead. But the radio writer can neither follow his incidents nor his characters; he must lead them and control them or else his script will not be buttoned and tucked away at the end of thirty minutes. The radio writer must know clearly beforehand how his script will end or else he may not get much beyond his beginning.

To give a script momentum and direction it is sometimes a good idea to write the last scene or the last narration immediately after the opening is completed. *The Battle of the Warsaw Ghetto* was done this way as was, to cite another example, *A Second Exodus*. It will happen occasionally that opening narration becomes a summary rather than an introduction, and, therefore, it is discarded as an introduction but salvaged later as a peroration.

The radio plot is a straight line. Deviation from the line is distraction. The plot may accommodate a hundred scenes, if the writer is so inclined, but those scenes must be consecutive, they must be coherent, and they must follow a direct path beginning at a point marked 1 to a point marked 100. A digression must be clearly labelled a digression and the listener must be brought back to the story line without too much delay or else he will have forgotten it.

Sub-plot under these circumstances becomes rather hazardous. It will rarely be found in the non-comedy half-hour radio drama. And in the comedy program its justification is the element of confusion which it introduces for the sake of hilarity. In adapting a novel, a play, or a long short story for radio, the writer must invariably eliminate the sub-plot and simplify the main plot.

Part of the simplification consists of reducing the number of characters. Experience has shown that there may be any number of bit characters in a script but that more than four or five leading characters will create confusion. Confusion or ambiguity is always to be avoided.

For this reason an experienced director in casting a show will never engage for the same script two actors who sound even remotely like one another. For the same reason the radio writer tries very hard to limit dialogue at any one time in a given scene to two or three or four characters at the most. And if the number is four then the writer will be at great pains to set up voice difference through age or sex. As Erik Barnouw points out in his excellent *Handbook of Radio Writing* the family group is a favorite casting arrangement in the daytime serial and one reason, although not the most compelling, is that father's baritone, mother's alto, daughter's soprano, and Junior's fluctuating tenor can never be mistaken for one another.

When characters do not readily stand apart from one another, they must be identified. This accounts for the constant use of names, something which is quite foreign to the film or the stage play, where the audience can always see who is addressing whom. In the radio play the writer must learn to do this:

VOICE. Get my hat, Joe, will you?

He does not write:

VOICE. Get my hat, will you?

This is not a small thing. It is an important technique of radio writing. Radio characters must constantly identify one another to prevent any confusion in the listener's mind.

Why this emphasis on the prevention of confusion? Why does the radio script constantly repeat a point, or emphasize identity, or eliminate sub-plot, or strive so heroically to prevent characters from sounding like one another? The answer is that there is no pleasure in confusion to the blind man. And a radio listener is blind. He sees through sound. Therefore, the sound must be clear, ideas must be instantly comprehended. Motivation may be subtle, but it must be a subtlety without evasiveness. If there is complexity or ambiguity, the consequence for the listener is uncertainty, a sense of loss. Being uncertain the listener will pause and wrestle with himself for clarification. But in the act of pausing he will snap the thread of the story which continues and passes him by. If he is not discouraged, he will make a mental dash in pursuit, but if the exertion is too great, or if he has missed too much, illusion will be shattered. The listener's vexation with himself will be transferred to the play. And his irritation will prompt him to tune to another station or shut off his radio completely.

How different this is with the reader of a book. A book is

a costly investment. If it has been borrowed, it has been borrowed at the expense of time and trouble. Thus, the reader may be dismayed by a dull first page or an unpromising first chapter, but he will hang on a bit longer in the hope that he will get something for his money or his trouble.

Unlike the book and a seat in the theatre which represent an outlay of cash, the seat next to the radio has cost nothing. Things that are free are seldom prized and a twist of the dial costs no great exertion.

These are things which the radio writer learns each day. His best teacher is the radio rehearsal. From this he will discover what the playwright and the novelist have also discovered—that dialogue cannot be entirely true to the natural speech of natural people. It may approximate it and suggest it but not slavishly imitate it. For people in their homes, in trolley cars, on sidewalks, do not bounce dialogue back and forth like a rubber ball. They do not finish sentences. They do not even engage in dialogue but in alternating monologue; and monologue and radio drama are incompatible.

They are incompatible because, if speeches are not short, or apposite, or progressive in terms of plot, the radio play loses its conflict. Good radio dialogue should sound like a pair of boxers trading blows, short, swift, muscular, monosyllabic. Each block of dialogue and each scene must create its own tensions. The conflict need not be violent, it need not be physical; it may be latent, or implied; but there must be a continuous opposition of resolution and irresolution, thesis and antithesis.

Hence, speeches may not be long. A biblical Joseph on the stage may harangue his brothers for as long as he chooses. On the air, his brothers must interrupt him. They must make their presence known to the listener. If their presence is not made known, so far as the listener is concerned Joseph stands alone making a speech and his brothers are dead. This doesn't mean that no radio dialogue ever contains a long speech. But the speech will invariably come at the close of a scene and it will come only after it has been carefully foreshadowed and after the listener has been fully prepared to receive it. In *Moses Mendelssohn,* the second script in this volume, the long speech comes at the end of the play, and the little scene that precedes it has been introduced almost solely for the purpose of setting the stage for its delivery.

To put it another way, speeches may not be long because the ear does not remember. There is quick forgetfulness of everything except the last phrase or the last word spoken. This fact has influenced radio writing. The last word becomes the important word, the climax of each line. It is the last word that will be heard last and forgotten last. Therefore, a radio character could say:

VOICE. What are we going to do, Ben?

if he means to single out Ben from a group of other characters. But if he is alone with Ben, he will say instead:

VOICE. Ben, what are we going to do?

If the last word is the key word in the line, the last line is the key line in the scene. It is called a tag-line and it is important because it is a summary of what has transpired, or a statement of what will ensue, or a resolution of action, or the cue for a transition. A tag-line is a climax to a scene and its meaning and its tension are underscored by the music or the sound effect or the dead air which invariably follow. This music, or sound, or silence is the writer's way of giving the climax idea a chance to sink in and be absorbed.

Not so long ago a poet dismissed radio drama as a progression of tag-lines separated by dialogue. He said it to disparage the medium, but it would have made equal nonsense to disparage the sonnet by dismissing it as a pattern of rhyme confined in a rigid format. The sonnet, depending on its tag-rhymes as it does, can nevertheless achieve an effect of wholeness and completion; so can the radio play which is dependent on its tag-lines.

It will happen then that if a radio play contains ten scenes it will in effect become a dramatic whole composed of ten lesser but component dramas. That it is so divided does not constitute a depreciation of its art. Quite the contrary.

Narration was also once considered to be a confession of dramatic weakness. It was held that the dramatist's skill was demonstrated in his ability to *dramatize,* and narration was deemed to be exposition. This conception of narration was compounded of prejudice, tradition, and a complete misunderstanding of narration. Expository narration is exposition but expository narration is only *one* of the narrative forms.

Before examing narration it is interesting to see how the narrow traditional concept limited the radio play.

Dialogue is expansive whereas narration contracts. In the non-narrative drama, where dialogue was the carrier of characterization and plot, the canvas chosen had to be small, because a large canvas demanded explanation, and explanation through dialogue is undramatic, protracted, and murderous to characterization. The longer the period to be covered, the more emphatic the plot. Scenes had to become more numerous, and therefore scenes had to become shorter. But when scenes are short, and preocupied with plot, what becomes of characterization? It has to be sacrificed. Hence the fiction arose that the radio drama was an inferior creature because it allowed within the confines of its alloted time room for either plot or characterization, but never both. Of course, this isn't true. Not only must the radio drama be scrupulously plotted, but it must be equally attentive to characterization.

The fact is, to return to the subject of narration, that narration can be as dramatic as dialogue. *Hunger* is dramatic narration in the third person. *The Day of the Shadow* is dramatic narration in the first person. Narration can be effective in many forms. And narration allows the writer an opportunity to choose a big canvas, to write historical drama, the documentary, biography. Narration is one opportunity in radio for "good" writing; not pretentious writing, although this has been frequently true, but writing that is sensitive to the rhythms of speech and the texture of words. The narrative form is the only dramatic radio form which allows poetry without creating a wall of embarrassment between the listener and the actor. Poetic dialogue always seems contrived and mannered, but poetic narrative, as Archibald MacLeish and Stephen Vincent Benét proved, can be as natural to radio drama as color is to painting.

Behind their barricades in advertising agency offices there are still to be found program editors who assert the supremacy of pure dialogue. But they are a declining breed. It is not accidental that in a representative anthology* of "best" radio plays written during the war, twenty-four of the twenty-five plays included illustrated almost every form of narration possible. The one non-narrative exception was a daytime serial.

Not only does narration admit good writing to radio drama, it also admits good music. For one way of keeping narration distinct from dialogue is to keep it against a backdrop of music.

First-person narration has its rules. These are neither binding nor universally accepted but they are worthy of consideration. The first-person narrator should not complete his narration and open an ensuing scene with a line of dialogue. Nor should he be given a tag-line and go from it to narration. There must be separation of narration and dialogue. The way to accomplish that separation is to open dialogue with a character other than the narrator and to close it the same

---

* *Radio Drama In Action*, edited by Erik Barnouw

way. Thus in *A Rhode Island Refuge*, it would have been possible for Mordecai, who is the Narrator, to conclude his narration and begin the following scene:

> MORDECAI. I was ordered to join the 8th Massachusetts Regiment and before I went my father took his musket and gave it to me. (*Music out*)
> MORDECAI. I'll try to use it well, Father.

But as written and performed the separation was made between narration and dialogue in this way:

> MORDECAI. I was ordered to join the 8th Massachusetts Regiment and before I went my father took his musket and gave it to me. (*Music out*)
> FATHER. Take it, Mordecai.
> MORDECAI. I'll try to use it well, Father.

It should be noted that this last sentence of narration leads directly into the scene and clearly informs the listener of the identity of the first voice to be heard.

There are times, however, when it is essential for the sake of the mood to combine narrator-narrative and narrator-dialogue, as in the concluding scene of *The Battle of the Warsaw Ghetto*. This places a heavy burden on the actor since his transitions must be sharp and clearly offset. The two Isaac Davidsons, Raymond Massey and Arnold Moss, did this by quick shifts of perspective to the microphone and by giving more voice to the dialogue. As a result there was never any question of ambiguity.

Dialogue and narration are obvious ingredients of drama. But, to the writer fresh to radio, music and sound-effects are not. It is easy and understandable for him to become infatuated with the devices and to mistake them for the drama, which essentially belongs to the word and to nothing else.

Sound is like salt. A very little suffices. But in his infatuation with its possibilities, an inexperienced writer will drown his script in sound-effects. He will cause his characters to whistle, to blow their noses, to scrape chairs, lift pots, pour water, and ring doorbells. He will have them opening doors but forgetting to close them, lifting the telephone receiver but forgetting to hang it up, walking on gravel, trotting on cobblestone, throwing bricks through windows, and causing small explosions while dogs bark agreement and birds sing. He will have a fine time and happily exhaust the sound-effects man. But it won't be worth it. For the listener will be combing the noise out of his inner ear and wondering what became of the story.

The best rule is to use sound when it is absolutely necessary but not otherwise. With the exception of those sounds which identify themselves—footsteps, doors opening and closing, etc.—the other sounds must be identified *in advance*. And the identification in advance will neutralize the effect of surprise.

Every sound effect requires rehearsal. The sound of water dripping in the facsimile script appended to this volume required many minutes of precious rehearsal time. If it were not for the fact that in this one case the narration hinged on the sound, it would have been more advantageous to dispense with it altogether. As it was, there were two productions of the script, and in the first production, Frank Papp gave the dripping effect to the music and Morris Mamorsky's score was spectacular.

Music produces its own intoxication. But music is only a frame. It should not call attention to itself except when it is assuming the function of a character in the drama, e.g., except when music is "in the clear" or featured alone.

Background music, a narrative theme behind a narrator, must be neutral. If it is lively or if it is full of musical figures, it will call attention away from the narrator to itself. In the competition that will follow the listener will be aware of neither but only of conflict.

These are things that the experienced radio composer knows. But the new writer does not; nor does the new writer quite know how to phrase his musical directions. His intoxication with music may cause him to neglect the essential business of dramatic creation in favor of addressing solemn directions to the composer. Here is an example in the best between-symphony manner:

> (MUSIC. Maestoso, with pride in the brasses and dignity in the woodwinds, then a two-toned tympani beat repeated once, after which the violins enter shimmering and fade underneath)

If the composer is belligerent, he will immediately, to put the writer in his place, start to rewrite the script. If the composer is not belligerent, he will merely stop laughing and write a musical cue which in his opinion the script needs—probably a ten-second bridge carried by the cellos and double basses.

But sooner or later the radio writer comes to accept the competence of the composer. He will allow the director to cast the script and the composer to create its cue music with only the briefest of directions. In time he will indicate a bridge with a laconic:

> (Music: . . . .)

The little black dots say to the composer, "Use your own judgment." Composers appreciate this. It allows the initiative demanded by self-respect.

A radio script is only a cue for drama. Drama begins when

the actors assemble and the director assigns the parts. The actors sit around a table and read the lines through for meaning and for a sense of drama. Then it happens. Something indefinable and collective in the cast reaches out and touches the pages of the script. By some alchemy, inanimate words quicken and become warm. The cast is standing now. The lines are read into a microphone. An actor, who has read a line through once or twice or three times, suddenly adds a nuance of his own. In the control room the director nods. Nothing else. But the script has become fleshed with personality and each of its words is a nerve-ending.

The comments of the director are casual. "Play against the words," he says. The cast knows what he means. And a scene that is perilously close to sentimentality achieves dignity and credibility. Carefully, the director builds up tensions. Each block of narration is nailed to a scaffolding of emotion. Each sound effect is framed by silence. Something which was only a script has now evolved into something else—a script in the process of becoming a play. Director and actors have discovered overtones of meaning never contemplated by the author and which he will hear later as a revelation of his own inner intention.

Now the musicians enter the studio and tune their instruments. The conductor flicks his baton against his music stand, he signals the beat, and a score which superimposes the composer's creative intelligence upon the script comes to life. The musicians are playing at sight, it is a first reading, and for one who does not understand the meaning of the word "professional," it is a magical thing. They rehearse the score and the conductor does for the notes of music what the director has done for the words of the script.

It is time for the dress rehearsal, time for music and sound-effects to be added to the words of the script and blended with them. Now something new will happen. For the musical background will electrify the narrator and charge a line of prose with the incandescence of poetry. Ten seconds of musical transition will bridge two scenes with laughter, or suspense, or terror, or fantasy.

For the next few minutes until air time, the director will race the clock, making a cut, transposing a line, altering a reading, shifting a voice perspective. He will eliminate one sound effect and add a new one. He will slow a musical bridge or accelerate it or even replace it by a few bars from a narrative theme. Then, in the control room, an engineer will throw a switch and outside the studio a red light will go up, "On the Air." The red hand will go around the clock. In the control room the pig-squeal of the time-check will sound very loud. "On the nose," says the engineer. The director throws a cue. And from this second and for thirty minutes after something will happen that will be drama.

I wish to acknowledge the contribution of Dr. Louis Finkelstein, President of the Jewish Theological Seminary and of Dr. Moshe Davis, Dean of the Teacher's Institute of the Seminary and Program Editor of *The Eternal Light*, to the creation of these scripts. Many of the good things here belong to them. They have been friendly teachers and forbearing ones. They have always been ready with praise and diffident with censure.

Dr. Davis, who began by reading these scripts with a wary eye for theological solecism, was swiftly metamorphosed into a radio editor of no mean competence. He is probably the only radio editor in the United States who can recommend a parable from the Talmud while altering a music bridge. There are texts in these scripts that originate with Dr. Davis. They were shamelessly appropriated and no acknowledgment given until this moment. But he has never seemed to mind. We have had script conferences before breakfast and beyond midnight, and if he has ever been impatient or unsmiling, I cannot recall the occasion.

Dr. Davis is responsible for the key to the English transliterations from the Sephardic and Ashkenazic Hebrew. The transliteration is intended to assist the reader in pronouncing the words as they are spoken in their Palestinian and Western accents. The actual laborious translation into Roman characters was done by Howard Singer, a student in the Rabbinical School of the Jewish Theological Seminary of America. For this and for other generous favors I am deeply grateful to Mr. Singer and to Mr. Gershon Cohen, his fellow-student.

Every radio production is a result of team work. *The Eternal Light* team has been fortunate in including Milton E. Krents as producer for the Seminary; Frank Papp, one of NBC's and radio's very best directors; Morris Mamorsky, a truly original and gifted composer, and conductor Milton Katims, whose talents are becoming increasingly known. For each of them and for Cantors David Putterman and Robert H. Segal I have affection and admiration.

At the certain risk of doing an injustice to the scores of fine actors who have been heard on the program, I should like to single out Alexander Scourby and Roger De Koven. They are actors who do not read a script, they perceive it. And they are constantly illuminating an author's words with their own intelligence.

Thanks are due, for help rendered, to Bertha Krantz and Edmund Fuller, of the editorial department of Crown Publishers; and to Mildred Freidenreich, secretary to Milton E. Krents.

Finally, I wish to thank my wife. Her critical influence is evident in every line I have written. She has saved me from the embarrassment of self-importance and she has prevented these radio characters from losing their humanity in verbal pieties.

MORTON WISHENGRAD

THE TENDER GRASS

THE TENDER GRASS

A little boy was once taken to the ballet and his little boy's soul was seized by an illusion of grace which unaccountably diminished as the ballet progressed. The dancers represented spirits but somehow, for spirits, they were too lifelike; or perhaps the boy's imagination was too earthbound. In any case he suddenly found himself wondering if their muscles ached. The illusion evaporated and was gone forever.

Radio fantasy has no tired muscles because there are no dancers representing spirits. There are only spirits. Gravity and rubbing alcohol tie the ballet to the ground; but a voice soars easily on the air and loses its body. Dreaming, as the little boy knew, is always best when your eyes are closed.

In The Tender Grass *the Fledgling had a fledgling's voice. Listeners said so. They complimented Frank Papp on his sensitive production and accurate casting. How did they know it was accurate? Had they ever heard a fledgling speak? Of course they had heard. For their eyes had been closed. They knew. This is fantasy and if radio has any superiority as a medium of drama over the stage or screen, it is here.*

The Tender Grass *was produced on April 14, 1946. The script was suggested in part by D. Bergelson's* The Seven Birds, *which Gershon Cohen, a student in the Rabbinical School of the Jewish Theological Seminary, remembered as a children's story told him by his mother. Alexander Scourby was the Narrator, Juano Hernandez was Shalom, and Cantor Robert H. Segal sang the role of Elijah. Others in the cast were Michael Artist, Daniel Ocko, Frank Garry, Richard Keith, Doris Rich, Abby Lewis, Joseph Wiseman, Guy Spaull, Stuart MacIntosh, and Hester Sondergaard. Donald Bain produced the sound of the birds. A musical score by Morris Mamorsky was conducted by Milton Katims.*

THE TENDER GRASS

(Music: Tinkling and frail)

NARRATOR. There are so many questions that no one ever asks. Like how is April and when does the night-time sleep? I like such questions. They are rounder than gladness and very important. No one thinks of that. I will ask you a question. Suppose once upon a time there was a boy who never was and who lived in a story that never happened. And perhaps he cried a long time because he wanted you to hear the story that never happened. Wouldn't it be terrible to let him cry? Isn't that important? I think so. I will tell you his story.

(Music: Up and down)

NARRATOR. Shalom means peace and Shalom was his name. But there were bad things in his heart. *(Music Fading)* Once upon a never-time when the forest ferns were lit by the moon and the rain was hiding from April, this boy Shalom found a bird's nest which had fallen from a tree. And in the nest were seven little birds who did not know how to fly.

(Sound of birds peeping)

SHALOM. One, two, three, four, five, six.

FLEDGLING. Little boy, count me, I'm the seventh.

SHALOM. Where's your mother?

FLEDGLING. We lost her. *(Pause)* You should be home sleeping.

SHALOM. I don't like to sleep and it's none of your business.

FLEDGLING. Little boy, I don't like you.

SHALOM. You're ugly.

3

FLEDGLING. Please put me back in the nest.

SHALOM. You have an ugly voice.

FLEDGLING. You're hurting my wing.

SHALOM. Your wing is ugly.

FLEDGLING. Please put me down. (*Pause*) Little boy, why are you staring at me?

(*Pause*)

SHALOM. I don't like you. I don't like you, I don't like your brothers, I don't like your sisters.

(*Peeping up frantically*)

SHALOM. Shut up. I said shut up. All of you, shut up. I'll make you shut up.

(*Peeping high on mike and ... cut*)

(*Pause*)

NARRATOR. (*Close*) He took each of the seven little birds and he tore out each of the seven little tongues. There was no sound left, nothing except the sound of nothing. And the boy went home to grow a day older.

(*Music: Narrative theme and down*)

NARRATOR. The mother bird flew back and a neighbor bird told her what had happened. Then all the crickets beat their breasts, and the wind whimpered and the animals of the forest began to cry because seven little birds would never sing again.

(*Music: Up and segue to something with a great whirring sound of many birds' wings and down*)

NARRATOR. And all the birds of the forest flew to the top of the mountain where the great lone eagle lived.

(*Music: In the clear and fade out under*)

NARRATOR. The birds of the forest sat as a court, and the eagle was judge.

EAGLE. Let the mother bird speak.

BIRD. "When the hay is mown, and the tender grass showeth itself, and the herbs of the mountains are gathered in," all

(*Pause*)
SHALOM. Now sing it with me. (*He repeats*)
CHILDREN. (*They hum in accompaniment*)
(*Pause*)
SHULAMITH. Shalom, they carry the melody splendidly.
SHALOM. I don't want the melody. I want the words. Sing it again, sing the words.
CHILDREN. (*They hum*)
(*Pause*)
SHULAMITH. Shalom, why do you torment yourself? It isn't any use, it never will be any use.
SHALOM. They have harmed no one. Shulamith, why were they afflicted?
SHULAMITH. I don't know. When the Lord smote the Egyptians, he punished only the first-born. Who can explain this, Shalom? Can you, Shalom, can I, can anyone?
(*Music: Bridge to Passover Kiddush and hold in the clear with:*)
CHILDREN. (*Hum in the clear with music and then fade under*)
NARRATOR. The Passover came. For it always comes and it may not be held back. And the seven sons of Shalom sang with the muted singing that has never found words. And hearing them Shalom thought he heard the crying of birds from a great distance, dimly, sweetly, with the sadness of lost memory. And he was troubled and did not know why he was troubled. (*Music and children fading out*) Then Shalom broke the middle cake of unleavened bread, and he lifted the matzoh for all to see and spoke the immemorial invitation to the stranger.
SHALOM. This is the bread of affliction which our forefathers ate in the land of Egypt. Let those who are hungry enter and eat with us; let those who are forlorn come and celebrate the Passover with us.
(*Knocking on door*)

SHULAMITH. Shalom!

SHALOM. I thought I heard it, too.

(*Knocking*)

NARRATOR. There was a stranger at the door. A beggar. They made him welcome and gave him a place at the festal table.

ELIJAH. Won't you continue with the service? (*Pause*) I see, my presence embarrasses you. Perhaps I should go.

SHALOM. Oh no. Stay. Please stay. We have very little but you are welcome to all we have.

ELIJAH. Thank you. (*Pause*) You have reached the Four Questions.

SHALOM. Yes.

ELIJAH. With seven fine sons like these you are blessed sevenfold.

SHALOM. My sons do not sing.

ELIJAH. It is not necessary to sing. The questions may be spoken.

SHALOM. I said my sons do not sing.

SHULAMITH. Shalom! Excuse him, please. Our children . . . they . . . they . . . were born without the gift of tongue. They are mutes.

(*Pause*)

ELIJAH. Forgive me. I did not mean to add to your pain. (*Pause*) I am a beggar. I am older than you. I am younger than you. Let me sing for your youngest son. Please?

(*Pause*)

SHALOM. It will make us very happy.

(*Cantor: Sings "Mah-nish-tah-naw . . ."*)

CHILDREN. (*Come in and hum with him . . . Hold under*)

NARRATOR. The voice of the beggar was the voice of the never-old. In the house of Shalom there was such singing that Passover as to make the angels envy. And the voices of the seven children were like the young birds in the forest . . . wordless yet filled with strange joy. Silently, Shalom relinquished his place at the head of the table. And the beggar took his place. (*Cantor and children fading*) It was something inevitable, preordained, wonderful. The meal progressed. The questions, the answers, the parables, the digressions, so new and yet so timeless . . . and always, the singing.

(*Cantor: Register "V'hee sheh-awm-daw . . ." children humming . . . establish as beginning of montage . . . hold under*)

SHALOM. Shulamith, do you not sing?

SHULAMITH. It is so strange, Shalom. I cannot sing. I am suffocated with happiness. I want only to listen.

SHALOM. Shulamith, I feel the same way. Who is he? Shulamith, he was sent to us. Why?

(*Cantor: Segue to "Hallel" . . . children humming as before . . . and down*)

SHALOM. Shulamith, there are birds singing.

SHULAMITH. I cannot hear them.

SHALOM. Oh, distinctly. Shulamith, can't you hear them? There are birds singing . . . all the birds of creation. Why are they singing? What does it mean?

(*Cantor: Segue to "Migdol" . . . children as before and down*)

SHALOM. I hear a flapping of wings. A flapping of a hundred million wings. Shulamith, what are they trying to say to me?

SHULAMITH. Shalom, you have taken too much wine. There are no wings.

SHALOM. There are, Shulamith . . . and I have barely sipped the wine.

(*Cantor: Segue softly . . . softly to "Nah-ahr Haw-yee see . . ." Hold in clear as long as possible and down*)

NARRATOR. And then a curious thing happened. Shulamith took the cup reserved for Elijah the Prophet, the cup prescribed by custom. She filled it with wine and set it on the table. And then the candles, which had been guttering, burst into terrible flame. Magical and terrible was the light in the room ... and Shulamith shielded her eyes against the light and Shalom and the speechless children of Shalom.

(*Cantor: Cuts*)

NARRATOR. (*Softly*) Behold, the goblet of Elijah the Prophet was drained dry! And the beggar was gone!

(*Music: Register "Eh-lee-yaw-hoo Hah-naw-vee ..." and down*)

NARRATOR. A miracle of the Passover in the house of Shalom! Do the hallelujahs rise from those who have gone down in silence? Only the living praise the Lord. Shalom and his children lifted up their eyes and they praised the Lord for the presence of Elijah the Prophet, Elijah the Tishbite, Elijah of Gilead, Elijah the enigma, the messenger of God, the bringer of redemption, the beloved of man.

(*Music: Up and segue to narrative theme and under*)

NARRATOR. The Passover was gone. The moons waxed, the moons waned. The sun climbed his ladder by day and came down the steps by night. An owl hooted in the forest, a locust shrilled in the field. And the year turned again to the day "when the hay is mown, and the tender grass showeth itself, and the herbs of the mountains are gathered in."

(*Music fading*) And the man Shalom who had lost remembrance of the boy Shalom, came into the field with his seven sons who were without speech.

(*Piping of birds*)

SHALOM. Gently, gently. (*Pause*) Seven little fledglings. And their wings have been broken. Who could have done such a thing? Children, carry them home. We must help the birds. We must make them strong, we must heal them. We must help them to fly. They are God's creatures. They must fly into the open firmament of heaven. Carry them gently, children.

(*Music: Bridge*)

(Birds singing)

SHULAMITH. I am pleased with you, children. So is your father.

SHALOM. Yes. You have made the birds well.

(Birds louder)

SHULAMITH. Children, they are thanking you. *(Pause)* Shalom, open the window and let them fly away. Children, you do not mind? *(Pause)* I'm glad, a house is not for birds.

(Pause)

SHALOM. God created man on the sixth day. But on the fifth day He created these. Children, I open this window for them. It is no longer a window. It is the door to the fifth day.

(Window opens)
(Birds sing into)
(Music: With birds and down)

NARRATOR. Who opens the door to any day? Who heals the night and pledges the rain? Who numbers the gossamer of the spider's web, and drops down the dew into the cup? And the rabbit startled in the hedge and gave no answer, and the dogstar blazed in the southern sky and kept his silence, while by meadow stiles the purple flower smoldered into bloom and would not speak.

(Music: Up and down)

NARRATOR. Shalom! The word means peace. And peace was the name of Shalom and Shulamith was his wife. They came again to the Passover. But the new had become old and the old was as new. For Elijah the Prophet spoke to the raven and the raven spoke to the owl. The owl held conversation with the woodlark and the eagle sent forth the herald birds to make a convocation upon a mountain. And all this on the Passover. *(Music out)* Yes, of course, it had to be. That is the best thing about a story that never happened. The end of it is foreseen and always good. *(Music out)* Once again the eagle spoke upon the mountain.

EAGLE. "For that which befalleth the sons of men, befalleth beasts; ... yea, they have all one breath." *(Pause)* Does my brother, the raven, wish to speak?
RAVEN. I wish to say that "gentleness allayeth great offenses."
EAGLE. Spoken well. What does the woodlark say?
WOODLARK. If the eagle does not object, I yield to the owl.
EAGLE. Modesty is becoming. The owl will speak if he is ready.
OWL. We sat upon a mountain top once, far removed from men and we judged a judgment. Now let us unjudge that judgment, seeing that it is come to the season of Passover, a day of liberty. Freedom gave birth to the Passover and Passover gave birth to freedom. There are seven sons who wait. Let them be told.
(Pause)
EAGLE. The owl, as usual, is wise. "A bird of the air shall carry the voice, and that which hath wings shall tell the matter." I instruct the raven to carry the news to his old friend Elijah the Prophet.
(Music: Bridge)
(Sound of birds singing)
SHALOM. You have come again?
ELIJAH. Yes, wherever it is the Passover, Elijah must now go. To each house, to each table, to each place where there is reverence and song.
(Sound of birds up)
(Whirring of many wings)
SHALOM. Look, the birds remember my sons. You never would have thought their wings were broken once.
(Sound briefly and out)
SHULAMITH. We are about to make a blessing over the Passover wine.
SHALOM. Yes, of course. I have forgotten my duties to my guest. Shulamith, fill the goblet of the Prophet Elijah and let him sing the Kiddush in the house of Shalom.
(Sound of wine poured)

SHULAMITH. Children, stand round. Your tongues may never be able to speak it, but let your eyes see and your ears hear how Elijah the Tishbite sings the Kiddush on the Passover. (*Cantor: Sings "Sahv-ree Maw-raw-nawn . . ." When he reaches the blessing the children sing:*)

CHILDREN. Amen.

(*Pause*)

SHALOM. (*Close . . . awed*) Shulamith . . . Shulamith, you heard? They spoke. Please say that you heard it also?

CHILDREN. Amen.

SHULAMITH. I heard it, Shalom. They spoke. And their first word was Amen!

(*Music: Register "Chahd Gahd-yaw" . . . hold in the clear for Cantor and children*)

(*Cantor: With children . . . Leader . . . and Choral Answers . . . Registers for fifteen to twenty seconds and then under*)

NARRATOR. I shall tell you a secret. I said to you that this was a story that never happened. But that wasn't true, was it? Of course it happened. It happened long, long ago in a place called Anywhere. You do not remember it, of course, because it happened before your day . . . when time was a zero and the first bird fledged. (*Singers fading*) So tomorrow evening, when the Passover table is spread with fine matzoh, and the wine is in the cup, and the father sits at the head of the table, you and I, we shall sing.

(*Music: Up and segue to "Eh-chawd Mee Yoh-day-ah"*)

(*Cantor: With children . . . register and down*)

NARRATOR. And, of course, without any doubt, we shall sing "Eh-chawd Mee Yoh-day-ah" . . . it's a fine song. "Who knows the answer to One. I know the answer to One. One is the Lord our God. On earth and in heaven above."

(*Music: Curtain*)

MOSES MENDELSSOHN

MOSES MENDELSSOHN

Perhaps the most obvious advantage of radio as a medium of drama (critics insist that it is the only advantage), lies in economy of production. A script may contain twenty scenes, yet not a single set is required. Playwrights are constantly warping their themes and artificially squeezing their action into one or two sets because of the prohibitive cost of stagehands and settings. The radio writer can allow his plot to develop naturally and follow its internal impulses. A bridge of music will carry the listener across time or distance without any measurable cost. Similarly, there are no problems of costuming or make-up in radio. Thus, in Moses Mendelssohn, *a hero afflicted by a curvature of the spine presents no great difficulty to the director. The Narrator declares that the hero is a hunchback and, listening, you will accept Peter Capell's voice as the voice of a hunchback.*

This acceptance is an act of faith. Indeed, every radio script is an act of faith—the faith of a writer in the ability of your imagination to create for itself an image out of a voice, and to endow that image with attributes of flesh, color, dimension, and moral texture.

Moses Mendelssohn *was broadcast on February 24, 1946, with Peter Capell in the title role and a cast that included Charlotte Holland, Martin Wolfson, Joseph De Santis, Daniel Ocko, Elmer Lehr, and Delmar Nuetzman. Cantor David Putterman was the soloist and Milton Katims conducted the score composed by Morris Mamorsky. The production was directed by Frank Papp.*

On February 16, 1947, Moses Mendelssohn *was performed in a Yiddish translation by DP actors over the Frankfurt radio.*

MOSES MENDELSSOHN

NARRATOR. He was a hunchback. And he was ugly. Ugly, awkward, shy, sickly. And there was something strange in this. For the deformity was upon his back only and not upon his mind, which was transfigured with beauty, and rare. He lived two hundred years ago. His name was Moses Mendelssohn. "The prophet that hath a dream, let him tell a dream."
(*Music: Mendelssohn's "On Wings of Song"*)
NARRATOR. Do you know this melody? Mendelssohn. Felix Mendelssohn—grandson of Moses, the hunchback. But fame does not rest there. For Moses Mendelssohn, ugly, shy, awkward, sickly, hunchback—this man who lived in Berlin in the time of Frederick the Great—he was something also. First he was a Jew. Then he was a philosopher. And finally, if you looked further, he was the universal man.
(*Music: Up and down*)
NARRATOR. On a summer's day in the year 1760, the hunchback went to the King. The philosopher-King had summoned, the philosopher-Jew obeyed. (*Music fading*) All Berlin held its breath. The only person unimpressed was the warder of the King's gate, who blew his nose into a discolored rag . . .
WARDER. (*Blowing*)
NARRATOR. . . . and coughed into the philosopher's face . . .
WARDER. (*Coughing*)
NARRATOR. . . . and unceremoniously demanded . . .
WARDER. Who are you?

MENDELSSOHN. My name is Moses Mendelssohn.
WARDER. Fine, now go away.
MENDELSSOHN. You don't understand.
WARDER. That's good. Now go away.
MENDELSSOHN. I should like to. But I can't. The King sent for me.
WARDER. You!
MENDELSSOHN. Me.
WARDER. What for?
MENDELSSOHN. I really have no idea.
WARDER. What do you do?
MENDELSSOHN. I am a theologian.
WARDER. Impossible. The King doesn't want to see you.
MENDELSSOHN. Very well.
WARDER. One moment. What's a theologian?
MENDELSSOHN. A pugnacious man who belligerently proclaims peace. A juggler of morals.
WARDER. Did you say juggler? Like in a circus?
MENDELSSOHN. In a manner of speaking, life is a circus.
WARDER. Why didn't you say so before. Enter, juggler. The King will see you.
 (*Music: Bridge*)
KING. Mendelssohn, how dare you?
MENDELSSOHN. How dare I, Your Majesty?
KING. Don't pretend. You wrote this. You wrote this about my poetry.
MENDELSSOHN. Did I, Your Majesty?
KING. You did. "If no one will correct the King's philosophy, at least some one must venture to correct his grammar."
MENDELSSOHN. Your Majesty . . .
KING. Don't try to explain it away.
MENDELSSOHN. Whoever makes verses, Your Majesty . . .
KING. Indeed?
MENDELSSOHN. . . . whoever makes verses plays at ninepins. And whoever plays at ninepins, be he king or peasant, must

have the pinboy tell him how he bowls.

KING. (*Chuckles*) I can't say I wasn't warned about you. You may be seated, philosopher.

MENDELSSOHN. Your Majesty is most condescending. Thank you.

KING. I have a question, Mendelssohn. Which form of government is the best?

(*Pause*)

MENDELSSOHN. Sire, I cannot answer.

KING. You will answer, if I command it.

MENDELSSOHN. I cannot, Your Majesty. It is like asking which food is the most wholesome. Every climate and age, every sex and profession requires a different answer.

KING. Go on.

MENDELSSOHN. That is all, Sire. Each stage of civilization requires a new form of government.

KING. How will you know whether government is good in each stage?

MENDELSSOHN. No government is good, Your Majesty.

KING. (*Chuckles*) Take care, Mendelssohn. You will become a reformer and then I shall have to relieve you of your head.

MENDELSSOHN. I do not care much for reformers, Your Majesty.

KING. No? Glad to hear it.

MENDELSSOHN. They are ruthless people. They must be. Every reformer is a fanatic who lacks consideration for other people's feelings.

KING. I dare say. Only, Mendelssohn, where was your consideration for my poetry when you wrote your criticism?

(*Slight pause*)

MENDELSSOHN. Your Majesty, where was your consideration for literary criticism when you wrote your poetry?

KING. (*Chuckles . . . then roars with laughter*)

(*Music: Bridge to narrative theme and down*)

NARRATOR. Such was Moses Mendelssohn ... sickly, awkward, spindle-legged, curved of spine ... but a mind transfigured with beauty ... and rare. In the dark path on which man is to walk here on earth, his mind provided light for each step of the way. He was the friend of Gotthold Lessing, of Immanuel Kant, of Christopher Nicolai; they hailed him as the Socrates of Germany, and in return he tried to show them God in every rising sun, in every fall of rain, in every blowing flower. And yet, this man was lonely. (*Music out*) And then in the year 1762, Moses Mendelssohn saw Fromet.

MENDELSSOHN. You are very plain.

FROMET. I know.

MENDELSSOHN. But, Fromet, I am worse than plain.

FROMET. I know.

MENDELSSOHN. It's absurd.

FROMET. Is it?

MENDELSSOHN. What can you see in me?

FROMET. You.

MENDELSSOHN. No, Fromet, I can't allow it. I am a caricature of a man.

FROMET. Moses Mendelssohn, I see you.

MENDELSSOHN. Fromet, I am ugly.

FROMET. Once, Moses Mendelssohn, there was an ugly man named Rabbi Joshua. And when a Roman Princess saw him, she marvelled that God had seen fit to put so much wisdom in so unbeautiful a vessel.

MENDELSSOHN. But, Fromet ...

FROMET. And he answered, "Why does your father keep his wine in an earthen vessel?" So she persuaded her father, the king, to transfer the good wine to vessels of gold and silver; and the wine turned sour. (*Pause*) Don't you see, Moses Mendelssohn, she discovered what I know. Goodness and wisdom are like wine. They keep best in a plain vessel ... like you.

(*Pause*)

MENDELSSOHN. Thank you, Fromet.

FROMET. Moses Mendelssohn, will you ask me?

MENDELSSOHN. It's impossible.

FROMET. Ask me.

MENDELSSOHN. I can't find the words.

FROMET. Then I shall ask you. Moses Mendelssohn, I'm a plain, silly, poor girl. I wish to cook for you, to mend your clothes, to tidy your books, to ask you foolish questions, to annoy you, to scold you. I think I snore at night—I'm not sure. I'm moderately stupid, I'm illiterate in several languages, and I wish to be your wife.

(*Pause*)

MENDELSSOHN. Fromet, I've never noticed . . . but you have blue eyes.

(*Music: Bridge*)

RABBI. Blessed art Thou, O Lord our God, King of the Universe, who hast created joy and gladness, bridegroom and bride, mirth and exultation, pleasure and delight, love, brotherhood, peace and fellowship. Soon may there be heard in the cities of Judah and in the streets of Jerusalem the voice of joy and gladness, the voice of the bridegroom and the voice of the bride, the jubilant voice of bridegrooms from their canopies, and of youths from their feasts of song. Blessed are Thou, O Lord, who makest the bridegroom to rejoice with the bride. (*Pause*) Bridegroom.

MENDELSSOHN. Yes.

RABBI. We come now to an ancient marriage custom. Even on this day of your gladness, you may not forget the yearning of Israel for its ancient home. This glass is a symbol of the Temple of Jerusalem. Step on this glass and crush it. For so was the Temple destroyed. And let this knowledge temper your joy.

(*He steps down hard*)
(*Cantor: Sings the benediction*)

(*Music: Cover ... hold for bridge*)

FROMET. What are you writing?

MENDELSSOHN. I'll be finished in a little while, Fromet.

FROMET. More coffee?

MENDELSSOHN. No, thank you.

FROMET. Then I'll have some.

(*Sound of coffee poured*)

FROMET. Must you write?

MENDELSSOHN. Yes, of course. Why, Fromet, this is for the prize competition of the Berlin Academy of Sciences.

FROMET. Is it? What's the subject?

MENDELSSOHN. Are metaphysical truths susceptible to mathematical demonstration.

(*Pause*)

FROMET. Well, if you ask a foolish question, you generally get a foolish answer.

(*They laugh*)

MENDELSSOHN. Fromet, I know this is a curious way to spend a honeymoon. But the second prize is twenty ducats. That's a good deal of money.

FROMET. And the first prize?

MENDELSSOHN. I can't hope for that. Immanuel Kant is entered in the competition.

FROMET. What's the first prize?

MENDELSSOHN. Fifty ducats. But that's impossible.

FROMET. Moses Mendelssohn, I plan to have six babies. Three sons and three daughters. We need the fifty ducats.

(*Pause*)

MENDELSSOHN. Fromet.

FROMET. Yes.

MENDELSSOHN. I have ... I have to work.

FROMET. No. Tell me what you were going to say.

MENDELSSOHN. I couldn't, Fromet. I seem to have words for everything ... but no words for that.

FROMET. That's good enough. Go back to your writing. I promise not to disturb you. I promise . . . not for at least ten minutes.

(Music: Narrative theme and down)

NARRATOR. In June, 1763 . . . Fromet Mendelssohn received fifty ducats from a philosopher. The Berlin Academy of Sciences had announced its awards. Moses Mendelssohn the victor over Immanuel Kant. And now an ungainly little man who, each morning, donned the traditional prayer shawl and phylacteries . . . now this man, skull-capped, retiring, shy of adulation, became the most sought-after scholar in Europe. Socrates in a prayer shawl. This was the Age of Enlightenment. But it was also the age of prejudice. Prejudice refined—tinged with scholarly courtesies—and, therefore, more dangerous. *(Music out)* Moses Mendelssohn was a marked man.

(Door shuts)

MENDELSSOHN. Pray be seated, Baron.

BARON. Thank you, Mendelssohn.

MENDELSSOHN. May I offer you some wine?

BARON. Thank you, no. *(Pause)* Mendelssohn, I spoke to King Frederick this morning. I found him reading your latest work.

MENDELSSOHN. I am flattered.

BARON. Prussia is proud of you, Mendelssohn. I wish we could be even prouder.

MENDELSSOHN. I do not understand you, Sir.

BARON. You are a Jew. If you were not a Jew . . . well . . .

MENDELSSOHN. Has the King suggested this visit?

BARON. It's my own idea. No, that isn't so. A great many people have the same idea. Influential people—if you understand what I mean.

MENDELSSOHN. My dear Baron, have you come to discuss a religious matter?

BARON. Your religion is a state matter.

MENDELSSOHN. I believe that Church and State must be separated. My religion cannot concern you, Baron.

BARON. Nevertheless, it does.

MENDELSSOHN. We appear to differ.

BARON. There is no difference between the State and the Church, Mendelssohn . . . no difference at all.

MENDELSSOHN. Baron . . . no. You are wrong. The State dictates and coerces; religion teaches and persuades. The State enacts laws; religion suggests commandments. The State is armed with physical force; religion has no force but benevolence . . . benevolence and love and truth.

BARON. Well, I'm not a philosopher, Mendelssohn. I can't argue with you.

MENDELSSOHN. I'm very glad. I do not molest any man for his religion. I ask in return that no man molest me for mine.

BARON. Good day, Herr Mendelssohn.

MENDELSSOHN. Good day, Baron.

(*Music: Bridge*)

KING. Mendelssohn, I am surprised at your stubbornness.

MENDELSSOHN. Are you, Your Majesty?

KING. This is the State of Prussia. A state cannot abide differences. I cannot.

MENDELSSOHN. Your Majesty, how manifold is God's world? How varied, how multi-colored? Each man has his own peculiar countenance and speech.

KING. Well?

MENDELSSOHN. Your Majesty, this is not for nothing. Difference is the design of creation. Sameness would frustrate that design.

KING. I have to consider the welfare of the State. You are arguing away from the point, Mendelssohn.

MENDELSSOHN. It is the point, Your Majesty. Be strict as to the life and conduct of men; make wise laws for them; but leave speaking and thinking to us. Can't you see, Your

Majesty, the height of civilization will only be attained when there is universal forebearance among men, not otherwise.

KING. Mendelssohn, you are away from the point.

MENDELSSOHN. You must forgive me, Sire, but I am not. Do I disturb the welfare of the State?

KING. No.

MENDELSSOHN. Am I obedient to the civil government?

KING. Yes, you are.

MENDELSSOHN. Do I act righteously toward you, toward my countrymen?

KING. Well?

MENDELSSOHN. Then let me pray to God after my own fashion. Let me seek eternal salvation where I think I may find it. Your Majesty, do not become, and do not suffer anyone to become, a searcher of hearts and a judge of opinions. These are rights which God has reserved to Himself.

KING. Mendelssohn, you are stubborn.

MENDELSSOHN. Your Majesty, I am right.

(Pause)

KING. Philosopher, you have not heard the last of this.

MENDELSSOHN. I beseech Your Majesty. Laws do not alter persuasions; arbitrary punishments improve no morals; fear and hope are no criterions of truth. Your Majesty, I beseech you, leave supremacy of opinion to God.

KING. Thank you, Mendelssohn. You may leave now.

MENDELSSOHN. Good day, Your Majesty.

KING. Good day, philosopher.

(Music: Narrative theme and down)

NARRATOR. It was not to end. In the year 1769, Dr. Johann Caspar Lavater translated into German a work entitled, "An Inquiry into the Evidences of Christianity." And Dr. Lavater did a strange thing—he dedicated the work to Moses Mendelssohn. *(Music out)* And the dedication contained a challenge.

LAVATER. Permit me to read the inscription, my dear Mendelssohn: "I beseech you to read this work . . . either for the purpose of publicly refuting the arguments in support of the facts of Christianity or else, should you find those arguments conclusive, to do what love of truth demands—what Socrates would doubtless have done."

(*Pause*)

MENDELSSOHN. Why do you want to make this challenge, Doctor? I do not wish to engage in religious controversy.

LAVATER. I am terribly sorry, Mendelssohn. But I am afraid it is too late . . . too late now. The volume has been published. People will expect an answer. Naturally, people will expect an answer.

(*Music: Bridge*)

FROMET. Moses, you must stop pacing back and forth. You are making yourself sick.

MENDELSSOHN. Why can't people leave me alone? Have I harmed them?

FROMET. Your face is flushed.

MENDELSSOHN. I can't be silent now. People will think I'm indifferent.

FROMET. Drink this. It's good for you. Your head is hot.

MENDELSSOHN. When will they understand? He that planted the ear, shall He not hear? He that formed the eye, shall He not see? He that instructeth nations, shall He not correct, even He that teacheth man knowledge?

FROMET. You will make yourself worse. Please go to bed.

MENDELSSOHN. How can I? I want to stand in the window. I want to shout to them. I want them to hear . . . the whole world to hear. I want to say, the house of God is accessible to all. God alone knows our secret thoughts; God alone searches the heart. We are but of yesterday. We know nothing.

(*Pause*)

FROMET. Drink this.

MENDELSSOHN. I'm sorry, Fromet. My head is hot.
FROMET. Drink it all down. All of it. (*Pause*) Feel better now?
MENDELSSOHN. Yes, yes I feel better. Listen, Fromet.
FROMET. Yes.
MENDELSSOHN. The entire thing is a subterfuge. It is a trap, not only for me but for all men.
FROMET. Then answer them. It's simple.
MENDELSSOHN. If I answer, they will call me presumptuous and blasphemous.
FROMET. Then don't answer. That's even more simple. Keep still.
MENDELSSOHN. But that's the trap. If I keep still, they will smile and say that I am afraid or that I have no faith to defend.
FROMET. What are you going to do?
MENDELSSOHN. I don't know. If people would only see that belief is something which no man can compel. Once belief is compulsory, men believe not through honesty but through fear of penalty and religion then becomes a dead work.
(*Pause*)
FROMET. You will know what to do. I have faith in you. Now please go to your bed. Please.
(*Music: Bridge*)
FROMET. Herr Lessing, where are you taking him?
LESSING. He must go, Frau Mendelssohn.
FROMET. My husband is ill.
LESSING. Mendelssohn, shall I read your answer for you?
MENDELSSOHN. No, thank you. I must not involve you in this. Lessing, my coat. (*Pause*) Thank you.
LESSING. It's time. They are waiting. A great many of them.
FROMET. Take this scarf for your throat, Moses.
MENDELSSOHN. Thank you, Fromet. All right. I am ready.
(*Music: Bridge*)
(*Crowd up and then fade out*)

(*Pause*)

MENDELSSOHN. There are some of you present who admit to an unflattering opinion of my religion. I wish to shame that opinion . . . but through virtue and not through controversy. Yet you insist on controversy. Then listen. My religion does not believe that only through Judaism is there salvation. The Rabbis teach that the righteous of all nations shall have a part in the rewards of the future world. Suppose sitting here there were a Confucius or a Plato. I could, consistent with my religious principles, love and admire such a man. But would I propose to convert him? What for? I believe that he who leads mankind on to virtue in this world cannot be damned in the next world. These are my principles. (*Pause*) So long as I live I will adhere to them. I do not wish to force those principles upon you; I shall not let you force your principles upon me. I shall not admit your right to rake into the innermost recesses of the human heart in order to compel avowals which yield only misery to society. Men are born for each other; either teach your neighbor or bear with him. Principles are free. He who has eyes, let him see; and he who has sense, let him examine and live according to his convictions. Let us combine wisdom with goodness and call it justice. Among all the laws of the Bible, and the Talmud, you will find none which imposes belief. Belief cannot be imposed. The laws do not state: Thou shalt *believe* or not *believe*. Only thus: Thou shalt do and Thou shalt not do. I believe that I have found these truths and that anyone can find them who seeks with his eyes open and does not stand in his own light.

(*Music: Bridge to narrative theme and down*)

NARRATOR. End of a controversy that has not ended. But at least during the lifetime of Moses Mendelssohn it was not raised again. And now this man, universally honored, was acclaimed chief representative of the Jews—the First Jew of

Europe. (*Music fading*) He was the first in Germany to plead for separation of Church and State, the first to plead for freedom of belief and conscience. He belonged to the Age of Enlightenment. He was the universal man.
(*Music: Curtain*)

THE BATTLE OF THE WARSAW GHETTO

THE BATTLE OF THE WARSAW GHETTO

Compression is the distinctive mark of one kind of radio writing. This is the half-drama, half-documentary whose object it is to telescope a lifetime of emotion into a single scene, a people's history into a montage, a morality into a line of dialogue, and a philosophy of life into a phrase. These elements must be fused dramatically within a space of thirty minutes. The writing must be lean. Yet standing mutely behind each spoken word there must wait a hundred words unspoken and unutterable.

The Battle of the Warsaw Ghetto *tried to capture the tragedy of the most heroic resistance in Jewish history since the Maccabees and to precipitate from it a concentrate of ethical indignation and exaltation.*

The script was given three NBC productions over a period of two years. During the war it was broadcast overseas by Armed Forces Radio to troops stationed throughout the world. It has been performed in Yiddish by inhabitants of DP camps in Europe, in Hebrew over the Palestine radio, and it has been given hundreds of amateur productions in American universities and secondary schools.

The Battle of the Warsaw Ghetto *owed a great deal to the patience and encouragement of Milton E. Krents, producer of* THE ETERNAL LIGHT *for the Jewish Theological Seminary since the inception of the program. It was also indebted to performances by Raymond Massey and Arnold Moss, to a fine musical score by Morris Mamorsky, and to able direction by Frank Papp and Anton M. Leader. Mr. Papp directed the initial NBC production for the American Jewish Committee on the eve of the Day of Atonement in 1943. Mr. Leader directed the subsequent broadcasts. Cantors David Putterman and Robert H. Segal sang the liturgical music.*

THE BATTLE OF THE WARSAW GHETTO

(*Cantor: "Ayl Maw-lay Rah-chah-meem," unaccompanied and fade under following*)

VOICE. (*In close, softly*) It is a prayer for the dead... "Ayl Maw-lay Rah-chah-meem." Hear him with reverence, for it is no ordinary prayer and they are not the ordinary dead. They are the dead of the Warsaw Ghetto—the scapegoats of the centuries. Once the priest robed himself in linen and stood on Sinai in a convocation of Israel and they brought unto him a live goat, chosen by lot. And he laid his hands on the goat's head and confessed over it the iniquities of the people. And he released the goat, and its name was Azazel—scapegoat; and it fled into the wilderness. But for them in the Ghetto of Warsaw there was no release... there was only the abyss. In the Ghetto thirty-five thousand stood their ground against an army of the Third Reich—and twenty-five thousand fell. They sleep in their common graves but they have vindicated their birthright. Therefore, let him sing and hear him with reverence, for they have made an offering by fire and an atonement unto the Lord and they have earned their sleep.

(*Cantor: Up and finish*)
(*Music: Establish theme almost as a segue and then fade under following*)

NARRATOR. (*Simply*) My name was Isaac Davidson and I lived in the Polish city of Lublin with my wife, Dvora, and Samuel, our son. When Poland fell, they herded us into a cattle car and transported us to the Ghetto of Warsaw. It was a place in purgatory and around that purgatory they had built a brick wall and another wall of barbed wire and beyond the wire stood a third wall of soldiers armed with bayonets.

(*Music: Out . . .*)
(*Fade in shuffling of feet and hold under*)

NAZI I. All right there, move on. Next, next, next. Lively.

NAZI II. Your name?

NARRATOR. Isaac Davidson.

NAZI II. Who are they?

NARRATOR. Dvora Davidson, Samuel Davidson. My wife, my son.

NAZI II. (*Stamping three cards in rapid succession*) Three blue cards. Get along.

NAZI I. Next, next, next, move on. Pick up your feet. There's no funeral.

(*Shuffling of feet up and take out with*)
(*Music: Fade narrative theme under*)

NARRATOR. Three blue cards stamped with the letter J. Bread cards. Each card . . . a pound of bread a week. As precious as life. Dvora held the cards in her hand and we went to the tenement in the Twarda District (*Music out*) to the place where we were to live. (*Footsteps going up*) We went up the stairs of the tenement, and Samuel and I waited in the hall, while Dvora spoke to the woman who lived there.

DVORA. They said you would know where we are supposed to stay.

WOMAN. Come in, this is where you stay—in this room.

DVORA. But you live here.

WOMAN. In this corner. The other corner is yours.

DVORA. But I thought . . .

WOMAN. You don't know how lucky you are. This room has a window.

DVORA. Perhaps we shouldn't trouble you. Maybe . . . some other place.

THE BATTLE OF THE WARSAW GHETTO

WOMAN. (*Laughing bitterly*) You'll find out. Before they walled the Ghetto, fifty thousand people lived in these slums.

DVORA. Yes, but . . .

WOMAN. Do you know how many are here now? Five hundred thousand! A half-million! I know a man who sleeps in a vault in the cemetery. Don't be a fool, come in. It's still better than the cemetery.

(*Music: Theme and under*)

NARRATOR. That was our room. And because Dvora lived in it, it was also our home. There was no soap; but she cleaned it. There were no needles, but she made a cloth for the table. There was no lamp in it, yet she filled it with light. And then when she found a box, our son Samuel scrabbled up some earth and a few pathetic blades of grass (*Music out*) and Dvora put the box on the sill of the window.

(*Thump of box coming to rest*)

DVORA. There. Now our house has a garden.

NARRATOR. Yes, Dvora. Our house has a garden.

DVORA. You say it as though it is not true. Look, Isaac, look at the sun. There is no land where the sun doesn't shine. Now let it shine here on something green in the Ghetto.

(*Music: In under*)

NARRATOR. Green grass in the Warsaw Ghetto . . . a few pathetic blades of green in the scrabbled earth. But a sign of living spirit and a proof that where the spirit lives there can be no degradation. There in this place of death, shut-off, walled-in, foredoomed, there were things of the spirit done by men and women like Dvora. (*Music out*) In the Ghetto of Warsaw there was beauty and comradeship and learning.

TEACHER 1. (*Rabbinical—Fade in*) There are seven marks of an uncultured man and seven marks of a wise man. Do you know what they are, Samuel?

BOY. The wise man does not speak before him who is greater

in wisdom; and does not break in on the speech of his fellow; he is not hasty to answer; he questions according to the subject matter, and answers to the point; he speaks upon the first things first; and upon the last last; regarding that which he has not understood, he says, I do not understand it, and he acknowledges the truth.

TEACHER. And the mark of an uncultured man.

BOY. The reverse of all these things.

TEACHER. *(Fading)* Very good, Samuel. You are a good boy.

(Cross fade with classroom voices ad lib)

GIRL. *(She is struggling to make herself heard)* Weismann's theory of germinal continuity . . . Teacher, I can't finish the recitation when they talk.

TEACHER II. Please, all of you. This is a classroom in the Ghetto. It is different from other classrooms. We must be an example. *(Murmur out)* Thank you. Go on, Esther. The theory of germinal continuity.

GIRL. The germ contains living material which has come down in unbroken continuity ever since the origin of life and which is destined to persist in some form as long as life itself. *(Fading)* While Weismann's name is chiefly associated with this theory, other . . .

(Cross fade with laughter)

INSTRUCTOR. I thought this was a class in sculpture. Apparently, I'm wrong. What's this supposed to be?

PLUMBER. I don't know. Maybe I'm one of those surrealists.

INSTRUCTOR. *(Laughing)* Well, don't give up, I'll make a sculptor out of you yet.

PLUMBER. It's all right with me. If you're willing, I'm willing. But my father made me a plumber and I guess I'll always be a plumber. Now if I had my tools and a piece of brass pipe, I'd show you some real sculpture.

(Both laugh and fade out of laughter into:)

DOCTOR. Say, Ah. Ahhh!

BOY. *(Almost gagging)* Aah, aah.

DOCTOR. Wider . . . a little more . . . there, that will do, boy. Why didn't you bring him earlier?
DVORA. It's my fault. I didn't know there was a clinic.
DOCTOR. His tonsils are badly infected, they'll have to come out.
DVORA. I don't have any money to pay you.
DOCTOR. There's nothing to pay here. Money can't buy what no one will sell to us.
DVORA. No?
DOCTOR. No. We need drugs, instruments, anaesthesia.
DVORA. Then—you operate without anaesthesia?
BOY. Please, Doctor, will it hurt?
DOCTOR. Yes, it will hurt. In the Ghetto, everything hurts. Perhaps tomorrow it will be different.
(*Music: Short bridge*)
NARRATOR. The Ghetto waited for tomorrow. It tried to do so with dignity and self-respect. Sometimes it was hard. But the Ghetto tried. In the cellars of the tenements the children went to classes; and wherever there was a patch of dirt the older boys studied agriculture; carpenters taught their trade to clerks with thin chests; the watchmakers and the leather workers opened trade schools; the artists taught their art. And all of this was free. Whoever wanted to learn was welcome. It was a somber, grim, melancholy place, heavy with the foreboding of death, but we encouraged each other to work and to study and to laugh. Yes, to laugh also—we organized four theatres. But our greatest pride, our finest symbol, was our orchestra—The Ghetto Symphony.
(*Fade in tuning of instruments*)
(*Rapping of baton*)
VOICE. We'll try it again. From the same place. Now watch me. Please! (*Rapping baton again*) Please, watch the stick. We're going to start together and finish together. All right now. Watch the stick.

(*Orchestra: Air from Smetana's "Fatherland Suite"—Register and then hold under dropping out instruments to solo violin*)

NARRATOR. We sat and listened to the Ghetto Symphony, feeding our hunger on the clear, sweet sound. But since the Herrenvolk, the Master race that erected the walls, since they intended that we should be hungry, they came and confiscated some of the instruments. First they took only a few, then more. Our orchestra dwindled. It became an ensemble. And then the Herrenvolk came again and stole more instruments. The ensemble became a quartet. And then . . . a single solo violin was left. Why did they do it? Perhaps it irritated them—Jews satisfying a hunger. (*Music out*) We were left with hunger. And where there is hunger, the plague always follows. The plague came and 17,800 persons died of spotted typhus in Warsaw. And of these 15,758 were Jews. A pestilence imprisoned behind a brick wall, a great achievement of medical science; I say it without irony. Yes, 15,758—and Dvora Davidson, my wife . . . 15,759.

(*Sound of boy sobbing softly*)

NARRATOR. (*Gently*) Samuel, leave her. You cannot help her any more.

BOY. Mamma, Mamma!

NARRATOR. Come here. Come here, Samuel. She cannot hear you. (*Pause*) You are a big boy. You mustn't cry. (*Pause*) Here let me wash your face. She wouldn't like to see you with a dirty face. Stop crying now.

BOY. I'll try. (*Pause*)

NARRATOR. Will you do something for me, Samuel?

BOY. Yes, if I can.

NARRATOR. I want you to go to your corner; I want you to try to go to sleep.

BOY. I couldn't . . . I couldn't sleep, Papa.

NARRATOR. Then go to your corner and turn your face away.

THE BATTLE OF THE WARSAW GHETTO

Mind me. Do as your father says. (*Pause*) That's right, to the wall. You are a good boy, Samuel.

BOY. (*Off mike, suggesting face turned away in his following speeches*) You will not hurt her, Papa?

NARRATOR. No one can hurt her. (*Pause*) I am taking off her clothes. Her apron, her dress, Uncle Avrum's shoes—everything—Naked came I out of my mother's womb and naked shall I return thither.

BOY. (*Sobbing*) You are going to carry her into the street!

NARRATOR. Yes, after dark I am going to carry her into the street . . . and I will leave her there . . . cold, naked, nameless. You know why I must do this, Samuel. They must not be able to identify her. They must not know who she is.

BOY. (*Sobbing*) It's because of the bread card, Papa?

NARRATOR. Yes, it's because of the bread card. If they identify her as Dvora Davidson, they will take it away. They must not be able to identify her.

BOY. Please, Papa, please. Let them take it away. Not in the street.

NARRATOR. It is her last wish, Samuel. The bread card is for you. Honor her last wish. The blue card with the letter J—a pound of bread a week for her son.

BOY. I won't take it, I can't.

NARRATOR. You must, Samuel. Once you took her milk. Now you must take her bread. She leaves you nothing else. You must take it, Samuel—it is your inheritance.

BOY. (*Sobbing louder and hold under prayer*)

VOICE. (*Very slowly*) Yis-gah-dahl v'yis-kah-dahsh shmay rah-baw b'awl-maw dee v'raw chir-oo-say, v'yam-leech mahl-choo-say b'chah-yay-chohn oo-v'yoh-may-chon oo-v'chah-yay dee chawl bays yis-raw-ayl bah-ah-gaw-law oo-veez-mahn kaw-reev v'im-roo aw-mayn.

(*Music: Fade narrative theme in above and hold under*)

NARRATOR. This was our degradation. In the Ghetto of Warsaw we divided dead men's bread. Have you tasted dead men's bread? The taste is bitter, and it is dry in the mouth because the saliva will not flow. This is what we ate and this is how we lived . . . the five hundred thousand at the Warsaw Ghetto. But not five hundred thousand for long. On June 22, 1942 armored cars escorted a convoy of black trucks into the Ghetto. They seized men and women and children and packed them into the trucks and these were the uncoffined dead who never returned. And each day thereafter the black trucks came. And each day when they left, there was weeping in the Ghetto. I have seen the faces of the men that did these things. They were men like other men. Some were old. Some were young, with eyes, with skin and flesh and nails and the requisite number of fingers. I looked into their faces and did not believe. But the trucks continued to come. (*Music out*) And it must be said that if the thing that they did was monstrous; it was a monstrous thing done with order and method; for *they* take pride in order.

(*Sound of trucks and under voices*)

VOICE I. July 22, 1942.

VOICE II. Six thousand two hundred and eighty-nine.

VOICE III. Destination . . . Tremblinka.

VOICE I. July 23rd.

VOICE II. Seven thousand eight hundred and twenty.

VOICE III. Destination . . . Oswiantzem.

VOICE I. July 24th.

VOICE II. Seven thousand four hundred and forty-four.

VOICE III. Destination . . . Belzec.

(*Voices and truck sounds hold under narrator*)

NARRATOR. Done with method, precise, efficient, recorded. To Tremblinka, Oswiantzem, Belzec, Sobibor, Majdany—a lethal gas chamber, an electric furnace, a poison pit, an execution field, a cemetery. And add also ten thousand brave, hopeless, tragic men who seized sticks and stones and knives and bare fists and charged the tanks and tried

to halt the trucks. Add their bodies to the list for the ten days of June, 1942. Make your total and then add two precise, methodical, documented months in August and September, 1942. Reckon it. Do it carefully. You cannot do it on your fingers. No! Let me give you the sum. Listen, 275,954 fewer bread cards in the Ghetto! Swift, accurate, final. Quicker than typhus, surer than hunger.
(*Rumble of tanks and sound of trucks up for bridge and take out with:*)
(*Music: Register second narrative theme and fade under*)
NARRATOR. They sent the black trucks because the hunger and pestilence were too slow and too merciful. When we were starving, we beseeched the civilized world for food, and when the plague struck us, we appealed for simple things—for soap, medicine, for tools for our physicians. But when the black trucks came, we no longer asked for rescue, we no longer asked for mercy—we asked for weapons. Through the Polish underground which carried our appeals we asked England, Russia and the United States for weapons. And there was silence. You did not answer. And then through the Polish underground there came your answer: resolutions of sympathy, phrased with felicity. It was a greater injury than silence. I who know can say to you that the grave does not yield its tenant for such coin, nor will such coin inspire the enemy to lie down and crimson the gutter with his blood. We waited for weapons that did not come. Five hundred thousand waited. (*Pause*) Three hundred thousand waited. (*Pause*) One hundred thousand waited. And finally thirty-five thousand who did not know where to look . . . (*Music out*) but the answer came from under their feet—from the sewer under the Warsaw Ghetto.
(*Echo chamber*)
(*Footsteps*)
POLE. Carry it gently, Pan Meyer. Don't let it fall.

MEYER. I'm carrying it as though it were a case of eggs.
POLE. More gently than that, Pan Meyer.
MEYER. What could be more fragile than a case of eggs?
POLE. A case of dynamite.

(*Music*: *Accent*)

VOICE. The rifles are already distributed. Our men want to know if there will be any machine guns.
POLE. If we can get some through, there'll be machine guns. But don't count on it. You'll have to make out with rifles.
VOICE. It won't be much against tanks and mortars.
POLE. It will be better than bare hands.
VOICE. Yes—better than bare hands—much better.

(*Music*: *Accent*)

VOICE II. The Ghetto Council would like to know your name.
POLE. What difference does it make?
VOICE II. They want to thank you.
POLE. Tell them to thank the Polish underground. (*Pause*) Take good care of those barrels. There are enough grenades in them to blow up every Jew in the Ghetto.
VOICE II. Then there must be enough grenades in them to blow up every German in Warsaw.
POLE. I'm glad you see it that way.
VOICE II. What do you think we've been waiting for?

(*Music: Bridge and segue to narrative theme and under*)

NARRATOR. April 19, 1943. Thirty-five thousand men, women, children stood ready. It was the day. Trenches were dug during the night. Every house, every room, every cellar, every roof was prepared. At 4 a.m a detachment of Storm Troopers in light tanks escorted the black trucks to the walls of the Ghetto. They came as usual on their daily errand. (*Music up higher*) We waited until the vehicles were within range.
VOICE. Fire!

(*Blast of rifle fire and top with rattle of machine guns—then distant scream of pain*)

THE BATTLE OF THE WARSAW GHETTO

(*Music: Crashing finish*)
NARRATOR. The entire detachment was wiped out. In a few hours they came again. SS troops. Our snipers manned the Ghetto Wall itself. We were ready.
(*Burst of fire, rattle of machine guns under narrator*)
NARRATOR. They brought up a loudspeaker.
NAZI. (*Through loudspeaker*) Jews, put down your guns. You haven't a chance in the world against us. Put down your guns, Jews. We will give you fifteen minutes to make up your minds and then we'll come after you. Jews, put down your guns. It's your last chance.
(*Guns as before*)
NARRATOR. That was the answer. That and the flags of the United Nations which floated over the roofs of the Ghetto.
(*Sound of dynamite explosions one after another rapidly*)
NARRATOR. More answers. (*Explosion*) Eight hundred answers. Eight hundred factories producing material for Germany—blown up by our engineers. (*Explosion*)
NAZI. (*Loudspeaker*) You still have another chance. Jews, put down your guns. Put them down and come out of the buildings and you will be treated with mercy. (*Ping of single shot*) (*He gasps and coughs as though he has been hit*)
NARRATOR. They brought up the regular army. The Ghetto had defeated the Storm Troopers and now it was the Ghetto against the German Army. We retreated slowly from our positions as they sent flame throwers, mortar, cannon, tanks and planes against us.
(*Build up volume of sounds, planes diving, machine guns, bombs, etc.*)
VOICE. April 20th . . . April 25th . . . May 2nd . . . May 6th . . . May 10th . . . May 14th . . . May 18th . . . May 20th . . . May 22nd . . . May 25th . . .
(*Increase volume of sound*)
NARRATOR. They planted land mines under the tenements

(*Explosion*) and blew them up one by one. The tenements crumbled but from the rubble of the shattered cellars the snipers kept up a continuous fire. The surviving men and women and children retreated slowly from house to house, erecting barricades in the streets, paying with their lives for every tenement, every room, every step of the way. When their ammunition ran out, they used broken furniture as clubs and hurled stones. On the twentieth day the enemy shut off the water supply and planes dropped incendiary bombs.

(*Tremendous crackle of flames added to sound*)

The entire Ghetto was in flames. Those who were not burned alive were slaughtered by the Nazis.

(*Fade sound to background*)

MEYER. (*Gasping*) Isaac Davidson. Isaac . . . here . . . in the trench.

NARRATOR. His right arm had been blown off at the elbow. I spoke to him. (*As Isaac*) Let me tie a tourniquet around your arm.

VOICE. Don't waste the bandage on me. Tell me how it is going.

NARRATOR. We're still fighting.

VOICE. After thirty-seven days. A few Jews with guns fighting a Nazi army for thirty-seven days.

NARRATOR. (*Narrating*) The blood ran from the shattered stump and soaked the ground. But he smiled.

VOICE. They are really very foolish. They should have known that the Ghetto would explode.

NARRATOR. (*As Isaac*) They know now.

VOICE. How many did we kill?

NARRATOR. Some say a thousand, some say twelve hundred. (*Pause—Narrating*) The smile lingered on his lips even as his eyes began to glaze—and he spoke an epitaph for the Warsaw Ghetto.

VOICE. It is not for thee to complete the work, but neither

art thou free to desist from it. Tell them to mark that on my grave.

NARRATOR. Yes, tell them to mark it on our graves—It is not for thee to complete the work, but neither art thou free to desist from it.

(Cantor: Singing unaccompanied solo "Ayl Maw-lay Rah-chah-meem" . . . Fade under narration)

VOICE. Hear him with reverence. For he sings a prayer for the dead—twenty-five thousand dead. It is no ordinary prayer and they are no ordinary dead. For they are the dead of the Warsaw Ghetto—in the year nineteen hundred and forty-three. Tonight they sleep in their last trench, their choirs dispersed in ashes, their holy books sodden in the seventh-month rain, the rubble deep on the thresholds of their houses. They were Jews with guns! Understand that—and hear him with reverence as he chants the prayer. For on the page of their agony they wrote a sentence that shall be an atonement, and it is this: Give me grace and give me dignity and teach me to die; and let my prison be a fortress and my wailing wall a stockade, for I have been to Egypt and I am not departed.

(Cantor: Up and finish)
(Music: Curtain)

THE PARABLE OF REB YISROEL

THE PARABLE OF REB YISROEL

Fantasy leans heavily on music. In The Parable of Reb Yisroel *two kinds of music were needed, one for the scenes in heaven, the other for earth. It was necessary to make the distinction very clear and so an unaccompanied chorus of "angelic" voices backed the heavenly narration and supplanted the orchestra for transitional bridges. The orchestra took over as soon as the inquiring angels descended to earth, and so long as the action was confined to Bialystok Morris Mamorsky's music set the tone.*

In casting, Frank Papp used fantasy as license to make his humans sound occasionally angelic and his angels sound like longshoremen. In radio parlance this "paid off" when the chastized angels, played by Joseph Di Santis, Norman Rose and Joseph Boland, returned home and made heaven seem like a Sabbath day in Bialystok.

The Parable of Reb Yisroel had two performances. Both times Reb Yisroel was played by Juano Hernandez. For the performance on January 13, 1946 the Narrating Angel was Melchor Ferrer. In addition to the chastized angels mentioned above, the cast included Harold Huber, Martin Wolfson, Charme Allen and Will Geer. Alexander Scourby was the Narrator in a repeat performance on September 29, 1946. Cantors David Putterman and Robert H. Segal sang the liturgical music. Milton Katims conducted the orchestra and chorus.

This script and A Chassidic Tale *and* The Broken Sabbath of Rabbi Asher, *which appear further in the volume, owe a great deal to the growing literature in English of Chassidic legend and history, especially to the writings of Martin Buber. Most of the legends and sayings included in these scripts may be found in* A Hasidic Anthology, *edited by Louis I. Newman in collaboration with Samuel Spitz.*

THE PARABLE OF REB YISROEL

(Cantor: Register with choir)
NARRATOR. That morning in question I happened to be standing outside the Heavenly Gate. As usual there was a great throng waiting to be tried by the Heavenly Tribunal. Some groaned and bit their fingernails; others radiated an aura of confidence. Now it has been my experience founded on four hundred and sixty-two years of personal observation that sinners who await the heavenly trial are frequently expectant and self-assured while righteous men and women invariably tremble at the imminent prospect of judgment. On this particular morning one hundred and twenty years ago, I observed two men who had died that very hour, and who were now awaiting trial.
(Cantor: And choir fading)
One had been a wealthy man; the other had been a thief. And both had come for judgment directly from the city of Bialystok.
(Fading) The thief spoke first.
THIEF. Menachem . . . before you go in there . . .
MENACHEM. Yes?
THIEF. I want you to know . . . it's hard to put into words . . . I . . .
MENACHEM. It was nothing.
THIEF. Oh, no, Menachem, it was a good deal. I was starving. Everyone said I was nothing but a thief. But you sent me food, you and Reb Yisroel. Do you call that nothing?
MENACHEM. Well, thank Reb Yisroel . . . it was his example.

50   THE ETERNAL LIGHT

ANGEL. (*Off and Projecting*) Next case, Menachem Aaronson.
THIEF. Wait, Menachem . . . I must tell you . . .
MENACHEM. The Angel is calling me.
THIEF. All I want to say . . . I mean . . . that is . . .
ANGEL. Menachem Aaronson of Bialystok.
THIEF. Menachem, what I'm trying to say, I mean, well . . . good luck to you, Menachem Aaronson. May you be admitted to Paradise.
MENACHEM. There is little chance, my friend. On earth . . . I was a rich man. Not a good man—only a rich man.
THIEF. Well . . . good luck, Menachem.
   (*Cantor: Up with choir and fade out under:*)
   (*Pounding of gavel*)
JUDGE. Menachem Aaronson, stand before the bar.
MENACHEM. Yes, your honor.
JUDGE. Do you have anything further to say in your own behalf?
MENACHEM. No, your honor. The record in your hands is correct.
JUDGE. Hmm. Too bad.
MENACHEM. You mean . . .?
JUDGE. The list of your iniquities is very great. They outweigh your good deeds many times . . . very many times.
MENACHEM. I can't say that I wasn't warned. Back in Bialystok, Reb Yisroel used to speak to me all the time. He used to plead with me.
JUDGE. You will have to leave Heaven and go to . . .
MENACHEM. (*Hurriedly*) I know. (*Sighs*) Yes, of course. All right, I know the way.
JUDGE. (*Gently*) Sinners generally do.
MENACHEM. I wonder if you could spare me pen and ink; I want to send a letter to Bialystok and tell Reb Yisroel that . . .
JUDGE. Absolutely out of the question.
MENACHEM. Oh! Well . . . all I wanted to tell Reb Yisroel

THE PARABLE OF REB YISROEL

was that I've had a fair trial. Well, thank you very much that is . . . thank you.
(*Cantor: With choir for bridge*)
(*Footsteps running on gravel path*)
ANGEL. (*Panting*) Menachem . . . Menachem Aaronson of Bialystok . . . hold on.
MENACHEM. Oh . . . I really know the way. You didn't have to follow.
ANGEL. Stop. Don't go any further.
MENACHEM. But I was told to . . .
ANGEL. The order has been countermanded.
MENACHEM. What! Oh, Reb Yisroel, thank you. Thank you for interceding for me.
ANGEL. Fiddlesticks. Reb Yisroel, whoever he is, had nothing to do with it. You've been ordered to reappear before the Heavenly Tribunal . . . it seems something unusual took place during the trial of your friend, the thief.
MENACHEM. I hope he hasn't taken sick.
ANGEL. Don't speak nonsense, Menachem. No one gets sick here. Come on. You're going back.
(*Cantor: With choir and fade out under gavel*)
(*Sound of gavel*)
JUDGE. Menachem Aaronson of Bialystok.
MENACHEM. The same, your Honor.
JUDGE. A man was starving . . . you fed him.
MENACHEM. I did what Reb Yisroel told me to do. Reb Yisroel is a holy man . . . a real Tsaddik. When after a hundred and twenty years, he comes to Heaven he will not be an ordinary angel. No. He will take his place among the seraphim.
JUDGE. Menachem Aaronson, you are impertinent and presumptuous.
MENACHEM. I beg your pardon, but Reb Yisroel said that a thief is also a human being and that it was my duty to feed him.

JUDGE. (*Wearily*) The court will discuss Reb Yisroel on the proper occasion. The court now informs you, Menachem Aaronson, that your sentence has been reversed.

MENACHEM. Reversed?

JUDGE. Reversed.

MENACHEM. But the list of my iniquities . . . you said . . .

JUDGE. I did.

MENACHEM. You ordered me to leave Heaven and go to . . .

JUDGE. (*Quickly*) I did.

MENACHEM. But the list of my iniquities . . . you said . . .

JUDGE. There is no list.

MENACHEM. No list?

JUDGE. It's gone.

MENACHEM. Oh, thank you, your Honor.

JUDGE. Don't thank me. Thank your friend, the thief.

MENACHEM. (*Not understanding*) Oh!

JUDGE. He stole the list.

MENACHEM. (*Softly*) Reb Yisroel, oh, Reb Yisroel, you should know what has happened.

JUDGE. Menachem Aaronson of Bialystok, not another word about Reb Yisroel . . . not a single word. And be good enough to close the door as you leave. There's a terrific draft! (*Rap of gavel*) Next case.

(*Cantor: With choir and fade under*)

NARRATOR. A very unusual incident. Even for Heaven . . . The Judge ordered a thorough investigation, you can be sure, but Menachem Aaronson remained in Paradise, blessing the name of Reb Yisroel, who had taught many men to love each other. Now I must tell you that Reb Yisroel became something of a problem because due to his earthly influence, many irregular things began to take place with alarming frequency within the precincts of the Heavenly Tribunal. Immediately there was politics. One party of angels declared that Reb Yisroel was a saint who was surely destined to sit among the seraphim. A second party insisted

THE PARABLE OF REB YISROEL

that he could only take his place in the lesser rank among the ordinary angels. And a third party declared that Reb Yisroel wasn't a saint at all and that he was not even sure of admission to Paradise.

(*Cantor: And choir fading*)

NARRATOR. It became very disturbing. The angels commenced to quarrel. So measures had to be taken.

(*Voices quarreling*)

JUDGE. Quiet! Quiet! I ask the angels to behave as gentlemen.

(*Voices out*) Phineas.

PHINEAS. I didn't say a word.

JUDGE. I didn't ask you. Now listen . . . all of you. There will be no peace until we send messengers down to earth and investigate this Reb Yisroel of Minsk.

ABNER. Bialystok.

JUDGE. Bialystok, thank you, Abner. We must put him to the test. Determine whether he is qualified to sit among the angels . . . to say nothing of our superiors, the seraphim. I need two angels for the mission.

PHINEAS. I'm willing.

ABNER. So am I.

JUDGE. Good. Now step closely and listen. We've got to put Reb Yisroel to the test. Now the plan is . . . (*Conspirational mumbling*) That's test one. Is that clear?

PHINEAS. Absolutely.

JUDGE. Very good. The second test is . . . (*More business*) You understand?

ABNER. Perfectly.

JUDGE. Very good. May you both have a quick passage to Bialystok. I will expect you to report back every fortnight. Good luck.

(*Cantor: With choir and take out with:*)
(*Music: A segue from the Heavenly Chorus to an earthly theme and down*)

NARRATOR. The Heavenly Chorus faded into the distance.

Phineas and Abner descended through the atmosphere toward the place where the fifty-third meridian intersects the twenty-third parallel . . . or to be more specific, exactly where the Synagogue stands in the city of Bialystok. For an Angel, I must say that Phineas had a most peculiar disposition. There sat Reb Yisroel and a number of men deep in study. (*Music fading*) But Phineas insisted on creating a disturbance.

(*Door slams*)

ONE. (*Sotto*) Sssh. Not so loud; we are studying.

PHINEAS. (*Loudly*) Which one is Reb Yisroel?

ONE. Hush, my friend. We spend this hour in silence.

PHINEAS. Never mind that; which one is Reb Yisroel?

TWO. (*Quietly*) If you cannot behave properly, I'm afraid I shall have to ask you to leave.

PHINEAS. You, over there, are you Reb Yisroel?

(*Pause*)

YISROEL. Yes, my son, I am Yisroel.

PHINEAS. I want to ask you a few questions.

YISROEL. I should be glad to answer, my son. Will you return in an hour?

PHINEAS. No. I want my answers now.

TWO. Shall I make him go, Reb Yisroel?

YISROEL. No. No. Let him stay. Very well, my son, what are your questions?

PHINEAS. The Talmud declares that when a man runs away from honors, honors pursue him. Is that so?

YISROEL. It is so. What is your question?

PHINEAS. I have run away from honors but no honors pursue me. What is the reason, Reb Yisroel?

YISROEL. The reason, my son, is you keep looking backward.

(*Laughter*)

ONE. Now will you let us study in peace?

PHINEAS. I'm not done. Reb Yisroel, why is it that the pious man is not eager to persuade others to become virtuous

THE PARABLE OF REB YISROEL

while wicked people always seek companions in wickedness?
YISROEL. Why?
PHINEAS. That's my question.
YISROEL. A man of piety walks in light. He is not afraid to walk alone.
PHINEAS. Well?
YISROEL. A wicked man walks in darkness. He is anxious for company because it is dark. (*Pause*) May we resume our study now?
PHINEAS. Not yet. One last question. You pray a good deal, don't you?
YISROEL. I try to.
PHINEAS. Have you succeeded through your prayers in bringing it about that the rich should be more generous in their gifts to the poor?
YISROEL. Not altogether, my son. But I have accomplished half my prayer. The poor are willing to accept them.
(*Laughter holding under first few bars of:*)
(*Music: Narrative theme and down*)
NARRATOR. They laughed while Phineas bit his lip. I might say that it does not pay to antagonize an angel who possesses a peculiar disposition. For Phineas immediately quit the Synagogue and spoke to Abner, who had been waiting near the Rabbi's house. At once Abner put on the garments of a beggar, waited until the Rabbi returned to his house (*Music fading*) and then he knocked on the door.
(*Knocking on door*)
(*Door opens*)
YISROEL. Yes, my son?
ABNER. I'm a poor man. Give me alms. Alms, for the poor man.
YISROEL. Come in, my son. (*Door shuts*) I have no money to give you.
ABNER. Then you refuse to give charity?

YISROEL. I did not say that, my son. I said only that I have no money. But perhaps . . . (*Reflectively*) . . . perhaps I can find something in this chest of drawers. One moment please.

(*Sound of drawers—opening, shutting*)

ABNER. You're only pretending to look.

YISROEL. Pretending? I'm sure I don't know what's come over people today. (*Pause*) Here. Take this and may God go with you.

ABNER. What is it?

YISROEL. It is a ring. It belongs to my wife. You may have it. Take it, my son, and go in peace.

(*Music: Bridge*)

WIFE. Good Heavens! What has happened here? Yisroel, pick your head out of the book. Look at my chest of drawers!

YISROEL. What is it, my dear?

WIFE. Yisroel, how can you sit there? The drawers are open . . . ransacked. There have been burglars!

YISROEL. Hmm?

WIFE. I said burglars. Look, my ring! It's missing!

YISROEL. Oh, no, my dear. It isn't missing.

WIFE. I put it here myself.. If it isn't missing, where is it?

YISROEL. A man came. He asked for alms. I had no money. So I gave him your ring.

WIFE. You did what?

YISROEL. Your ring, my dear. I gave it to him. It is a sin to turn a man away who requests alms.

WIFE. Yisroel, do you know what you've done? That ring is worth fifty dollars.

YISROEL. That's a great sum, isn't it, my dear?

WIFE. Yisroel, put down that book! I want you to run after that beggar! I want you to run after him this very moment!

(*Music: Bridge*)

YISROEL. (*Panting*) Oh, I'm glad I caught up to you. I've got a stitch in my side.

ABNER. I thought so. Well, I expected it. What do you want?
YISROEL. That ring . . . my wife says . . .
ABNER. Yes, what did your wife say?
YISROEL. She says the ring is worth fifty dollars.
ABNER. What about it?
YISROEL. I came to warn you.
ABNER. What's that? You came to . . . *warn* me?
YISROEL. Yes, of course. My wife does not lie. If she says the ring is worth fifty dollars, we may both believe her. Don't let anyone cheat you.
ABNER. Cheat *me?*
YISROEL. Yes. When you sell it, make sure you get fifty dollars. Don't take anything less than that . . . not a single penny.
(*Music: Bridge to:*)
(*Cantor: With choir, register and hold under*)
NARRATOR. It became necessary for Phineas and Abner to return to the Heavenly Tribunal and make a preliminary report. The temptation of Reb Yisroel was not proceeding according to plan. And where there had formerly been three parties of angels, now there were six. Two parties insisted that at Reb Yisroel's death, he would take his place among the seraphim. Two other parties protested that Reb Yisroel was worthy only of a place among the ordinary angels. The remaining parties went into separate caucus . . . and there were sounds of argument, contention, and strife. I must say that for a while it was difficult to know what Heaven was coming to. (*Cantor and choir fading*) Phineas and Abner were recalled. In their place a single angel was sent to Bialystok . . . a certain Reuben, who was notoriously hot-tempered . . . and . . . ingenious in a nasty sort of way. For Reuben set himself up as a rich man and then . . . he caused a terrible famine to come to Bialystok.
WIFE. Yisroel, we're foolish to come here. Reuben won't help.
YISROEL. He must, my dear. There's no one left to turn to.
WIFE. He's a violent man, Yisroel. Let's go home.

YISROEL. You may go home if you wish. But someone must appeal to him. People are starving.
WIFE. Please, Yisroel, come home with me.
YISROEL. No, my dear.
WIFE. Very well, if you stay, I stay.
(*Door opens*)
(*Footsteps come on*)
REUBEN. Well!
YISROEL. Reuben, my wife and I . . .
REUBEN. What about it?
YISROEL. People are starving in Bialystok.
REUBEN. So?
YISROEL. Everyone has helped but you.
REUBEN. So?
YISROEL. My son, I am here to ask you for alms.
REUBEN. Good day.
YISROEL. You turn us away?
REUBEN. I do.
YISROEL. Are you human? You can't turn us away. I will not leave, Reuben.
REUBEN. You won't, eh?
YISROEL. Not until you give me something.
REUBEN. Very well, Reb Yisroel, come here. (*Pause*) Closer. (*Sound of hard slap*) (*Pause*)
WIFE. (*Softly*) You struck him. You really struck him. Oh, Yisroel!
YISROEL. My son.
REUBEN. Well!
YISROEL. That slap, my son—that was evidently meant for me. Now what will you give for the poor of Bialystok?
(*Music: Bridge . . . Fade out under narrator*)
NARRATOR. Reuben stood there and it was as though he himself had been slapped. And so another chastized angel returned from Bialystok to the Heavenly Tribunal. And for once there was no bickering, no tumult of contending

THE PARABLE OF REB YISROEL

angelic voices. That was very significant. Even the Heavenly Choir was silent. And one voice sang. Only one voice. And it was significant also that he sang Reb Yisroel's melody, a song without words.

(*Cantor: A Chassidic song without words . . . In the clear for fifteen to twenty seconds and then hold under*)

NARRATOR. There was a hasty consultation. This could never do. Reb Yisroel was influencing Heaven. The angels were becoming very solicitous of their observance of Heavenly decorum, as though they were ashamed of their past behavior. And suddenly, each Heavenly day became transformed . . . it was like the Sabbath day in Bialystok . . . only every day a Sabbath day. Phineas would meet Abner.

PHINEAS. Gut Shabbas, Abner.

NARRATOR. And Abner would meet Reuben . . .

ABNER. Gut Shabbas, Reuben.

NARRATOR. And Reuben would meet Menachem of Bialystok . . .

REUBEN. I bring you regards from Bialystok. Your grandson Jonas has become the best marble player. They say also that he's a fair scholar.

NARRATOR. There was such sweetness, such amiability on all sides . . . it was unearthly . . . and rather becoming. Still . . . there was one small group of angels . . . insignificant in number, really, but quite vocal . . . who were not convinced that Reb Yisroel could take his place among the seraphim. Among the ordinary angels, yes, without a question. But the seraphim? Well, they demanded more evidence.

(*Cantor: Finishes and is covered by choir in "Kol Nidre." They fade down*)

NARRATOR. It happened that in Bialystok Reb Yisroel and the townsmen were observing Yom Kippur, the Holy Day of Atonement.

(*Choir: In the clear and down again*)

And Reb Yisroel and the congregation asked forgiveness for the sins they had committed against one another, and they asked God to forgive them for the sin they had committed against Him. I must tell you that even in Heaven, when the chant of "Kol Nidre" rises on the Day of Atonement, there is much solemnity and even tears. So all of us looked down on the congregation of Bialystok and especially upon Reb Yisroel. (*Choir fading out*) We could see everything going on . . . hear every prayer, observe the actions of every man and woman and child. You must judge of our astonishment when we heard the angry words coming from the mouth of Nachum, the tailor. And so we waited for the end of the services—waited for Reb Yisroel to rebuke the tailor.

YISROEL. Nachum, I do not wish to rebuke you; each man prays to God in his own way, but it is quite wrong to . . .

NACHUM. Wrong to do what, Reb Yisroel?

YISROEL. To scold God.

NACHUM. I thought about it, Reb Yisroel. I'm sorry I was angry with Him.

YISROEL. I'm glad to hear that. It seemed to me I heard you arguing with God.

NACHUM. I was.

YISROEL. On Yom Kippur?

NACHUM. Is there a better time? I declared to God. You want me to repent of my sins. All right, I repent. But what do I repent?

YISROEL. Yes?

NACHUM. Small sins . . . very minor things. I said to God, all right, I may have sewed a button with a single thread when I should have used a double thread. I kept left-over cloth, all right. Perhaps I ate a meal without first washing my hands and making the benediction, but You, O Lord, You commit great sins. You take babies away from their mothers. You take mothers away from their babies. So, Lord,

THE PARABLE OF REB YISROEL

let's be even. If You forgive me, I'll forgive You.
(*Pause*)
YISROEL. That was your argument with God?
NACHUM. Are you going to scold me, Reb Yisroel?
YISROEL. Scold you, Nachum? No, I'm not going to scold you. For the things you said, you said with simplicity and with faith. I shan't scold you. Only, Nachum . . .
NACHUM. Yes, Reb Yisroel?
YISROEL. Nachum, Nachum, my son . . . why did you let God off so easily? The things you said were not entirely false. Why did you let him off so easily? Why didn't you press your advantage? Nachum, don't you see, you could have forced Him to forgive all of mankind.
(*Cantor: With choir and down*)
NARRATOR. Very irregular, I admit. But there wasn't a single member of the Heavenly Court who uttered a word of protest. And for the remainder of Reb Yisroel's life on earth, there were no disputes among the angels. Many days were left to him, and he lived each one with goodness. And then, when his spirit rose to Heaven . . .
(*Choir: Out and Cantor segues to song without words*)
. . . there was a sound of singing outside the portals of the Heavenly Tribunal.
(*Cantor: Briefly in the clear and down*)
JUDGE. Reb Israel of Bialystok!
YISROEL. I await my judgment, your Honor.
JUDGE. Nice to see you, Reb Yisroel.
NARRATOR. It was this very hour, this precise minute and second one hundred and nine years ago, that the soul of Reb Yisroel flew straight to Heaven and took his place among the seraphim. Not among the ordinary angels. But among the seraphim. I tell you this as a fact.
(*Cantor: Up and finish with orchestra*)

THOMAS KENNEDY

THOMAS KENNEDY

Often the best source for the kind of fact that makes drama is not the historical text but the historical footnote. A footnote is a scholarly aside, and a scholar's small-talk tends to be less pedantic and more human than his weightier utterances.

Thomas Kennedy's name first appeared as such a footnote in a volume read for another research project. Reference led to cross-reference, and cross-reference led to the deepest files of the American Jewish Historical Society. Needless to say the original project paled and was forgotten.

Thomas Kennedy has received three NBC performances. Two productions were directed by Frank Papp for THE ETERNAL LIGHT; *a third, by Garnet Garrison for a special Brotherhood Week program on February 22, 1947.*

The title of the script was changed to Liberty in a Featherbed *by the Writer's War Board, which named it the script of the month and sent it to nearly a thousand amateur radio groups for production. It received a first prize at the 10th American Exhibition for Education by Radio conducted by Ohio State University.*

The script was first performed as a Thanksgiving Day program on November 25, 1945. Ian MacAllister was featured as Kennedy and the cast included Guy Repp, Norman Rose, Philip Foster, Len Sterling, Horace Braham, Burford Hampden, Alfred Shirley, Delmar Nuetzman, Elmer Lehr, Edward A. Wright, Richard Keith and Robert Craven.

Horace Braham was Kennedy in the second production; Carl Swenson, in the third.

THOMAS KENNEDY

(*Music: Register and down*)
NARRATOR. "Blessed are Thou, O Lord, Who has kept us in life and sustained us unto this day." A prayer of thanksgiving.
(*Music: Up and down*)
NARRATOR. Offer thanksgiving on this day for the uniqueness of America. Offer thanksgiving for the nameless heroes who took the words of the fine declarations, and believed them, and fought to make the word a deed. Offer thanksgiving to the memory of men who were not ashamed to be good, who sought no refuge in cynicism, who did not fear to stand alone.
(*Music: Out*)
Listen, this is your story.
(*Sound of gavel*)
NARRATOR. (*In close*) 1818 . . . The House of Delegates . . . Annapolis, Maryland . . . The Clerk of the House . . .
CLERK. Mr. Speaker, I have the credentials of the elected member from Washington County.
SPEAKER. Are they in order, Mr. Clerk?
CLERK. They are, Mr. Speaker.
SPEAKER. His name, if you please.
CLERK. The Honorable Thomas Kennedy.
SPEAKER. Come forward, Mr. Kennedy, and take the oath.
(*Pause*)
CLERK. (*Close*) Do you, Thomas Kennedy, solemnly swear or affirm that you will protect and defend the Constitution of the State of Maryland?
KENNEDY. I do.

CLERK. Upon the true faith of a Christian.
(*Pause*)
SPEAKER. Complete the oath, Mr. Kennedy.
KENNEDY. I should like to, Mr. Speaker, but I'm rather troubled by the form of the oath.
SPEAKER. I was not aware that there is anything in the oath to cause difficulty. Mr. Clerk, are you troubled?
CLERK. Not at all, Mr. Speaker.
SPEAKER. Proceed then . . . unless Mr. Kennedy is not a Christian.
(*General laughter*)
KENNEDY. Mr. Speaker, I was born in Scotland. The sect in which I was bred is the Presbyterian Church. (*Dryly*) I have no doubt a person may get to Heaven that way.
(*Laughter*)
SPEAKER. We are gratified to hear you say that, Mr. Kennedy. But let us get on with the oath, shall we?
KENNEDY. Mr. Speaker, Article Six of the Constitution declares, "No religious test shall ever be required as a qualification to any public office or public trust under the United States."
SPEAKER. You are asked to uphold the Constitution of the State of Maryland. I might inform the Gentleman from Washington County that the Constitution of Maryland is older than the Constitution of the United States.
KENNEDY. This oath of office makes it impossible for citizens who are not Christian to be seated here.
SPEAKER. Mr. Kennedy, I was not aware that Jews and Mohammedans are numerous in your constituency.
KENNEDY. Sir, is it the custom of this body to insult new delegates?
SPEAKER. Not at all, Mr. Kennedy. I was merely making an observation.
KENNEDY. There is not a single Jew resident in Washington County. In fact, I have not met a single Jew in Maryland.

VOICE. *(Off)* Then, in Heaven's name, take the oath and be done.

SPEAKER. Exactly, Mr. Kennedy. Take the oath and be done.

(Pause)

KENNEDY. I cannot, Mr. Speaker.

SPEAKER. Why not?

KENNEDY. Because I am an American and a Christian. Article Six, Mr. Speaker, of the United States Constitution. Chapter Twenty-five, verse ten of the third book of the Bible: "Proclaim liberty throughout all the land unto all the inhabitants thereof."

SPEAKER. Mr. Kennedy, I ask you again . . . do you swear the oath?

KENNEDY. You ask me to hold my hand on the Bible . . . the Bible that declares the oath to be false and injurious.

(Pause)

SPEAKER. Mr. Clerk, you will proceed with the next order of business. Mr. Kennedy does not take the oath. Mr. Kennedy is not a member of this Legislature.

(Sound of gavel)

(Music: Bridge to narrative theme and down)

NARRATOR. Incident in the House of Delegates in the town of Annapolis, Maryland in the year of 1818—but an incident that was not closed. It could not be closed; for a man called Jefferson had said: "We are not to expect to be translated from despotism to liberty in a featherbed." Jefferson said it and Thomas Kennedy was of the party of Jefferson. *(Music out)*

The incident was not closed. Now Thomas Kennedy received a visitor.

SULLIVAN. The name is Sullivan, Mr. Kennedy. Jeremiah T. Sullivan.

KENNEDY. What can I do for you, sir?

SULLIVAN. Go back to the House of Delegates and take the oath.

KENNEDY. Mr. Sullivan, I don't know why you came. I don't know who sent you, but I'll trouble you to mind your own business.

SULLIVAN. Spoken like a man. (*Chuckles*) A fine temper like that and you're not Irish! What a pity. (*Pause*) You ask me to mind my own business?

KENNEDY. I do, Mr. Sullivan.

SULLIVAN. This is my business. It wasn't so many years ago a Catholic couldn't sit in the House of Delegates. Did you know that now?

KENNEDY. Yes, I do. What do you think I'm trying to do.

SULLIVAN. Kennedy, in Maryland before the Revolution, a Catholic, because he was a Catholic, paid twice the land tax. A Catholic servant from Ireland paid a tax of twenty shillings. If a Catholic man died the law said that his children could be taken from the widow. You see, Mr. Kennedy, I'm minding my own business now.

KENNEDY. It's not altogether clear, Mr. Sullivan.

SULLIVAN. I'm coming to the point. Why did it take so many years to change the law?

KENNEDY. You tell me.

SULLIVAN. I'll do that. Because laws are written and changed in the Legislature; you can't change a law when you don't sit in the Legislature.

KENNEDY. That's why you want me to take the oath?

SULLIVAN. That's why.

KENNEDY. It's a good reason, Mr. Sullivan.

SULLIVAN. Think it over.

KENNEDY. All right, Mr. Sullivan, I'll think it over.

SULLIVAN. I'll shake your hand now. (*Pause*) One more thing.

KENNEDY. Yes, Sullivan?

SULLIVAN. Kennedy . . . that's a fine name.

KENNEDY. Thank you.

SULLIVAN. You're sure now?

KENNEDY. Sure? Sure of what?

SULLIVAN. Was it Scotland you really came from and not Ireland? Kennedy, are you sure?
(*Music: Bridge*)
(*Sound of Gavel*)
SPEAKER. Proceed, Mr. Clerk.
CLERK. Do you, Thomas Kennedy, solemnly swear or affirm that you will protect and defend the Constitution of the State of Maryland?
KENNEDY. I do.
CLERK. Upon the true faith of a Christian.
KENNEDY. (*Slowly*) Upon the true faith of a *Christian*.
SPEAKER. I congratulate you, Mr. Kennedy, on your good sense.
KENNEDY. Mr. Speaker.
SPEAKER. You have the floor.
KENNEDY. I offer a resolution.
SPEAKER. What is your resolution, Mr. Kennedy?
KENNEDY. I offer a resolution calling for the appointment of a committee to consider placing all citizens on an equal footing in this state.
(*Voices up, ad lib protest*)
VOICE. (*Off*) The Gentleman from Washington County is entirely out of order.
ANOTHER. (*Off*) If Mr. Kennedy does not like Maryland, let him return to Scotland.
THIRD. (*Off*) The question is out of order.
KENNEDY. Mr. Speaker, I ask you to put the resolution before the House.
VOICE. (*Off*) Mr. Speaker, I move we adjourn.
KENNEDY. I protest, sir. There is a question before the House. The motion to adjourn is out of order.
SPEAKER. Mr. Kennedy, you are new in this body and entitled to your ignorance. I must inform you, that a motion to adjourn is never out of order.
BRECKENRIDGE. (*Off*) I rise on a point of special privilege.

SPEAKER. What is your point, Mr. Breckenridge?
BRECKENRIDGE. *(Moving on)* I confess to a sense of shame. Mr. Speaker, Gentlemen of the House of Delegates, we may abuse Mr. Kennedy here, but we abuse ourselves more. This is the Legislature of the people of Maryland. Mr. Kennedy is entitled to an honorable hearing. He is entitled to our courtesy. He is entitled to every privilege of this legislature. I appeal to your sense of decency.
VOICE. *(Off)* Mr. Speaker, motion to adjourn.
(Rap of gavel)
SPEAKER. The motion is to adjourn. All those in favor will say "Aye."
THREE VOICES. Aye.
SPEAKER. Only three for adjournment. Apparently, there is no need to call for the negative. The House of Delegates remains in session. Mr. Clerk, the roll-call on the resolution.
(Music: Bridge to narrative theme and down)
NARRATOR. The resolution carried. A first small step in a Maryland incident. A Committee of three was appointed to report. On December 9, 1818, Thomas Kennedy rose before the House of Delegates.
(Music: Out)
(Rapping of gavel)
KENNEDY. Your committee introduces a bill, a bill entitled: An Act to extend to those professing the Jewish religion, the same rights and privileges that are enjoyed by Christians.
(Rapping of gavel)
(Music: Narrative theme and down)
NARRATOR. Incident in the Maryland Legislature—and an incident which was not closed. The Bill was defeated. Yes, Jefferson was right: "We are not to expect to be translated from despotism to liberty in a featherbed." During the ses-

sion of the Legislature in the following year, once again the bill was introduced, and once again it was defeated. (*Music out*) Kennedy and Breckenridge continued the work of the committee.

BRECKENRIDGE. Mr. Kennedy, I believe you've already met Mr. Sullivan.

SULLIVAN. He's practically married to me, Mr. Breckenridge . . . and he can't forgive me because I'm not somebody else's wife.

(*Laughter*)

BRECKENRIDGE. Will you be seated, sir.

SULLIVAN. That I will.

(*Pause*)

KENNEDY. Sullivan, Mr. Breckenridge tells me you're not happy over the Bill I've introduced.

SULLIVAN. You're right there. I don't like it.

KENNEDY. You're a hard man to please, Sullivan.

SULLIVAN. It's the Dublin blood in me.

KENNEDY. I'm trying to remove the religious test. Sullivan, I thought that was what we both wanted.

SULLIVAN. Sure. But your bill does not remove the religious test.

KENNEDY. What in Heaven's name does it do?

SULLIVAN. It substitutes tolerance for intolerance.

KENNEDY. Good Lord, and is there anything wrong with that?

SULLIVAN. Sure.

KENNEDY. How?

SULLIVAN. Tolerance is no virtue, Mr. Kennedy. A man tolerates the other fellow only when he thinks the other fellow is less than he. I think tolerance is a rotten word.

(*Pause*)

KENNEDY. Yes, you have something there, Sullivan.

SULLIVAN. The Maryland Legislature can't give me permission to worship God as a Catholic. I'd spit clean in their eye. They can't give Breckenridge here permission to worship as an Episcopalian. And they can't give my good friend Captain Reuben Etting permission to worship as a Jew, because when did the Maryland Legislature last speak to God?

KENNEDY. You are absolutely right, Sullivan. What do you propose?

SULLIGAN. Take out the word "Jew" from your Bill. Put the word "all" in its place.

KENNEDY. Breckenridge, do you agree?

BRECKENRIDGE. You better go slow, Kennedy. You'll be attacked as irreligious.

KENNEDY. I won't let them. Religion is in my bones. It's in the Declaration of Independence. It's in the American Constitution. Breckenridge, I'm a religious man; government without the spirit of religion is like a bird without wings, but, by Heaven, we're not going to allow the Legislature to make a political club out of religion.

(*Pause*)

SULLIVAN. Kennedy, now don't deceive a believing man. Are you sure it's Scotland you come from?

(*Music: Bridge to narrative theme*)

NARRATOR. Thomas Kennedy amended his Bill. For the third time, the Bill came before the House of Delegates and for the third time the Bill was defeated. Then Thomas Kennedy returned to Washington County to stand for reelection. (*Music out*) And now he was a marked man. (*Build crowd, swell and hold under*)

GALLOWAY. (*Shouting above crowd*) I tell you, Tom Kennedy wants to strike from our laws the last protection of true religion. (*Crowd down*) This bill is the spawn of the devil. That's what it is. Where does he come from? Scotland ... a country flooded with infidels. And I'll tell you where he's not going. He's not going back to the Legislature.

VOICE. Good for you Galloway. Give him both barrels.

GALLOWAY. I tell the people of Washington County, I tell you Tom Kennedy is half Jew and the other half ain't Christian.

(*Raucous laughter*)

VOICE. (*Off*) Shut up, Galloway.

(*Voices ad lib, menacing.*)

GALLOWAY. Shucks, I don't mind that, he's Kennedy's man and what do you expect from a pig but a grunt?

(*Laughter*)

KENNEDY. (*Off*) He's not my man, Galloway.

(*Pause*)

KENNEDY. (*Coming on*) I don't need anyone to talk for me. Mr. Gabby, you can put down that shotgun, I've got no weapons on me. You too, Joe Merrick. (*Pause*) Seems to me our state has been advancing backwards for a long time. We seem to get one day older and two days worse.

GALLOWAY. Kennedy, I don't like you and I don't like your Bill.

KENNEDY. Mr. Galloway, that's your inalienable right as an American.

GALLOWAY. Now, get out.

KENNEDY. I'll say what I have to first.

GALLOWAY. I said get out.

VOICE. (*Off*) Let him talk, Galloway.

KENNEDY. Thank you. (*Pause*) I want you to understand that I'm against the religious test because I'm an American. That test reminds me that I'm a Protestant and that another man is a Catholic. That test divides us. That test justifies the Massachusetts Puritans who drove out the Quakers. That test justifies the Virginia bigots who drove out the Catholics.

GALLOWAY. Are you done, Mr. Kennedy?

KENNEDY. No, I'm not done. Galloway, go home and pick up your Bible and show me one word in it that justifies the proscription of any man because of his religious sentiments.

GALLOWAY. Kennedy, don't tell me to read the Bible.

KENNEDY. Galloway, at Christmas time you say "Good will to men." To what men? Galloway, it's either to all men or to no men.

VOICE. (*Off*) Now, Kennedy, we've heard enough.

KENNEDY. No you haven't. You can't take a religion which flames with justice and make it an excuse for bigotry. You can't use it to cover the narrowness of your own heart. (*Pause*) All right, Galloway, it's your meeting.

(*Music: Narrative theme and down*)

NARRATOR. Washington County voted . . . and Thomas Kennedy was defeated for re-election. But in the other counties of Maryland there were also changes. From Frederick County and Montgomery, from Carroll and Prince George Counties, there were new faces in the House of Delegates. For one year Thomas Kennedy remained at home and carried the fight to his own constituency.

(*Music: Up for montage theme and down*)

ONE. Kennedy, there's a new Speaker in the House. They say he wants you back.

KENNEDY. I'll be back. Come on. We've got work.

(*Music: Up and down*)

(*Voices*)

KENNEDY. I read to you from the First Amendment of the United States Constitution: "Congress shall make no law respecting an establishment of religion or prohibiting the free exercise thereof."

(*Music: Up and down*)

TWO. Kennedy, what's Jefferson got to do with it?

KENNEDY. Listen: "Our civil rights have no dependence on our religious professions any more than our opinions in physics or geometry."

(*Music: Up and down*)

KENNEDY. People of Washington County . . . We've got to prove to the whole world that it's wrong for men to have only enough religion to hate.

(*Music: Up to narrative theme and down*)

NARRATOR. The citizens of Washington County returned Thomas Kennedy to the Maryland Legislature. Once again he stood before the Speaker's Table in the House of Delegates.

(*Music: Out*)

(*Gavel*)

KENNEDY. I speak as an American citizen. I beg leave only to remind this House that the honors of office in our republic are not assumed but conferred; not usurped but bestowed by popular confidence. I say to you that to disqualify any class of citizens is for the people to disqualify themselves. This same principle of disqualification stains nations, tramples the charities of life, places arms in the hands of men for bloody war.

VOICE. (*Off*) Mr. Kennedy, it is not expedient to make innovations in the Constitution of Maryland.

KENNEDY. Sir, that is the language of prejudice. The American people were an innovation. The sun that shines each day is each day's innovation.

ANOTHER. (*Off*) I am not convinced. Mr. Speaker, I say to the Gentleman from Washington County, that no man has a right to complain of being excluded from office if he does not conform to the prevailing religious sentiment of the State.

A THIRD. (*Off*) Answer that, Kennedy.

KENNEDY. I do. What sort of God do you worship? Is the God you worship a fool? Does the smell of your persecution rise up to Him as incense? I tell you again . . . opinion should be answered by opinion. Religion is the opinion of a man's conscience. The interposition of the state in matters of opinion is improper.

VOICE. (*Off*) All right, Kennedy . . . suppose we do exercise a compulsion. It's mild enough. We don't molest any one.

KENNEDY. It's not the degree of compulsion, sir, which renders it improper; the act of interposing your authority is improper. Religion is a matter between man and his God. Gentlemen, this is the right of conscience which is so badly understood throughout the world, and which I regret to say is so little understood here.

ANOTHER. (*Off*) Gentlemen, this debate has taken up too much of the Legislature's time.

KENNEDY. Sir, the only way to close the debate is to vote for the Bill.

THIRD. (*Off*) Call the question, Mr. Speaker.

(*Voices ad lib . . . Call the question*)

(*Gavel pounding*)

SPEAKER II. Gentlemen, the Bill before the House of Delegates is to amend the Constitution by extending to all the citizens of Maryland the same civil rights and religious privileges that are enjoyed by all under the Constitution of the United States. (*Pause*) Mr. Clerk, you may proceed with the roll call. Gentleman, the question. Shall we pass the Bill?

CLERK. Harris.
ONE. No.
CLERK. Gantt.
TWO. No.
CLERK. Garner.
THREE. No.
CLERK. Grubb.
FOUR. No.
CLERK. Dalrymple.
ONE. Yes.
CLERK. Hughlet.
TWO. No.
CLERK. Kilgour.
THREE. Yes.
CLERK. Kennedy.

KENNEDY. Yes.
CLERK. Banning.
FOUR. No.
CLERK. Hawkins.
ONE. Yes.
CLERK. Welch.
TWO. Yes.
CLERK. Milliard.
THREE. Yes.
CLERK. Wickes.
FOUR. Yes.
CLERK. Estep.
ONE. Yes.

(*Music: Sneak in and hold*)

CLERK. Brooke.
TWO. Yes.
CLERK. Smith.
THREE. Yes.
CLERK. Chapman.
FOUR. Yes.
CLERK. Semmes.
SPEAKER. Yes.
CLERK. Rogerson.
VOICE. Yes.

(*Music: Up for bridge and down*)

NARRATOR. February 26, 1826. Thomas Kennedy's Bill . . . carried by the Maryland House of Delegates. (*Pause*) Incident in the history of the American people. But the incident is not closed. The incident never closes. Every generation must make its own fight for freedom—every generation in every age.

KENNEDY. Lord, who shall dwell in Thy tabernacle? Who shall ascend into the hill of the Lord? Even he that hath clean hands and a pure heart—he shall receive the blessing from the Lord.

NARRATOR. A prayer of thanksgiving. "Blessed art Thou O Lord, Who has kept us in life and sustained us unto this day." Yes, a prayer of thanksgiving.
(*Music: Curtain*)

A PITY FOR THE LIVING

A PITY FOR THE LIVING

Mention the name of Sholom Aleichem in any house where Yiddish is spoken and read and instantly you are among friends. There are tender smiles for you, a glass of tea which you may not refuse, and a nostalgic story of the old country. This is a tribute to the place occupied by Yiddish literature's great genius; a genius, incidentally, who could not tower above the people because he was the people.

A Pity for the Living is tragedy, as all sensitive childhood is tragedy. There are some children for whom living can be endurable only if the process of growth is also a process of callousing. In the Ghetto of which Sholom Aleichem wrote this was especially hard.

In adapting this story it was necessary to expand the slender original by creating characters, supplying the narration and inventing much of the dialogue. Ordinarily, this is not much of a problem; but Sholom Aleichem is all mood and mood is fragile. Adapting A Pity for the Living *was like translating a poem. The production was helped by Morris Mamorsky's delicate narrative score.*

Michael Artist was the Levi of the story. Others in the cast were Adelaide Klein, Daniel Ocko, Juano Hernandez, Eleanor Audley, Richard Keith, Ben Cooper, Charles Nevil, and Joan Lazer. Last but not least was Donald Bain. Mr. Bain never speaks through a microphone. His vocal organs are too busy making the sounds of birds crying, dogs barking, cats meowing, roosters crowing, lambs bleating, etc.

A Pity for the Living appears in this volume through the courtesy of Mrs. B. Z. Goldberg, daughter of Sholom Aleichem.

A PITY FOR THE LIVING

(*Music: Establish narrative theme and down*)

LEVI. Do you know something? Every grown-up was once a little boy or a little girl. It's hard to believe, isn't it? I find it very hard. Do you think the Czar of Russia was once a little boy? Teacher says so. Of course I believe Teacher, but I'll tell you something. Of all the grown-ups I know, the only one who was ever really and truly a little boy was Teacher. I know. (*Music out*) Because Teacher is very good. He sees certain things.

TEACHER. Levi, look at that little fly on the wall.

LEVI. This one, Teacher?

TEACHER. Don't hurt him, Levi.

LEVI. I won't, Teacher.

TEACHER. Levi, all creatures are dear to the Lord. That is why even a fly on the wall must not be hurt ... out of pity for the living.

(*Pause*)

LEVI. All creatures, Teacher? Even a spider?

TEACHER. Even a spider. If the spider deserved to die, then the Lord Himself would slay him. Levi, there is the pain of all living things and you and I must pity the living.

LEVI. Do you see why I know that Teacher once was a little boy? I believe the things that he tells me. Only I wish I could ask certain questions. If we are to have pity for the living, why do people slaughter cows and calves and little sheep every day of the week. And not only cows and other animals, but people. Don't men slaughter one another? Don't they ride on horses, and whip them and dig in their sharp spurs until blood comes? I have made up my mind. I will never do harm to any living creature. May God punish me if I ever do.

(*Music: Bridge into:*)

(*Sound of water poured into basin*)

LEVI. Mama, the fish is still alive. His tail is flapping in the water.

MOTHER. Out of my way, Levi. The fish has to be prepared for supper.

LEVI. Mama, the fish wants to go back to the river where he belongs.

MOTHER. Levi, stop that nonsense and get out of my way. There are a million things to do. Instead of standing around and talking, do something useful. Scrape the horseradish.

LEVI. Yes, Mama. Only, Mama . . .

MOTHER. Levi!

LEVI. Yes, Mama. Only it's a pity. It's a pity for the living.

MOTHER. Levi, what are you talking about? Of whom is it a pity?

LEVI. It's a pity for the little fishes.

MOTHER. Now who told you that?

LEVI. The Teacher.

MOTHER. The Teacher?

LEVI. Yes, Mama.

MOTHER. Levi, you're a little fool and your Teacher is a big fool. Scrape the horseradish. Go on, scrape the horseradish.

(*Music: Narrative theme and down*)

LEVI. Poor little fish. I'm not able to do anything for you. There you are. They're going to take you, and scrape away your scales, they're going to rip you open, cut you in pieces, put you in a pot, cover you with salt and pepper, put you on the fire, and let you boil and simmer, and simmer, and simmer, and simmer. Little fish, don't grown-up people have any pity for the living?

(*Music: Up and down*)

LEVI. They don't understand. No one understands except Teacher. Velvel the poultry butcher doesn't understand. Do you know what a poultry butcher is? He takes a sharp knife, and he says a blessing, and he kills chickens and roosters.

(*Music: Out*)

(*Rooster crowing*)

VELVEL. Be still, you little wretch.

(*Rooster crowing louder*)

VELVEL. Levi, stop pulling at me.

LEVI. (*Crying*) Please, let him run away. He wants to be free. He wants to live. He wants to talk to the hens and to eat corn and drink water. Don't murder him.

VELVEL. I will give you a spanking in one minute. How dare you call me a murderer?

LEVI. You are.

VELVEL. Go away before I brain you. I'm not a murderer. I am a butcher. I perform the commandment of the Lord. I speak His blessing. Now get away from me.

LEVI. Let go of the rooster. Murderer. You're a murderer.

VELVEL. Levi, people would go hungry without my work.

LEVI. They wouldn't.

VELVEL. Levi, don't make me angry. I'm not a murderer. Only a good and learned man is permitted to be a butcher. For instance, a man who cannot hear is not allowed to do the work. (*Rooster up*) Be still, I'm explaining about us to the boy.

LEVI. I don't want to hear your explanations.

VELVEL. I have to tell you. A man who cannot hear is not allowed to do this work. Because then he wouldn't hear the cry of pain, and he would become calloused to the work. Levi, where are you going?

LEVI. (*Crying*) I hate you. You have no pity for the living. You are a heathen.

(*Music: Narrative theme and down*)

LEVI. He put down the rooster and he spanked me. I didn't care. The rooster got away. I was glad. Without grown-ups this would be a good world.

(*Music: Up and out quickly under*)

LEVI. There is a woman who helps my mother with the cooking. She is blind in one eye. I call her "Fruma of the one eye." She has no heart.

(*Sound of blows*)

(*Cat meowing in pain*)

FRUMA. You filthy, thieving cat. That will teach you a lesson. And that. And that. And that.

(*Cat meowing and fades*)

LEVI. You shouldn't have beat the cat.

FRUMA. In one minute I will beat you.

LEVI. Fruma, you are a wicked woman. What did the cat do to you?

FRUMA. She stole a chicken liver from the board. Right from here.

LEVI. She didn't. There are the chicken livers.

FRUMA. Levi, have more respect for older people. I say the cat stole a chicken liver. I had seven chickens. There should be seven chicken livers. Count them. There are only six now. Wait till I get my hands on that thieving cat.

(*Pause*)

LEVI. Fruma!

FRUMA. What do you want?

LEVI. There are not seven chickens.

FRUMA. What?

LEVI. There are only six chickens. And if there are only six chickens, how can there be more than six chicken livers?

FRUMA. Hmm. (*Pause*) That's right. There are only six at that. Well, I made a mistake.

LEVI. Pss, pss, pss. Here, cat. Come here, cat, I won't hurt you.

(*Cat meows softly*)

LEVI. Nice cat. Good old cat. (*Pause*) Fruma, you accused the cat wrongly. You punished her. Now apologize.

FRUMA. In the name of the Five Books of Moses, what did you say?

LEVI. Apologize to the cat. You beat the cat for nothing. You committed a sin. It was a pity for the living. Apologize to the cat.

FRUMA. Out of this kitchen. Out of this kitchen this very instant.

LEVI. The Lord will punish you. Fruma, He will.

FRUMA. If you don't go away, I'll give it to you across the face with the towel.

LEVI. (*Moving off*) I'm going. But the pain of the living will rise straight up into the ear of God. You will be punished.

FRUMA. (*Shouting*) You little monster, don't you dare say that to me. I'm a pious woman, do you hear? (*Pause*) Lord Almighty! Where in the world do such children come from?

(*Music: Bridge to narrative theme and down*)

LEVI. Where in the world do the grown-ups come from? I do not believe that they were ever children. Not ever. And Fruma most of all. She was born a grown-up. She cuts fish up and puts it into a pot. She doesn't apologize to the cat and yesterday a pot slipped from her hands, and the dog Sirko was scalded with boiling water. (*Music out*) He moaned and muttered and licked his sores. My heart melted for the dog Sirko.

(*Dog yelping and crying*)

LEVI. Good old Sirko. Ssh. Ssh. Don't run away from me. I'm Levi. I won't do you any harm. Not me. Oh, no, Sirko, not me. Don't run away. Good dog. Please don't run away. I'm not a grown-up.

(*Dog barks slightly off*)

LEVI. (*Panting*) Sirko, don't make me chase you. I have pity for the living.

(*Dog barks a bit further off*)

LEVI. Sirko, wait, Sirko . . . Sirko, I have ointment for your burns.

FATHER. (*Projecting*) Levi! Levi! Stop chasing that dog.

LEVI. Papa, I want to .. . I've got . . .

FATHER. (*Off*) You little wretch. I saw it with my own eyes. Come here. (*Moving on*) Come right here. I saw you. To think that a son of mine would do such a thing!

LEVI. Papa, he's going to get away.

FATHER. Oh, you shameless one, you dog-beater.

LEVI. Papa, I'm not a dog-beater. I was running after him in order to . . .

FATHER. Not another word. Down across my knees.

LEVI. (*Protesting ad lib*)

FATHER. Not another word, you dog-beater. This will teach you. (*Sound of spanking*) And this also. (*Spanking*) Be still, you dog-beater. (*Spanking continues*)

LEVI. (*Crying*) Oh, Papa, Papa, have you no idea of the pain of all living things?

(*Music: Bridge to narrative theme and down*)

LEVI. There is no justice any place. When your own father won't listen to you . . . there's nothing left in the whole world. I have to take the ointment for the dog and rub it on myself.

(*Music: Up and out*)

(*Dinner sounds*)

MOTHER. Levi, we're all finished, and you haven't touched a thing.

FATHER. Don't talk to him.

MOTHER. But a boy has to eat.

FATHER. He's a dog-beater and a cry-baby and I'm thoroughly disgusted with him.

LEVI. Papa, I am not a dog-beater. I was running after the dog because Fruma the cook . . .

FATHER. And you are a tattle-tale. I do not like tattle-tales.

You may leave this table. We will sing the Grace after meals without you.

LEVI. Yes, Papa.

(*Pause*)

MOTHER. And be careful of your new clothes. I don't want you wandering in the fields and soiling them.

LEVI. Yes, Mama.

FATHER. Leave the room, Levi, you are excused.

(*Pause*)

(*Door shuts*)

MOTHER. I don't like the way he looks. I don't like it at all.

FATHER. If you please, we will defer all conversation until Grace has been sung.

(*Cantor: Sings Grace ... Hold in the clear and then down*)

LEVI. It isn't very good to have to stand outside a door when Grace is being sung. If Papa had ever been a boy himself, he would have realized that. May God keep me from ever being a grown-up.

(*Cantor: In the clear and start to fade*)

LEVI. I didn't want to stand and listen. I hated them. They didn't understand. They didn't understand anything. So I went to the Teacher's house. But on the way I had to stop. Because there were two peasant boys . . . and they were doing a terrible thing.

BOY. Give me that rock, I'll show you. (*Expels breath as he throws*)

ANOTHER. You missed. Now watch me.

LEVI. Don't throw the rock at the bird's nest.

ANOTHER. Beat it. (*He throws*)

(*Crying of birds*)

ANOTHER. (*Exultant*) Got it. I can throw, heh?

(*Birds high on mike and then cut*)

LEVI. You killed the birds. They're dead. They're dead. And you killed them. And you're not even grown-ups.

BOY. Do you know what he's talking about?

ANOTHER. Me? Nah. He must be sick or something.

LEVI. Why did you do it? Why did you do it? What did they do to you? What harm did they do?

BOY. It's none of your business. Beat it.

LEVI. Why did you throw that stone? They let you alone. Why did you do it?

ANOTHER. You little sissy, they weren't any more than birds. Ordinary little birds.

LEVI. What if they were birds? Have you no pity for the living?

(*Pause*)

BOY. You want to take care of him or do you want me to?

ANOTHER. We'll do it together.

(*Sound of blow*)
(*Another blow*)

ANOTHER. Hey, the little sissy hits back.

BOY. I'll fix him. (*Pause*) Now ain't that a pretty hat.
(*Sound of cloth tearing*)

LEVI. That's wicked. That's worse than hitting me. My mother made that hat.

(*Cloth tears again*)
(*Sound of blow*)

BOY. Hit back, will you? Hold him. Hold his arms.
(*Ad lib struggle*)

BOY. (*Panting*) Now ... let's see. That's a nice clean shirt.
(*Shirt is torn*)

BOY. And this jacket. (*Mimicking*) My, what lovely buttons! Do you want this button, you little sissy?

LEVI. Yes, I do.

BOY. (*Laughs*) Here it is, sissy, I'll give it to you.
(*Material tears*)

ANOTHER. Here's another button.
(*Material rips*)
(*Material rips as boys roar with laughter*)
(*Music: Bridge*)

(*Door opens and shuts*)
(*Pause*)
FATHER. Levi!
LEVI. Yes, Papa.
FATHER. (*Softly*) Come here.
LEVI. Yes, Papa.
MOTHER. (*On a gasp*) His fine new clothes. Oh, Levi.
LEVI. I'm sorry they're torn, Mama.
(*Pause*)
FATHER. My dear Levi, I think you are going to be sorrier in a moment.
MOTHER. How did your eye get blackened?
LEVI. There were some birds in a tree.
MOTHER. I see.
FATHER. And your shirt is in ribbons also because of the birds?
LEVI. Yes, Papa. It is the pain of all living things.
(*Pause*)
FATHER. I'm glad to hear it. Come with me, Levi. We shall investigate the pain of all living things.
(*Music: Narrative theme and down*)
LEVI. Naturally I got a good beating, which I deserved. Then when Papa was finished, Mama looked at my clothes.
MOTHER. You ragged fool.
LEVI. I forgave Papa because he beat me, but why did she call me a ragged fool? Why? (*Pause*) I am never going to cry again. Never. I have made up my mind. There's no use crying in this world. It doesn't do any good. From now on I shall have nothing to do with grown-up people.
PERALLE. You may play with me, Levi. I am not a grown-up.
LEVI. Yes, I played with Peralle. (*Music fading*) Because she was a little girl, and a cripple, who used to be put in the sun, and who never harmed anything. Not even a spider.
PERALLE. I like you, Levi.
LEVI. I like you, Peralle. I do not wish to become grown-up. But if I have to, I shall marry you.

PERALLE. I cannot marry any one. I can't walk, or stand, or do anything. I can only sit.

LEVI. Then we shall sit together.

PERALLE. Like this?

LEVI. Peralle, why are you so skinny?

PERALLE. I don't know, Levi.

LEVI. I know! It is because you have pity for the living?

PERALLE. I don't know, Levi. Is it good to have pity for the living?

LEVI. I'm not sure any more.

PERALLE. But you think so?

LEVI. Yes.

PERALLE. Then I have pity for the living.

LEVI. Even a chicken?

PERALLE. Yes.

LEVI. And you will not eat chicken fat smeared on bread?

PERALLE. Mustn't I, Levi?

LEVI. Never.

PERALLE. I shall never eat chicken fat smeared on bread. Never.

LEVI. Then we are engaged, Peralle. We are definitely engaged.

(*Music: Narrative theme and down*)

LEVI. Every day after that, I would sit in the sun with my Peralle, and I would explain to her about the pain of all living things, and what the Teacher said. When the sun moved, I used to pick her up and carry her. She was very light. She used to put her arms around my neck, and her fingers would touch my face, her small, skinny, little fingers.

PERALLE. I like you, Levi.

LEVI. I like you also, Peralle. You will be a kind wife. We shall never quarrel.

(*Music: Up and down*)

LEVI. She would hug me closer and closer and rest her head

on my shoulder. (*Music fading*) Every day like that. Then the pogrom started.

(*Voice shouting off mike . . . Add sound of mob*)

FATHER. (*Projecting*) They're burning the synagogue now. They'll be coming for the houses soon. Get the children into the woods. Get all the children. Get them to safety.

(*Music: Bridge*)

(*Voices briefly and cut on*)

FATHER. Levi, I asked you not to come here.

LEVI. Papa, I wanted to tell you that our house is still standing. They didn't touch very much.

VOICE. Send the boy away.

FATHER. Levi, go home and wait for me.

(*Pause*)

LEVI. Papa, what's that?

FATHER. It's not for children to see.

LEVI. Papa, who is that?

(*Pause*)

FATHER. Levi, please go home. Please.

LEVI. Papa, who is that? It's someone dead.

VOICE. They killed her. Poor innocent creature.

(*Pause*)

FATHER. Levi, don't look.

LEVI. I must look, Papa, you don't understand. We were engaged. (*Pause*) You see I'm not crying. I shall never cry again. I told that to Peralle. And now I have to keep my promise.

(*Music: Bridge*)

MOTHER. Levi.

LEVI. Yes, Mama.

MOTHER. I have made you a new suit of clothes.

LEVI. Thank you, Mama.

MOTHER. Levi, we must not weep. We must not sin. We must forget. We must forget.

LEVI. Yes, Mama.

(*Pause*)
MOTHER. Don't you want to go out and play?
LEVI. No.
MOTHER. Would you like to help me in the kitchen?
LEVI. All right, Mama.
MOTHER. Here's some horseradish. You can scrape if you want to, Levi.
LEVI. Yes, Mama.
(*Sound of horseradish scraped*)
MOTHER. Levi, Levi . . . oh, my little boy. You're crying.
LEVI. From the horseradish, Mama.
(*Sound out*)
MOTHER. Don't think of her, Levi. We must forget. Forgetting is so good.
LEVI. It's the horseradish.
MOTHER. Here is my apron. Go on, dry your eyes. Oh, Levi, it's such a pity for the dead and such a pity for the living. Wipe your eyes. Take my apron, and wipe your eyes. And blow your nose, too.
LEVI. (*He blows*)
MOTHER. Ssh. Ssh. Ssh. Don't cry, Levi. Don't cry, my Levi. Hush. Hush.
(*She hums softly*)
(*Music: Sneaks in and covers, hold under*)
LEVI. I let her hold me in her lap because it made her feel good. But grown-ups don't really understand. When grown-ups learn to become as serious as children then they will understand. First it was a fish, and then it was a rooster, and then a cat, and a dog, and two birds in a tree . . . and then it was Peralle. They don't understand. I don't ever want to be a grown-up.
(*Music: Curtain*)

A SOUND OF MUSIC
(The Story of Adolf Baller)

A SOUND OF MUSIC

In the summer of 1945 a reprint of Dean Jennings' Coronet *article, "Music Hitler Couldn't Silence," was given to me by Milton Krents, producer for the Jewish Theological Seminary of* THE ETERNAL LIGHT. *He explained that it was the story of Adolf Baller, a gifted young pianist whose hands were mashed to a pulp by Nazi sadists. I kept the reprint but didn't read it. Like many people I was tired of Nazi-persecution stories. Months later Dr. Moshe Davis, Program Editor of the series, mentioned the Jennings' article. It was a time when the newspapers were filled with revelations of systematic horror in Auschewitz and Buchenwald.*

A week later my wife and I sat among an overflow audience on the stage of the Brooklyn Academy of Music. The thousands present had come to hear Yehudi Menuhin; we had come to study the fingers of his accompanist.

I met Mr. Baller. He submitted to the interview with patient embarrassment, confirmed the facts in Mr. Jennings' article, added some additional data, and gave his reluctant permission for the dramatization, saying, "I don't want people to come to Yehudi Menuhin's concerts out of morbid curiosity. If they come, let it be for the music."

A Sound of Music *was produced on December 23, 1945. Mr. Baller's* Sonata in B Minor *supplied the inspiration for Morris Mamorsky's excellent score. Alexander Scourby portrayed Baller, Mitzi Gould was Edith. With an eye for dramatic irony Frank Papp cast Stefan Schnabel, son of the distinguished pianist, Artur Schnabel, as the Nazi intellectual. Others in the cast were Daniel Ocko, Joseph Boland, Gene Leonard and Luis Van Rooten.*

A SOUND OF MUSIC
(The Story of Adolf Baller)

(*Piano: Brahm's Intermezzo, Opus* 119, *No.* 3 . . . *Register and down*)

EDITH. He has good hands, hasn't he? Good hands to make a sound of music. And yet, they are not extraordinary hands. Rather small, in fact . . . delicate . . . with fingers slender. I think that whatever is unique in Adolf Baller comes from the spirit through those fingers. It's strange that I should say that. For a man's fingers are only flesh and bone. And bone is fragile and flesh bruises. But the human spirit is something more. It is like . . . like gold tried in the fire . . . it remains pure. Even in the furnace of adversity it remains pure. Once Adolf Baller was only a concert pianist with gifted hands. But today, I think that Adolf Baller is something more. And I think I know. Eight years ago I was his fiancée.

(*Piano: Up and down*)

EDITH. He was born in Poland, I lived in Austria. He was a pianist, I was a violinist. Our music brought us together. (*Piano fading*) In March 1938, Adolf Baller left my house in Vienna to rehearse the *Emperor Concerto* with the Vienna Philharmonic Orchestra. There was nothing strange in this. There was to be a concert at the Vienna Concert Hall, and Adolf Baller was a celebrated pianist. Nothing strange. Only the day was strange. It was March 11, 1938.

(*Footsteps hollow . . . Slight echo*)

BALLER. Johann, where is the orchestra? Am I too early?
JOHANN. The orchestra went home, Herr Baller.

95

BALLER. But we're supposed to rehearse.
JOHANN. The orchestra went home, Herr Baller.
BALLER. But, we have to prepare our concert.
JOHANN. No concert, Herr Baller. We're closing the concert hall. Take my advice and go home.
BALLER. Go home?
JOHANN. (*Projecting*) Ernst, see to the shutters. Make sure the lights are put out. (*Pause*) Go home, Herr Baller.
BALLER. Why? I don't understand.
JOHANN. Von Schuschnigg has resigned. Arthur Seyss-Inquart has succeeded him. (*Projecting*) Ernst, hurry with those shutters. Get a move on.
BALLER. Johann, what does it mean?
JOHANN. It means that the Nazis are here. Herr Baller, go home. Go home as fast as you can.
   (*Music: Bridge*)
   (*Car engine idling . . . Sound of cab horns far in background*)
ONE. Is that him?
TWO. Where?
ONE. Turning the corner.
TWO. That's the one. Signal the other car.
   (*Sound of horn*)
TWO. All right, let's go.
   (*Car roars in first, shift to high and stop with screech of brakes*)
   (*Door opens*)
ONE. All right, you.
TWO. We want to see you, Herr Baller.
BALLER. I don't know you.
ONE. Get into the car.
BALLER. What for?
ONE. Get into the car.
BALLER. I'm a Polish citizen, you can't do this.
TWO. (*Quietly*) I advise you, Herr Baller, to get into the car.

BALLER. You can't do this. I'll show you my passport. You've made a mistake.
TWO. Have we made a mistake, Heinrich?
ONE. Not at all.
BALLER. What authority do you have?
TWO. Heinrich, kindly show Herr Baller our authorization.
(*Sound of blow . . . Pause . . . Sound of second blow . . . Body falls*)
TWO. Good enough, Heinrich. Now give me a hand with the Jew.
(*Music: Chord as*)
(*Car engines race and build and are topped by*)
(*Music: Finish bridge and cut on:*)
(*Door slamming*)
THREE. (*He is an intellectual*) Who is this one?
TWO. Another Jew.
THREE. (*Casually*) All right.
TWO. This one is a pianist.
THREE. He is?
TWO. I thought you'd like to know.
THREE. Naturally, I like to know these things. (*Pause*) So, he is a pianist? Interesting.
BALLER. I am a Polish citizen. I demand to see the Polish Consul.
THREE. Do you?
BALLER. I demand that you notify my fiancée, Fraulein Edith Strauss.
THREE. (*Breaking in*) So you are a pianist, eh? (*Pause*) I should like to see your fingers, if you please. (*Pause*) I said I should like to see your fingers.
TWO. Do as he says.
BALLER. What are you going to do?
THREE. Oh, come . . . let's not be boorish. I am a man of aesthetic taste. I should like to see your fingers.
BALLER. Why?

TWO. Do as he says. Put your fingers on the table.
 (*Pause*)
BALLER. You don't talk like a hoodlum.
THREE. Thank you. (*Gently*) You will do as I say, please. Your fingers, if you please. (*Friendly*) That's better. (*Pause*) So these are the fingers of a pianist. Interesting. (*Pause*) Leave them on the table. I said leave them on the table. (*Pause*) All right.
TWO. Shall I hold his wrist?
THREE. Yes . . . if you will be so kind. By all means hold . . .
TWO. Herr Baller.
THREE. By all means hold Herr Baller's wrists. I wish to study his fingers.
 (*Music: Bridge to Bach . . . "Out of the Depths I Cry to Thee" . . . Hold under*)
EDITH. I waited for him. Tell me, have you ever waited? Have you ever sat in a darkened house . . . in the middle of a darkened city . . . waiting for a familiar step . . . for the clasp of a familiar hand . . . not a large hand . . . a hand with slender fingers . . . fragile fingers that make a sound of music? I waited. I waited through the night and I knew the meaning of the verse from the Psalm, "O Lord, out of the depths I cry to Thee."
 (*Music: Up and build . . . Then down*)
EDITH. My foster father went to the Polish Consul. (*Music fading*) Near Turkenschantz Strasse in the 18th District, they found Adolf Baller . . . Three days later the Nazis released him.
 (*Sound of car pulling up to curb*)
 (*Screech of brakes*)   (*Sound of horn*)
 (*Footsteps running on*)
DRIVER. Fraulein Strauss?
EDITH. (*Slightly breathless*) Yes, I'm Edith Strauss. Have you . . .
DRIVER. In the car.

(*Door opens*)
EDITH. He's in there?
DRIVER. All yours, Fraulein.
(*Pause*)
DRIVER. Well, what's the matter?
(*Pause*)
EDITH. There's been some mistake.
DRIVER. No mistake.
EDITH. I tell you there's been a mistake. I don't know this man.
DRIVER. No? Here. (*Crackle of paper*) His passport, Fraulein Strauss. No mistake.
(*Pause*)
EDITH. That . . . can't be Adolf Baller. I tell you . . . (*Scared . . . words mumbled*) That can't be Adolf Baller.
DRIVER. Do you want him, Fraulein, or don't you?
EDITH. That can't be Adolf Baller.
DRIVER. Fraulein, I haven't got all day. If you want your fiancée . . . well, you'll have to take him the way he is.
(*Music: Bridge*)
(*Sound of water poured into basin*)
(*Pitcher set down*)
(*Cloth dipped into basin . . . Then wrung out*)
BALLER. Is that you, Edith? I can't see.
EDITH. Yes, It's Edith.
BALLER. Edith, tell me about my fingers. Edith, find my hands.
(*Pause*)
EDITH. (*Dully*) They're not hands any more.
(*Pause*)
BALLER. They walked across my hands. (*Pause—Emotionless*) They beat me with clubs, they put their cigarettes out against me . . . they kicked me . . . but they walked across my hands . . . back and forth . . . back and forth.
(*Pause*)
(*Sound of cloth wrung out*)

BALLER. Edith, please speak to me?
(Pause)
BALLER. Edith, I can't see you. I can't open my eyes. I can't feel with my fingers. Edith, speak to me.
(Pause)
(Sound of cloth wrung out)
(Pause)
BALLER. All right, I know. My hands are broken. I'm never going to play again.
(Music: Bridge)
(Door shuts)
(Footsteps slowly and stop)
EDITH. Yes, Doctor.
DOCTOR. Sit down, Fraulein.
(Pause)
EDITH. Yes, Doctor?
DOCTOR. Fraulein, there appears to be a rupture of the kidney. *(Pause)* His eyes . . . are, well, I think he will see. Use this for the burns. *(Pause)* That's all, Fraulein.
EDITH. Doctor . . . his hands?
DOCTOR. I can't tell. His hands . . . they're not human hands now. I can't tell, Fraulein.
EDITH. You must tell me. Doctor, don't try to make it easy.
DOCTOR. Very well. The holes burnt in his hands . . . they'll heal, I think. I don't know how many fingers are broken. I don't know whether the bone is merely broken or entirely crushed. We'll have to wait till the swelling goes down. That's all, Fraulein.
(Pause)
EDITH. Doctor . . . will he . . .
DOCTOR. Fraulein, Adolf Baller will never be able to play the piano again.
(Music: Bridge to theme and down)
EDITH. Do you ever stand before the Sabbath candles? Do you ever say a Sabbath blessing? Do you open a holy book and

pray to God? Do you find consolation in words? Or in silence? Or in speech? Do you? But then your light has not gone out. What is yours is still yours. What is you is still you. But ten fingers . . . ten fingers, two hands . . . two hands of fragile bone and fragile flesh . . . that was Adolf Baller. Do you understand that? Those fingers were the altar of his synagogue. Those fingers were the expression of his spirit. And what was acceptable to God and good to men, was the sound of music from Adolf Baller's fingers. Do you understand that?

(*Music: Up and finish briefly*)

EDITH. We could no longer stay in Vienna. Even had they allowed it, the air of Vienna was acid on the tongue and dry in the throat. So we went to Budapest as soon as he was able to be moved. And in Budapest there were bone specialists.

DOCTOR II. So . . . so . . . so. Hmm. Herr Baller, you are also something of a composer, I understand? Try bending your fingers, Herr Baller. No . . . no pressure . . . don't strain. So . . . they do not bend?

BALLER. I can try again.

DOCTOR II. For today, it is enough.

BALLER. I'll try again.

DOCTOR II. No. No. Let us talk, Herr Baller. You are a composer also, yes?

EDITH. He's written a fine sonata for piano and violin.

DOCTOR II. It is good. Musical composition is fine.

BALLER. Doctor, I'm a pianist.

DOCTOR II. Still, to compose . . . that is even better. Is it not so, Fraulein?

(*Pause*)

BALLER. Why don't you say it, Doctor?

(*Pause*)

DOCTOR II. Herr Baller, I shall say it. It's no use.

BALLER. I'm going to play again.

DOCTOR II. You must face it, Herr Baller. It's no use. Be thankful that you have regained vision in one eye . . . your hands? I do not think so.

(*Pause*)

BALLER. Doctor, they didn't beat only me. They beat other people. When they brought me to the house near Turkenschantz Strasse the chairs and the furniture were floating. They were floating on human blood.

DOCTOR II. Why do you tell me this, Herr Baller?

BALLER. They didn't do it with passion, Doctor, don't you understand? They weren't angry. They were methodical.

DOCTOR II. Still, I do not . . .

BALLER. I don't know how to say it, Doctor. I've got to play again. If I don't play, they've killed me. We mustn't allow that, Doctor.

(*Pause*)

DOCTOR II. Can you bend your fingers, Herr Baller?

BALLER. Not today. But there's tomorrow.

DOCTOR II. Not tomorrow, Herr Baller.

BALLER. Doctor, we have to fight back. Music is the only thing I have.

(*Pause*)

EDITH. Doctor . . . will massage help?

DOCTOR II. Perhaps. In any case it will do no harm.

EDITH. I can do that then. I'll massage his hands. Every day . . . all the time . . . I'll massage until . . .

DOCTOR II. What is the good, Fraulein? You will waste your time and deceive each other with false hope. Some things are broken and are mended; some things are broken and are not to be mended. (*Pause*) I'm sorry. If you will excuse me, I must go now.

(*Footsteps*)

(*Door shuts*)

(*Pause*)

EDITH. I'll . . . I'll get you a cup of tea.

BALLER. No, Edith.
EDITH. It will be good for you.
BALLER. I don't want tea.
EDITH. I'll get a book then. I'll read to you.
BALLER. I don't want to be read to.
EDITH. You mustn't make it more difficult than it is. (*Moving off*) I'll be back in a moment.
BALLER. Don't go, Edith. Edith . . . come here . . . I want you to massage my hands . . . I want you to start now.
(*Music: Narrative theme and down*)
EDITH. How is it written? "Gold is tried in fire, and acceptable men are tested in the furnace of adversity." I massaged his hands. Fingers stiff, fingers no longer slender and delicate. The broken bones had come closer together but the flesh was numb and dull. Flesh no longer sensitive, flesh no longer willing to make a sound of music. I massaged the flesh. And Adolf Baller smiled. Can a man smile when his teeth are clenched? He smiled.
(*Music: Up and down*)
EDITH. Every day, every day of every week, every week of every month . . . the same smile. (*Music fading*) In Budapest, seven years ago, I married a man with broken hands.
(*Cantor: Wedding blessing—One Brocheh*)
(*Music: Sneaking in above . . . Up for bridge now and down*)
EDITH. One day soon after we were married . . . I came home . . . I put my key in the lock . . . I turned the key . . . but I did not open the door . . . because there was a sound . . .
(*Music out . . . Piano as a segue . . . Clumsily . . . Like a small child hitting the keys*) . . . it was a sound I heard . . . O Lord, it was not a sound of music . . . it was Adolf Baller's heart . . . (*Door opens . . . Sound louder*) His fingers were like clumsy childish hammers . . . but he was at the keyboard . . . and there was a look in his eyes. (*Cut piano*)
BALLER. Edith . . .

EDITH. Yes.
BALLER. You heard?
EDITH. I heard.
  (*Piano again*)
BALLER. I'm doing it.
EDITH. There's sweat on your face.
BALLER. Did you hear what I said . . . I can do it.
  (*Piano out*)
EDITH. Here's my handkerchief. Wipe your face.
BALLER. You'll see, Edith.
EDITH. On your forehead. It's all wet. Here.
BALLER. I said you're going to see. You're going to hear.
EDITH. Yes.
BALLER. Say you're glad. Edith, say you're glad.
  (*Pause*)
EDITH. I'm glad, darling.
  (*Music: Bridge*)
EDITH. Know what this is? An electric vibrator. Hold out your hands, darling. This is going to help.
  (*Sound of vibrator*)
  (*Piano: Register . . . Montage theme . . . Primitive scales and down*)
  (*Sound of vibrator*)
EDITH. They look better . . . even I can see that they look better. Hold out your hands, darling.
  (*Piano: Segue to chord scale . . . Chopped but strong and down*)
BALLER. Clench, unclench, clench, unclench . . . Dear Lord, but I'm tired.
EDITH. You can't stop now. You must go on.
  (*Piano: Segue to octaves and down*)
EDITH. I know it's only a wooden board. But that's the treatment. Now come on. Press. That's right. Press . . . stretch . . . press.
  (*Piano: Up full and down*)

DOCTOR. Here are the new x-ray plates. Mrs. Baller, I'd like to shake hands with you.

(*Piano: Scales full, vigorous and complicated, hold under*)

EDITH. Some things are broken and cannot be mended; and some things are broken . . . and while bone is fragile and flesh bruises, the spirit is strong. The human spirit stretching the bruised hands . . . hands and fingers pressing a wooden board, gaining strength . . . clenching, unclenching, stretching . . . days and weeks and months . . . and sweat on a man's face and a look in his eye . . . and a sound of music again.

(*Piano: Segue from scales to Baller Sonata and down*)
(*Violin: Enters below*)

EDITH. Sonata in B minor for violin and piano . . . sonata of Adolf Baller. And my violin no longer shut away in its case. Each man must affirm the human spirit for himself. Each man must render his testimony in his own time, in his own fashion. And this was Adolf Baller's testimony and his affirmation. We left Budapest for France. From France seven years ago we sailed as immigrants to America. Only the clothes we wore . . . only the music we brought . . . was all we could bring. A memory of pain and a sound of music.

(*Violin: Up with piano for twenty to thirty seconds and crossfade with:*)
(*Street noises, taxis honking, voices . . . cut on:*)
(*Door shuts*)

MANAGER. Mr. Baller, I can assure you that you'll like this concert tour.

BALLER. I hope so.

MANAGER. Take my word for it. I've been managing these things for a long time. I know a natural when I see one. People are going to come to hear you. Take my word for that.

BALLER. How do you mean?

MANAGER. Natural publicity, that's what. Your story isn't going to hurt at the box-office, if you know what I mean.
BALLER. I'm very grateful. But please . . . what has happened to me, has happened. I want to forget it.
MANAGER. But people will come to hear you because of it?
BALLER. I'm only one of thousands who came through it. I suffered much less than they. Besides . . .
MANAGER. Yes?
BALLER. I'm a musician. If people will come to hear the music, I shall be very glad. But I want them to listen to me only for the sake of the music.
MANAGER. Well . . .
BALLER. My wife and I have thought this through. It's how we want it.
MANAGER. All right . . . if you say so. (*Pause*) Now here's your itinerary. Complete list of train reservations, hotel reservations . . . the whole business. And . . . by the way, Baller . . .
BALLER. Yes?
MANAGER. Have you ever heard of Los Gatos?
BALLER. Is it something to eat?
MANAGER. (*Laughs*) No, it's a little town in California about fifty miles from San Francisco. How would you like to take a trip there?
BALLER. I don't know.
MANAGER. Man out there who'd like to see you.
BALLER. Is there?
MANAGER. Man called Menuhin . . . Yehudi Menuhin.
BALLER. He wants to see me?
MANAGER. That's right. Mr. Menuhin happens to need an accompanist.
BALLER. Me?
MANAGER. (*Laughing*) Here are your train reservations. I think you and Mrs. Baller are going to be happy in California.

(Music: Bridge to sonata . . . Orchestral . . . and down)

EDITH. Perhaps you received a letter this year, from your husband, or your son, or your brother? Perhaps they wrote to you that standing before the barracks, or in the crowded hospital wards, Yehudi Menuhin gave a concert. And perhaps they noticed the hands of his accompanist. There was nothing extraordinary about those hands. Merely the ten fingers of an American citizen called Adolf Baller. He made a sound of music and that was all. But this was his affirmation in his own time and his own fashion, that "gold is tried in fire and acceptable men are tested in the furnace of adversity." I would say more if I could. But when you stand on American ground . . . somewhere under the American sun . . . the words fill your heart and they choke your throat . . . and you are glad . . . and you do not speak.

(Music: The orchestra rises grandly in Baller's "Sonata in B minor" to curtain)

A RHODE ISLAND REFUGE

A RHODE ISLAND REFUGE

THE ETERNAL LIGHT *became a radio series with the broadcast on October 8, 1944 of* A Rhode Island Refuge. *It was probably as nervous an innovation as any in radio. There were many things against it. It had to overcome the entertainment industry's prejudice against religious drama. It had to overcome religion's uncertainty about radio. It had to break through the skepticism of the network's affiliated but independent stations. Finally, it had to build an audience not only in New York but in places like Bozeman, Montana and Jackson, Mississippi. The prospects seemed dubious.*

Nevertheless, A Rhode Island Refuge *was broadcast as scheduled. Present in the studio from the Jewish Theological Seminary were President Louis Finkelstein, Mrs. Cyrus Adler, Professor Saul Leiberman and Rabbi Moshe Davis, a circumstance which probably did not add to the composure of Director Ira Avery. However, for a first broadcast the script did rather well and a year later, on Armistice Day, when the program had more than doubled the number of stations carrying it,* A Rhode Island Refuge *received a second performance under the direction of Frank Papp.*

Both productions featured Alexander Scourby as the Narrator. Over a period of more than two years, during which time the series has employed radio's best talent, Mr. Scourby has remained a favorite. His performances are modest, clear, and perceptive. Others in the cast were Roger De Koven, Adelaide Klein, Gregory Morton, and Bernard Lenrow. Cantor David Putterman was the soloist, a role he has held ever since with Cantor Robert H. Segal in alternating cycles of thirteen weeks. Henri Nosco conducted the orchestra.

A RHODE ISLAND REFUGE

MORDECAI. They call it the Old Jewish Cemetery of Newport. From Narragansett Bay the land breeze rustles in the trees and the Rhode Island sun is clean and friendly on our graves.

(*Music: Sneak in narrative theme and hold behind*)

MORDECAI. They sleep so still beside me. Once so long ago they fled from Spain and Portugal, fled before the Inquisition and they wandered over the earth again. And here in Rhode Island they found refuge. And now they sleep . . . a final refuge . . . the last exodus. The headstones mellow in the rain . . . Lopez, Alvarez, Levy, Seixas, Touro. But over my grave there is no tablet. Only a nameless stone the color of earth. It does not matter. The grass is my comfort and it is warm and green and living. And yet, once I had a name and also a history. My name was Mordecai, a good name; and Benjamin was my father, a good man. And in the year 1760, when I was a boy, my father said to me:

(*Music: Out*)

FATHER. It hath been told thee, what is good, and what the Lord doth require of thee; only to do justly, and to love mercy and to walk humbly with thy God.

(*Music: Theme and under*)

MORDECAI. In Rhode Island there was reverence for God and reverence also for men, which is a fine thing. It was not so in the other colonies where Puritans persecuted Quaker and Anglican opposed the Catholic and both opposed the Jew. My father told me this and also how twenty-three Jews came to Peter Stuyvesant in New Amsterdam and were turned away. And how in despair they came to Rhode Island and Roger Williams said:

(*Music: Out*)

WILLIAMS. All men may walk here as their conscience persuades them, and every one in the name of his God.

(*Music: Theme and down*)

MORDECAI. And for five generations after Roger Williams we found sustenance in his words and the colony of Newport prospered greatly even beyond New York and Philadelphia. Aaron Lopez sent his ships far to the whale fisheries, Jacob Rivera introduced candles of spermaceti, James Lucena made soap such as had been made before in Castile, and some were silversmiths, and ironworkers, and merchants, and simple farmers. And Benjamin, my father, was likewise a merchant with a shop on Long Wharf. I remember still how he quarreled with Meyer Pollack (*Music out*) and why it came to pass.

(*Voices in background*)

POLLACK. Ten casks of nails.

FATHER. Check.

POLLACK. Fifteen bushels of wheat.

FATHER. Check.

POLLACK. One hundred pewter basins.

FATHER. Check.

POLLACK. One fine looking glass.

FATHER. Check.

POLLACK. Six barrels of molasses. (*Pause*) Benjamin, six barrels of molasses.

FATHER. I heard you.

POLLACK. Well?

FATHER. I don't like it.

POLLACK. To hear you talk, someone might think molasses isn't kosher.

FATHER. I want no part of it.

POLLACK. Are you crazy?

FATHER. Molasses means rum, doesn't it?
POLLACK. Of course.
FATHER. And rum means slaves, doesn't it?
POLLACK. What if it does? You're not trading in slaves.
FATHER. Why not, Meyer?
POLLACK. Who cares why not?
FATHER. I care. Because it is written thou shalt not abhor an Edomite for he is thy brother.
POLLACK. Many things are written and you can lose your mind trying to live up to it all.
FATHER. Meyer, are you a Jew?
POLLACK. What has that to do with it?
FATHER. You can't be half a Jew, or a quarter of a Jew, or a fifth of a Jew. You have to do what is written.
POLLACK. Look here, don't tell me what to do . . . I go to synagogue every day as good as any man. I don't mix milk and meat and I have faith in the Torah.
FATHER. Faith isn't enough. You cannot be a Jew only with your lips. You are a Jew every hour, every moment, in every act.
POLLACK. Excuse me, Benjamin, when I need a sermon, I'll listen to Rabbi Touro. And I think when I want to do business, I won't come here.
FATHER. I'm not quarreling with you, Meyer. But I won't deal in molasses when it's the blood of the slave trade.
POLLACK. Is that your last word?
FATHER. If you wish.
POLLACK. Good-bye.
FATHER. Good-bye, Meyer.
   (*Door slamming*)
   (*Music: bridge and segue to narrative theme and under*)
MORDECAI. They did not speak much to one another after that. And then they grew stiff-necked and did not speak at all. Can a man bear to see injustice done without crying out? Yet how can a man protest to one who will not listen?

My father's business did not go well, but Meyer Pollack prospered. His ships went forth to Jamaica and Barbadoes and they came back laden with good things. He dealt in molasses and in rum and once my mother said . . .

MOTHER. Perhaps he's in the slave trade, Benjamin.

FATHER. Bring the bread to the table, Rachel.

MOTHER. Well, it's only what people say.

FATHER. People should learn not to slander a good man's name.

MOTHER. Did you ever hear of a rich man who was good?

FATHER. (*Chuckles*) Or a poor man's wife who wasn't envious?

MOTHER. Oh, be still. Here's the bread.

FATHER. Wash your hands, Mordecai.

MOTHER. He's already washed. Say the blessing, Benjamin.

FATHER. Blessed art Thou, O Lord, King of the Universe, who bringest forth bread out of the ground.

MOTHER. Amen. Isn't it true about Meyer?

FATHER. No, it isn't true. We're no longer friends and I know he talks against me. But it isn't true. The Jews of Newport do not deal in slaves. Now go ahead and eat your supper, Rachel. (*Pause*) Well, Mordecai, do you need a special invitation? Eat your supper.

(*Music: Narrative theme and down*)

MORDECAI. My mother ate her supper and smiled into her plate. Then when she looked up and saw my father and saw that he saw her also, I was glad for him and for her and for myself that I was their son. And as I grew older and took my place with the men in the synagogue I saw that my father was as he was because he was bred in the Talmud, and my respect for the law of Israel did not diminish. It happened many years later that Meyer Pollack lost his ships at sea and all his merchandise with it—my father went to him.

(*Music: Out sharply on:*)

(*Slamming of door*)

POLLACK. Oh, it's you. What do you want?

FATHER. I've heard of your loss, Meyer.

POLLACK. Get out.

FATHER. Meyer!

POLLACK. Get out. Do your gloating outside.

FATHER. I am not gloating, Meyer.

POLLACK. No?

FATHER. No, Meyer. You're wiped out; let me help.

POLLACK. (*Laughs*) I really believe you mean it. Benjamin, you are a fool.

FATHER. I don't have much to give, but take it.

POLLACK. Thanks, Benjamin. I shouldn't have called you a fool.

FATHER. Why not, I suppose I am.

POLLACK. Well, a good fool, then. You didn't believe I dealt in slaves, did you, Benjamin?

FATHER. No, I didn't believe it.

POLLACK. I didn't, you know. I could have, but I didn't. Once I tried, Benjamin, and then one day I found the Book on a chair . . . open . . . and the page was Leviticus. It stared at me.

FATHER. I know the place.

POLLACK. Do you? It said something about not making your brother serve as your bondservant. Of all the pages in the Bible it had to be open at that one.

FATHER. "For they are My servants, whom I brought forth out of the land of Egypt; they shall not be sold as bondsmen."

POLLACK. That's it. Benjamin, I thought you ought to know that.

FATHER. I'm glad you told me.

POLLACK. You'd better go now. If you stay any longer, I'll become a fool.

FATHER. Like me, Meyer?

POLLACK. *(Softly)* Like you, Benjamin, God willing.
(Music: Bridge to narrative theme and down)
MORDECAI. There were many things my father said as I came to manhood, and I do not remember that anything he told me was false or insincere or said merely for the sake of pious display. Each morning after prayers he went to his shop on Long Wharf and I went with him. And on Sabbath eve my mother would light the candles and make the benediction and there was peace and serenity and a table laden with good things. I wonder sometimes whether we are ever fated to have peace and serenity for long. For the colonies were impatient under the restrictions and the taxes of the Crown. And soon there was a feeling of tension and a sense of impending trouble which made the Sabbath bitter as Marah.
(Voices loudly)
FATHER. Please, not all at once. That's better, isn't it? Let's do this thing democratically. We're here to make up our minds on some action. Definite action. Moses Seixas, you haven't said anything.
MOSES. I'll stand with the others, Benjamin.
POLLACK. You can count on me, Benjamin. We'll buy no British tea, pay no British taxes, import no British goods.
(Ad lib agreement)
FATHER. How about you, Isaac Hart? Do you go along?
HART. *(Off mike)* You know my opinion.
FATHER. I'm not sure that we do.
HART. *(Closer)* It hasn't changed.
FATHER. Suppose you tell us.
HART. *(On)* All right, I will. All my life I've known you. I've broken bread with you, our children have grown up together, we've liked each other, respected one another . . .
POLLACK. Get to the point, Isaac. Thy yes must be true and thy No must be true; one must not say one thing with his mouth and another in his heart.

A RHODE ISLAND REFUGE

HART. You've become quite a scholar of the Talmud, Meyer Pollack.

POLLACK. I'm no Tory, if that's what you mean.

HART. And I'm no rebel. I side with England. England is where I was born. England has done me nothing but good. What reason . . .

MOSES. You live in Rhode Island, Isaac.

ALL. Yes, Isaac. (*Ad lib*)

HART. I see, true democracy— everyone wants to talk and no one wants to listen.

FATHER. Let him speak. Go ahead, Isaac.

HART. You are all, at this moment, guilty of rebellion.

POLLACK. Can you tell us what liberty has ever been accomplished without rebellion?

HART. I see, Meyer, you are not only a scholar, you are also a philosopher.

FATHER. Meyer! Sit down, please. Isaac, let's speak without anger.

HART. Every Jew in Newport is turned against me. Why? Because I am loyal to England. Would Roger Williams have been able to found Rhode Island colony if not for English tolerance? Would Spain have permitted you to live here unmolested? Don't you see the consequence of your rebellion? There may be bloodshed.

POLLACK. Some things can only be settled in blood.

HART. The words roll so fast from your tongue, Meyer. Before you quoted the Talmud to me. I can also quote.

POLLACK. I'm listening.

HART. Look in the Talmud Sanhedrin. "If someone should say to thee, kill, or I will kill thee, it is better that thou should be killed than to commit murder." Why don't you answer, Meyer?

FATHER. Shall I answer for him, Isaac.

HART. Yes, if you can.

FATHER. Two answers, Isaac. The first, Moses said: "Shall

your brethren go into the war and shall ye sit here." The second you know also, Isaac. Separate not thyself from the congregation.

HART. You distort the meaning.

FATHER. No, Isaac. The meaning is plain. The American colonies are your congregation. This is our place. We came here as the others came. Pray God there will be no letting of blood. But if blood is to be spilled, our place is with the colonists.

(*Music: Bridge to narrative theme and down*)

MORDECAI. Lexington came. We began to drill. Meyer and Moses Seixas went among the townspeople collecting saltpetre and brimstone. The guns from Fort George were removed to Newport. Sentries were posted on the hills and two full months before the Declaration of Independence Rhode Island declared itself free and independent. And with Rhode Island, stood the congregation of Newport. The young men took up arms. Abraham Seixas and Solomon Rophee, and Moses Isaacs, and many more. And I with them. Then there were battles and many of the redcoats were slain. (*Music out*)

POLLACK. Rejoice, Isaac Hart.

HART. And why should I rejoice, Meyer?

POLLACK. Because a hundred redcoats have fallen.

HART. When the angels began to sing as the Egyptians drowned in the Red Sea, God said "Creatures of Mine are drowning in the sea; how can ye sing a song?"

(*Music: Narrative theme and under*)

MORDECAI. Meyer Pollack raised his hand to strike him, and then his hand fell to his side and he turned away. Isaac Hart loved the King, and he did not fear to say so. He could have held his tongue, yet he would not. It came about that he was set on by a mob and killed. And even we who had shouldered the muskets of the patriot army mourned the passing of a man who suffered death for loyalty's sake. But during the fight there is little time for mourning. It is only later, when the living go into the fields to count the dead, that men can truly mourn. I was ordered to join the 8th Massachusetts Regiment and before I went, my father took his musket and gave it to me. (*Music out*)

FATHER. Take it, Mordecai.

MORDECAI. I'll try to use it well, Father.

FATHER. When you were a little boy, I read you a few lines from the prophet Micah. Do you remember, Mordecai?

MORDECAI. I remember, Father. "It hath been told thee, what is good, and what the Lord doth require of thee; only to do justly, and to love mercy and to walk humbly with thy God."

FATHER. I'm glad you remember. Now say good-bye to your mother and do not let her cry. And Mordecai . . .

MORDECAI. Yes.

FATHER. Be a good soldier . . . for Israel and for America.

(*Music: Narrative theme and down*)

MORDECAI. These were the last words I ever heard from my Father's mouth. I went to war and the congregation of Newport dispersed before the British invasion. The goods were burned, the warehouses emptied, so that nothing could fall into the hands of the enemy. And then many years later, after the terrible winter at Valley Forge, Moses Seixas wrote me a letter. (*Music out*)

MOSES. My dear Mordecai, God be with you. My heart melts for you for I have nothing to give you but bad news. Benjamin, your father, and Rachel, your mother, are no longer among the living. They went to settle in another place and to help the patriots and a terrible sickness came like a plague and took them from the living . . . Mordecai, Benjamin was a good man. He was eyes to the blind and feet to the lame and a pillar to the synagogue. Truly it is said the hope of man is but the worm. May they rest in peace.

(*Music: Narrative theme and down*)

MORDECAI. I said the Kaddish. It is not an easy thing for a soldier to say the mourner's prayer for the departed when the feet are naked and the body is cold. Yet I tried to say it. I said it shivering in the mud and weary almost to death. And many years later, when the war ended, I returned to Newport and stood with Moses Seixas in the synagogue Yeshuat Israel.

(*Music: Out*)

MOSES. You see, the synagogue still stands. It will always stand, Mordecai.

MORDECAI. Your faith is very great, Moses.

MOSES. Why not? In America, faith is possible. President Washington came here and stood where you are standing. He saw the Ark of the Lord and the Holy Scroll and he was pleased.

MORDECAI. I'm glad.

MOSES. He gave me a letter, Mordecai. You have fought your country's war, now you have a right to hear why. This is Washington's letter.

MORDECAI. Will you read it to me, Moses?

MOSES. "To the Hebrew Congregation in Newport, Rhode Island. The citizens of the United States of America have a right to applaud themselves for having given to mankind examples of an enlarged and liberal policy: a policy worthy of imitation. All possess alike liberty of conscience and immunities of citizenship. It is now no more that toleration is spoken of as if it was by the indulgence of one class of people that another enjoyed the exercise of their inherent natural rights. For happily the Government of the United States, which gives to bigotry no sanction, to persecution no assistance, requires only that they who live under its protection, should demean themselves as good citizens, in giving it on all occasions their effectual support."

MORDECAI. (*Softly*) Don't stop. Read the rest of it.

MOSES. "May the children of the Stock of Abraham, who dwell in this land, continue to merit and enjoy the good will of the other inhabitants, while every one shall sit in safety under his own Vine and Fig tree, and there shall be none to make him afraid. May the Father of all mercies scatter light and not darkness in our paths, and make us all in our several vocations useful here and in his own due time and way everlastingly happy."
(Music: Narrative theme and down)
MORDECAI. They call it the Old Jewish Cemetery of Newport. From Narragansett Bay the land breeze rustles in the trees and the Rhode Island sun is clean and friendly on our graves. Yes, they sleep so still beside me. Once long ago they fled from Spain and Portugal. But here they found a refuge. The names on the head stones are mellowed in the rain. And if I have no stone, it does not matter. For the grass is warm and green and living, and something else. The words too are living. The words a man called Washington addressed to the little Congregation at Newport. The Congregation that sleeps beside me.
(Music: Curtain)

SCHECHTER

SCHECHTER

The best advice for the new radio writer is to shun all biographical assignments that involve people still alive. The laws of libel are operative, there must be a proper respect for rights of privacy, and an impersonation release must be signed and received.

While Solomon Schechter has been dead since 1915, in the precincts of the Jewish Theological Seminary he is more corporeal than some of last year's rabbinical graduates. Students not born when he was alive are full of Schechter legends. And among members of the faculty, above all those who were his colleagues and those who were trained by him, there is an affection for Dr. Schechter and a wealth of anecdote and information that can overwhelm a radio writer whose weekly chore it is to turn out one script and get on with the next. If in this script I have been unfaithful to his memory in any respect, I ask those who loved him to forgive me.

Schechter had two performances. The first featured Edwin Jerome and Sarah Burton in a cast that included Jack Manning, Bernard Lenrow, Katherine MacDonald, Joseph Di Santis, Sam Raskyn, Donald Bain, Richard Keith, and James Van Dyke. Ira Avery was the director and Henry Brant was responsible for the musical score. Frank Papp directed a second performance with Ann Sterrett and William Podmore in the roles of Mathilde and Solomon Schechter.

SCHECHTER

MATHILDE. His eyes were quite blue . . . and his beard was quite red. (*Laughs*) He had a most unrabbinical temper; and when he swore, which was quite frequent, it was like a catalogue of Biblical prophets. He was terribly untidy, he used his vest for an ashtray and the house was a chaos of manuscripts and books. It was 1890, and he was a lecturer in rabbinics at Cambridge University in England. His name was Solomon Schechter and I was his wife.
(*Music: Narrative theme and down*)
MATHILDE. There was something about Schechter irresistible to men of learning. Our house was rich in friendships . . . Israel Zangwill, the writer; Father Nolan, who came to argue the Apostles against the Rabbis; Professor Haddon, the anthropologist; James Frazer, the author of the *Golden Bough;* and the Reverend Charles Taylor, Master of St. John's College. Schechter quarreled with them by turns, taught them by turns, and warmed them constantly with his wit and affection. We were very poor, but the Cambridge Library was filled with books, and we felt no lack. (*Music out*) Once, I recollect, a student came to see Schechter . . . to say good-bye.
SCHECHTER. What's this nonsense about good-bye, Matthews, you haven't completed your studies.
STUDENT. I can't afford to stay on, Dr. Schechter.
SCHECHTER. That's absurd, we can't afford to lose you.
STUDENT. Thank you, sir.
SCHECHTER. How much do you need?
STUDENT. Please, sir, I didn't come for that.
SCHECHTER. How much do you need, Matthews?

STUDENT. I can't accept your help.

SCHECHTER. It's not my help at all. I have charge of a college fund for students who need assistance.

STUDENT. You, Dr. Schechter?

SCHECHTER. How much do you need?

STUDENT. Are you sure, sir?

SCHECHTER. Will fifty pounds be enough?

STUDENT. Thank you, Dr. Schechter . . . I . . . I don't know what to say.

SCHECHTER. Just forget this nonsense about leaving. (*Pause*) Tilda!

MATHILDE. Yes?

SCHECHTER. Please give Mr. Matthews fifty pounds.

MATHILDE. Fifty pounds?

SCHECHTER. Of course. (*Slow fade*) If you'll both excuse me, there's some work I have to do. See you in class, Matthews. (*Pause—Fading in*) Come now, Tilda, you don't have to look so anxious. It was only fifty pounds.

MATHILDE. It was nearly all we had. Why did you do it, Solomon?

SCHECHTER. That boy's a fine scholar. He's going to be a fine minister some day.

MATHILDE. Why didn't you refer him to the Episcopal Church Fund?

SCHECHTER. Matthews is proud. He wouldn't take charity.

MATHILDE. It wouldn't be charity. He could pay it back once they found him a pulpit.

SCHECHTER. Let's not talk about it, Tilda.

MATHILDE. I don't understand it. You're the only Jew on the faculty. It would be different if you were rich.

SCHECHTER. Tilda, no man has a right to more than bread and water and fuel for his stove as long as the poor are not provided with the necessaries of life.

MATHILDE. But this wasn't a necessity at all. It wasn't for bread, it was for tuition.

SCHECHTER. Learning is a necessity of life, Tilda. Now stop fretting—it's unbecoming.
(*Music: Bridge to narrative theme and down*)
MATHILDE. Schechter needed a new greatcoat; that winter and the next he had to wear his old one. When I complained, he bristled.
SCHECHTER. Tilda, I'm a scholar. You cannot be everything if you want to be anything.
MATHILDE. I knew he was right, but he did need a new coat. Schechter wasn't a saint. He detested what he called mental squinting. He loved Matthews who was a Christian because Matthews was an honest scholar. Once a would-be scholar bored him for two whole days, until he couldn't stand it any longer.
(*Music: Out*)
SCHECHTER. Sir, the vocal organs were not meant to cover up ignorance.
BORE. But . . . but Dr. Schechter . . . Maimonides says . . .
SCHECHTER. Excuse me, sir, you know as much about Maimonides as a monkey in a cage knows about evolution. Now, must you stay?
BORE. But . . . I wanted you to discuss this passage in Nietzsche.
SCHECHTER. You will do very well. It doesn't require deep thinking to misunderstand Nietzsche. Your hat, sir.
BORE. I'm afraid, Dr. Schechter, you don't appreciate my scholarship.
SCHECHTER. On the contrary, my dear sir, you have the encyclopaedic ignorance of the highly uneducated. The door, sir. I have an important paper to write. Please excuse me. And try not to fall down the stairs.
(*Music: Bridge to narrative theme and down*)
MATHILDE. I made him send a note of apology. We argued about it for a whole day. He grumbled like a bear and began his note. (*Music out*)

SCHECHTER. Sir: My wife informs me I have been a boor. I beg my pardon.
MATHILDE. That won't do.
SCHECHTER. No?
MATHILDE. Schechter, you apologize decently.
SCHECHTER. All right. (*Writing*) Sir: It has been my observation that one must love people very much in order not to hate them.
MATHILDE. Schechter!
SCHECHTER. What's the matter, Tilda?
MATHILDE. Solomon Schechter, you're the most exasperating, the most prejudiced man I've ever married.
SCHECHTER. Tilda, a man can't carry on the business of life without prejudices. My prejudice is that I am a Hebrew and I fear the Lord God.
MATHILDE. You've offended that man.
SCHECHTER. I tried for two days, it seemed to make no impression.
MATHILDE. He's probably so heartsick now he won't be able to eat for a week.
SCHECHTER. Oh, no, Tilda. He's a very holy man . . . full of misquoted Scriptures; but I think he's still got room for a good dinner which he will eat with great devotion.
MATHILDE. Solomon Schechter, are you or are you not going to send that man a civil note of apology?
SCHECHTER. But it might encourage him to be a Rabbi. Think what a horrible example of red-tape Judaism he would be?
MATHILDE. Solomon Schechter!
SCHECHTER. All right, my dear. Hand me the Bible.
MATHILDE. What do you want the Bible for?
SCHECHTER. I want to verify the passage that begins, "I am looking for my father's asses."
MATHILDE. You're hopeless, Schechter. I throw up my hands.
SCHECHTER. Do you, Tilda?

MATHILDE. I emphatically do.

SCHECHTER. In that case, give me another sheet of paper, please. I'll send a note of apology.

(*Music: Narrative theme and down*)

MATHILDE. That was very characteristic of Solomon Schechter. The only grievances he ever nursed were those against himself. And while Cambridge and London knew and admired him as the foremost Talmudical authority in the West, I knew him and loved him as a very shy, human man who was intoxicated with God. From all over the world learned scholars sent precious manuscripts to Cambridge . . . ancient manuscripts in Hebrew, in Aramaic, in Coptic . . . and Schechter studied them under his glass and wrote his opinions. Once I recall (*Music fading*) he uttered his credo to Dr. Taylor and to Father Nolan.

SCHECHTER. Every discovery of an ancient document giving evidence of a bygone world, if undertaken in the right spirit, that is for the honor of God and the truth, is an act of resurrection in miniature.

(*Music: Up and under*)

MATHILDE. Solomon Schechter believed that the Jewish ministry must be concerned with Jewish scholarship. And nothing distressed him more than what he called platform-Judaism. Many congregations offered him rabinnical posts but he preferred to remain at Cambridge, living precariously on the meager pay of a lecturer. He published his studies of the Talmud and to a small group throughout the world he was a famous man. Now a larger group was to hear of him. It began in May, 1896.

(*Music: Fading*)

MATHILDE. Two of our dearest friends, Margaret Gibson and Agnes Lewis, had just returned from the Near East. Now, Agnes Lewis held two ancient fragments of Hebrew manuscript out to him.

SCHECHTER. (*Excited*) Mrs. Lewis, where did you find this?

MRS. LEWIS. Margaret and I bought them from a book-dealer in Jerusalem.

SCHECHTER. Please . . . handle it very carefully.

MRS. LEWIS. What is it?

SCHECHTER. This one . . . this is a fragment of the ancient Jerusalem Talmud. But it's this one . . .

MRS. LEWIS. This scrap of paper?

SCHECHTER. Yes, Mrs. Lewis. This scrap of paper. Listen . . . I'll translate . . .

"The wise man will seek out the wisdom of all the ancients;
And will be occupied in prophecies.
He will serve among great men,
And appear before him that ruleth.
He will travel through the lands of strange nations . . ."
(*Pause*)
That's all I can make out; but it's enough.

MRS. LEWIS. Dr. Schecter, you seem very agitated.

SCHECHTER. Mrs. Lewis, this is a fragment from the Hebrew Book of Ben Sira . . . the Book Ecclesiasticus of the Apocrypha.

MRS. LEWIS. Is it very important?

SCHECHTER. The only original in existence is the Greek translation. Mrs. Lewis, the Hebrew original has been missing for a thousand years . . . more than a thousand years.

MRS. LEWIS. You're sure this is from it?

SCHECHTER. As sure as there is a God in Israel. And I think I know where this came from . . . there can be only one place.

MRS. LEWIS. Jerusalem?

SCHECHTER. No, not Jerusalem. The writings were destroyed by Titus in A.D. 70. The place must be the Genizah of Cairo.

MRS. LEWIS. Genizah, Dr. Schechter?

SCHECHTER. Yes, Mrs. Lewis, Genizah. The Genizah is a hiding place for old books and manuscripts. Among the Jews holy books are never destroyed. When they are torn or worn out, they are buried in the ground . . . or hidden away. . . . And we know there is a Genizah in Cairo. There can be no other place, Mrs. Lewis.

MRS. LEWIS. But if this is as old as you say, it would have been decomposed by now.

SCHECHTER. Not in the dry Egyptian air. Mrs. Lewis, I must get the rest of the Ecclesiasticus. I absolutely must.

(*Music: Bridge to narrative theme and down*)

MATHILDE. Schechter did not sleep that night. He was agitated, abstracted, and he immediately reported Mrs. Lewis's discovery to the Reverend Dr. Taylor, Master of St. John's College.

(*Music: Out*)

SCHECHTER. I must go to Cairo, Dr. Taylor.

TAYLOR. How do you know you'll find anything, Dr. Schechter?

SCHECHTER. I don't know. But if my assumption is correct, there's a treasure of hidden manuscripts in Cairo.

TAYLOR. Well, I'm sure the University will grant you a leave.

SCHECHTER. I have no funds, sir.

TAYLOR. You do, Schechter . . . you have all the funds I have.

SCHECHTER. I knew you'd say that, Dr. Taylor . . . that's why I came to you.

TAYLOR. I'll talk to Professor MacAllister and Professor Sedgwick . . . they'll supply what I don't have.

SCHECHTER. Thank you, sir . . . but I implore you . . .

TAYLOR. Yes?

SCHECHTER. We must keep this absolutely secret. Every unscrupulous book-dealer and collector in the Orient will be following me. For them this represents more wealth than the pyramids of the Pharaohs. We must find the manuscripts, sir, and preserve them for science.

(*Music: Narrative theme and down*)

MATHILDE. Taylor was as good as his word. For many years it had been known that somewhere in Egypt there was a careful campaign of pilfering from some secret storehouse. And Schechter was staking his reputation on the fact that the storehouse was Cairo. Taylor found the money, Schechter bid us all a hurried good-bye and sailed to Egypt. (*Music out*) Schechter laid his groundwork carefully ... the first man he saw was the Chief Rabbi.

SCHECHTER. Dear Tilda: I burn with impatience, but I must win the Chief Rabbi to my side. I flirt with him by the hour, and am taking Arabic lessons three times a week. You see how practical your old man is.

(*Music: Narrative theme. A few bars, fading out under*)

MATHILDE. His letters came every day ... reporting slow progress.

SCHECHTER. The Rabbi is very kind to me. He took me to the Cairo Synagogue where I suspect the Genizah is located. I'm afraid I nearly disgraced you. My foot caught against a cobblestone and I uttered an Anglo-Saxon monosyllable which begins with d and ends with n.

RABBI. Did you say something, Dr. Schechter?

SCHECHTER. Oh ... uh ... nothing at all, Rabbi, nothing at all.

RABBI. I thought I heard you say something in English.

SCHECHTER. Just a little word, Rabbi.

RABBI. Oh, you must explain its meaning then, Dr. Schechter.

SCHECHTER. Rabbi, we have a word in the English language, a little word of one syllable which is full of theological meaning and is used as a sort of charm against things that annoy us.

RABBI. Oh, is that all. I thought for a moment you were swearing.

SCHECHTER. Merely theologically, my dear Rabbi.

RABBI. I see. Well, Dr. Schechter. This is the Cairo Synagogue.

SCHECHTER. I know every room here. I'm afraid you've come for nothing.
SCHECHTER. Do you mind if I make my own inspection?
RABBI. Not at all, Dr. Schechter. I've asked the Beadle to assist you. I hope you find what you're looking for but, Dr. Schechter, I strongly doubt that it's here.
(*Music: Bridge*)
(*Sound of cane tapping against wall*)
SCHECHTER. Beadle . . .
BEADLE. Yes . . .
SCHECHTER. This wall is hollow.
BEADLE. Oh, no, it can't be.
SCHECHTER. Listen. (*Tapping again*) Definitely, it's hollow.
BEADLE. Nothing of the sort, Dr. Schechter. Please come this way . . . we'll try the basement.
(*Music: Bridge*)
DEALER. Oh . . . yes, you . . .
SCHECHTER. I believe I don't know your name, sir?
DEALER. That's all right. I have some advice to give you.
SCHECHTER. That's very kind of you . . . what advice, sir?
DEALER. Return to England.
SCHECHTER. I have no intention of returning.
DEALER. That's very unfortunate. The climate of Egypt can be rather unwholesome for foreigners.
SCHECHTER. I see.
DEALER. I've taken the liberty to book passage for you. A few of my friends have gotten up a purse to give you.
SCHECHTER. Your friends are extremely generous.
DEALER. Merely public-spirited.
SCHECHTER. Thank you again, sir, but if you don't mind, I rather like Cairo.
DEALER. Now that's a question. Dr. Schechter likes Cairo . . . the question is, though, does Cairo like Dr. Schechter?
(*Music: Bridge*)
SCHECHTER. That's the man, Rabbi.

RABBI. Oh . . . I know him. He's a speculator in rare books.
SCHECHTER. Do you still believe that I've come on a wild-goose chase?
RABBI. I'm beginning to change my mind. (*Pause*) Dr. Schechter.
SCHECHTER. Yes, Rabbi.
RABBI. Only the Beadle and I know that you are looking for a secret hoard of manuscripts.
SCHECHTER. Excuse me, Rabbi . . . only you, the Beadle and the book-dealer.
RABBI. That's my point. I didn't tell the book-dealer.
SCHECHTER. Rabbi, if you don't mind, I think I should like to pay a visit to our friend the Beadle.
(*Music: Bridge*)
(*Tapping on hollow wall*)
SCHECHTER. That doesn't sound hollow to you, does it, Beadle?
BEADLE. No, Dr. Schechter, it doesn't.
SCHECHTER. Listen again, Beadle. (*Tapping*) That doesn't sound hollow?
BEADLE. I can't say it does.
SCHECHTER. Then get me a pick-axe. I'm going to find out.
BEADLE. Now don't be stubborn, Dr. Schechter.
SCHECHTER. Hmm. That's what the book-dealers think, isn't it?
BEADLE. (*Quietly*) Yes, that's what they think . . . that's what I think.
SCHECHTER. Why don't you help me save the synagogue from desecration? I don't want to break the wall. How do you get in?
BEADLE. The way you get into Gehenna.
SCHECHTER. I'm sorry you won't help me, Beadle. But that doesn't matter. I'll manage myself . . . somehow.
(*Music: Bridge to narrative theme*)
MATHILDE. The synagogue at Cairo employed a new Beadle the next day. Schechter wrote me about it and I cabled him

to be careful. He was careful.
(Music: Out)

SCHECHTER. Psss, psss, psss . . . here, kitty . . . a nice bowl of milk.
(Sound of milk poured into bowl)
(Cat meows. Laps milk noisily)

SCHECHTER. Not so fast, kitty . . . it may give you indigestion.
(Cat howls)

SCHECHTER. *(Projecting)* Rabbi . . . Rabbi, quick . . . an emetic . . . quick, Rabbi . . . your cat's been poisoned.
(Music: Bridge)

RABBI. The salt did it, Dr. Schechter. I think she's all cleaned out.

SCHECHTER. I've sent for a veterinary, Rabbi. I'm afraid you nearly had a dead kitten.

RABBI. And a dead scholar.

SCHECHTER. Apparently the Egyptian climate does disagree with foreigners.

RABBI. What are you going to do, Dr. Schechter? Shall we have the book-dealer arrested?

SCHECHTER. No, there's nothing we can prove. There's only one way to stop him.

RABBI. Just tell me . . . I'll take the necessary steps.

SCHECHTER. I'll have to take the steps. Rabbi, I'll trouble you for a pick-axe.
(Music: Bridge and take out with:)
(Sound of pick-axe . . . masonry falling)

SCHECHTER. Look . . . Rabbi . . . look. *(Cut axe)*

RABBI. It's a room.
(Masonry falls)

SCHECHTER. More than a room, Rabbi. Careful of the masonry. See, a hole in the ceiling and a ladder. That's how they got in.
(Rumble . . . and cut)

RABBI. Can you see through the dust, Dr. Schechter?

SCHECHTER. I don't have to see, Rabbi.
RABBI. No?
SCHECHTER. No, I know. This is the secret Genizah of Cairo . . . the built over part of the ancient synagogue. Rabbi . . . here is our treasure-chest . . . the Genizah of Cairo.
(*Music: Bridge to narrative theme and down*)
MATHILDE. I could barely decipher his writing now . . . for the penmanship was worse than usual. It was feverish. I knew that Solomon Schechter had made a great discovery. Mrs. Lewis and Dr. Taylor had a cable . . . and our hearts and hopes were with Solomon Schechter in the airless, windowless Genizah of Cairo.
RABBI. Schechter, where are you, Schechter?
SCHECHTER. (*A burst of coughing*)
RABBI. In the name of God, man, you can't remain here day and night. It's stifling. Look at this thermometer . . . Schechter, 110 degrees.
SCHECHTER. Only a hundred and ten degrees, Rabbi. (*Coughs*) But a hundred thousand precious manuscripts, Rabbi . . . one hundred thousand lost manuscripts of an ancient Hebrew civilization.
(*A burst of coughing*)
(*Music: Bridge*)
TAYLOR. Read on, Mrs. Schechter.
MATHILDE. Ragged scraps of writing to make the hearts of European scholars glad. For centuries whitewash has tumbled upon them from walls and ceilings. The sand of the desert has lodged in their folds and wrinkles; water has drenched them; they have squeezed and hurt each other, whilst all the time some of them were keeping for us very precious secrets. Give Dr. Taylor my great and abiding affection. As soon as I know what I have, I am bringing my treasure back to Cambridge. Praise be to God.
TAYLOR. Is that the end?
MATHILDE. Yes, that's the end of the letter.

TAYLOR. But it's a beginning . . . a new beginning for Hebrew scholarship.

(*Music: Narrative theme and down*)

MATHILDE. Solomon Schechter returned with his manuscripts. He returned with one of the great discoveries in modern times. But he returned an old man. His eyes were filmed, his beard was fringed with white. Days and nights in an airless room under the blazing Egyptian sun had taken their toll. His lungs were thick with dust and residue of centuries . . . he had burrowed like a mole . . . breathing it in . . . hour after hour, day after day . . . And he knew that he had shortened a useful life by many years. But Solomon Schechter did not grieve. He was supremely happy.

(*Music: Out*)

SCHECHTER. Tilda . . .

MATHILDE. Yes?

SCHECHTER. Will you ask Dr. Taylor if he can step by. I think I'm well enough to see him.

MATHILDE. All right, I'll send Dr. Taylor a note.

SCHECHTER. You're happy, Tilda, aren't you?

MATHILDE. I rejoice to have you back.

SCHECHTER. Tilda . . . Tilda . . . whatever is in your mind . . . understand one thing.

MATHILDE. Yes?

SCHECHTER. There is a rabinnical injunction . . . every age must make its own contribution to the Temple of truth.

MATHILDE. All right.

SCHECHTER. If it does not make its contribution, Tilda, it must consider itself false to truth and to learning. Tilda.

MATHILDE. Yes?

SCHECHTER. I thank God He has given me strength to make my contribution.

MATHILDE. Please rest . . . please . . . I'll send for Dr. Taylor.

(*Music: Bridge*)

SCHECHTER. I know there's no need to thank you again. The

manuscripts speak for me, Taylor.

TAYLOR. I understand. (*Pause*) What will you do with them, Schechter? The decision is yours.

SCHECHTER. No, Taylor.

TAYLOR. Schechter . . . you don't mean . . . you don't mean you're going to sell them? Oh, I apologize . . . I have no right to tell a man in your financial position what to do.

SCHECHTER. How many millions of pounds do you think they're worth?

TAYLOR. It's a very great fortune, Schechter, that's all I can say.

SCHECHTER. That makes me supremely happy. (*Pause*) Take it, Dr. Taylor. The manuscripts belong to Cambridge University.

TAYLOR. You know what you're doing?

SCHECHTER. Yes. (*Pause*) Dr. Taylor . . . I was born in Roumania. When I was a little boy and came from the cheder, my body was covered with blood and with bruises. You see, I was a Jew. Then I went to Austria. I found the higher anti-semitism that does not bruise the flesh but lacerates the soul. In England I found happiness. A place to work. If you don't mind, Dr. Taylor . . . I want these manuscripts for Cambridge University and for England.

(*Music: Closing theme and down*)

MATHILDE. He was a man like a lion and he recovered. But now he was an aged lion. His beard was white, but his eyes were still blue. And when his tongue grew caustic, I knew that whatever had been taken from his life in years, nothing had been taken from his mind. We found much happiness in Cambridge . . . and when the call came from America, Solomon Schechter and I went to New York, where he became the second president of the Jewish Theological Seminary of America. England and America . . . they were the countries he loved. And I, Mathilde Schechter, I loved them also . . . with all my soul.

(*Music: Curtain*)

THE BLACK DEATH

THE BLACK DEATH

In the Fourteenth Century Jews were massacred in the cities of the Valley of the Rhine because of a blood libel born of plague, panic, and the necessity for a scapegoat. In the Nineteenth Century a man named Haffkine discovered a serum against plague. (See The Prayer Shawl and the Microscope *which follows this script.) But so far no one has discovered a serum against hate, hysteria and evil propaganda.* The Black Death *is propaganda analysis.*

The best preface to this script is contained in a brief talk which Dr. Mordecai M. Kaplan, Professor of Homiletics at the Rabbinical School and Dean Emeritus of the Teacher's Institute of the Jewish Theological Seminary, delivered at the close of the dramatization.

Professor Kaplan said: "For the good of our souls it is often necessary to dig up from the subconscious the remembrance of long forgotten events which have left deep scars on our spirits." And Professor Kaplan added, describing the aftermath of massacre: "Only few relieve the feeling of guilt by making proper amends. The rest suppress their guilty feeling because it hurts their self-esteem. They suppress it by working up a case against their victim. It is far easier for one who has been wronged to forgive the wrong-doer than it is for the wrong-doer to forgive his victim. This is because the wrong-doer keeps on persuading himself that his victim must have deserved all he got and more. He then proceeds to finish in cold blood what he has left undone when in a state of fury."

The Black Death *was broadcast on November 5, 1944. Joseph Wiseman was Judah, and others in the cast were: Shepard Menken, Sidney Slon, James Van Dyke, Bernard Lenrow, Jean Ellyn, William Adams, and Robert Ramsen. Anton M. Leader directed.*

THE BLACK DEATH

ONE. Bubonic plague: an acute infectious disease transmitted by the rat flea and characterized by inflammation and suppuration of lymph nodes, pneumonia, and cutaneous hemorrhage.

TWO. The septicemic form is very fatal; the pneumonic is even more so.

THREE. In the middle of the Fourteenth Century the plague swept out of the Orient like a destroying angel to ravage the weak and the strong, the guilty and the good.

ONE. According to Hecker and other authorities, one-fourth of the population of Europe ... twenty-five million people died.

JUDAH. I died also. I, Judah, in the year 1349 in the city of Mayence in the Valley of the Rhine ... I died also ... but not of the plague. I hate no one for that. Six hundred years is time enough to heal a wound or mend a scar. Moreover, it is written that he who hates his fellow man is unto one who sheds blood. And even in the grave I do not wish that. Believe this and believe also in my story; for before God I declare it is true.

(*Music: Narrative theme and down*)

JUDAH. In an evil hour for the world there came upon Europe a great pestilence. A man stood talking in the market place, smiling, seasoned, sound, and suddenly a palsy seized his tongue. And he opened his mouth and the tongue within was black. They carried him to his cot and there was no liquid to assuage the burning of his thirst. And he raised himself on his cot and coughed up his life's blood and died. Sometimes he fevered, sometimes he did not; but always he died. (*Music Out*) One of the first to die was a little boy. The priest stood over his coffin.

(*Church bells . . . dirge . . . and hold under*)

PRIEST. Et super nivem dealbabor. Misere mei, Deus, secundum magnam misericordiam tuam. Gloria Patri et Filio, et Spiritui Sancto. Sicut erat in principio, et nunc, et semper, et in saecula saeculoram. Amen. (*He coughs*)

WOMAN. Father Joseph!

PRIEST. My throat. Something's in my throat.

WOMAN. Merciful God!

PRIEST. I'm stifling . . . Water . . . Please. (*He coughs again*)

MAN. What are you doing, Martha?

WOMAN. Father Joseph . . . he wants water.

MAN. Don't go near him.

PRIEST. (*Coughing*) Quickly, please, water.

MAN. Martha, come away. I order you.

WOMAN. He's just buried our son. Do you want me to refuse him a cup of water?

MAN. Where are you going?

WOMAN. To take him this cup.

(*Sound of cup falling to floor*)

MAN. No cup. Priest or no priest. He's taken the plague. The contagion is in his breath. Do you want to die, you fool? Come away.

PRIEST. (*He coughs*) In the name of Heaven, mercy. Help me. Will no one help me? I'm your priest. (*Spasm of coughing*)

(*Church bells up and take out with*)

JUDAH. There was no mercy in Europe. The supplicant had no mercy for the priest, the father for the child, the child for the father. The dead lay where they died and the sweet stink of putrefaction rose from the cities of the dead. Even in the fields there was a murrain upon the cattle. And then men sought for the cause.

(*Voices strident off mike*)

The rich accused the poor, the poor accused the rich; the patricians blamed the commoners and the commoners found the blame in the rich. (*Music out*) (*Build voices*) And then the wrangling, discordant, hysterical voices were suddenly stilled.

(*Voices out*)

WOMAN. The Jews!

MAN. Eh! What's that?

WOMAN. The Jews!

MAN. Well, what about them?

WOMAN. Nothing. Only . . . I wonder.

MAN. Wonder? What do you wonder? Do—you—

WOMAN. Yes. Why not?

MAN. Hmm. You might be right. I didn't think of it. Yes . . . you might be right. I'm going to talk to Peter.

(*Music: Montage theme . . . buzzing . . . and venomous . . . and down for*)

(*Build hysteria through montage*)

MAN. Psst, Peter.

VOICE. Ay?

MAN. It could be the Jews.

(*Music: Up and down*)

VOICE. Psst, Old Man.

OLD MAN. Ay?

VOICE. Do you hear, it's the Jews.

(*Music: Up and down*)

OLD MAN. Psst, Hilda, Peter saw them do it.

WOMAN. Was it poison?

OLD MAN. He didn't say . . . but it could be, couldn't it?

(*Music: Up and down*)

WOMAN. The old man says it's poison.

MAN. Are you sure?

WOMAN. He said so, didn't he?

(*Music: Up and down*)

MAN. They poisoned the wells.

VOICE. How do you know?
MAN. She told me.
   (*Music: Up and cut*)
VOICE. Well, what are we going to do about it?
MAN. Yes, what are we waiting for?
OLD MAN. Make them confess.
WOMAN. That's it . . . make them confess.
   (*Music: Chord*)
   (*Sound of slap*)
MAN. Do you confess?
BOY. Please don't hit me.
   (*Sound of slap*)
MAN. You put the poison in the well.
BOY. I swear on the Torah I didn't.
   (*Sound of slap*)
MAN. We know you put it there.
BOY. I don't know anything.
   (*Sound of slap*)
MAN. That's nothing. That's only a taste. Peter, put him to the torture. Get the thumbscrews. We'll make him talk.
PRIEST II. (*Fading in*) In the name of the Merciful God do not do this, my son.
MAN. Go away, Father, we didn't send for you.
PRIEST II. I'm your priest.
MAN. Go back to your church.
PRIEST II. My son, this is evil. This boy is innocent. You are committing a great wrong.
MAN. Peter, bring the thumbscrews.
PRIEST II. Wait. You cannot torture him. You must not.
MAN. Only a little, Father . . . until he talks.
PRIEST II. I know the boy, I tell you. I know his mother. She is not of our faith, but she is a virtuous woman. You can't do this.
MAN. He poisoned the well.
BOY. I swear on the Torah I didn't.

THE BLACK DEATH

PRIEST II. Wait, my son . . .
MAN. You can't stop us.
PRIEST II. I ask you . . . did you drink the water of the well?
MAN. That's not important.
PRIEST II. It is important. I drank the water. Today and yesterday and the day before.
MAN. You lie.
PRIEST II. I am your priest.
MAN. I say you lie. Go away now. Go away before we have you stoned. What are you waiting for, Peter? Bring the thumbscrews, I say.

(*Music: Bridge to narrative theme and down*)

JUDAH. He was a Jewish boy. Agimet was his name. You will find it written down. They tortured him only a little. Then a little more. The priest tried to interfere. They stoned their priest. He was not of my religion but he was a man of God. I prayed for his soul. But the boy was only a boy and the flesh is very weak. (*Music out*)

MAN. You confess now.
BOY. (*Lifeless*) I confess now.
MAN. You put the poison in the well?
BOY. Yes, I put it in.
MAN. What was the poison?
BOY. Anything you say.
MAN. Spiders and frogs.
BOY. All right.
MAN. Human flesh and lizards.
BOY. All right.
MAN. The rabbi made it into a powder for you.
BOY. You'll let me alone now, won't you?
MAN. Swear to it.
BOY. I swear it.
MAN. Swear it by your law, and on your Torah, and on the Pentateuch.
BOY. They're the same thing.

MAN. Swear it anyhow.
BOY. I swear it.
MAN. Take that all down, Peter.
BOY. Will you let me go to my mother now?
MAN. *(Softly)* No. That would be wrong. You must accept your punishment. Yes. You confessed, didn't you? Peter, take the murderer away.
(Music: Bridge softly to narrative theme and down)
JUDAH. By three things is the world preserved, said Rabbi Simon, the son of Gamaliel; by justice, by truth, and by peace. In the year 1348 there was no longer truth in Europe, no longer justice, no longer peace. There was a tumult over the earth, a corruption of the flesh, a rottenness of the mind. And even as men coughed in the death rattle, other men raised gibbets, and took cudgels and sharp knives until the water of the River Rhine ran red with Jewish blood. In Strasbourg on St. Valentine's Day in the year 1349 they built a platform in the Jewish cemetery and burned the Jews. Two thousand men, women and children. In Erfurt, the Jewish population was 3000. Not one survived. There is something you must know. In the city of Avignon resided the Pope, Clement, the Sixth, and the Pope wept and he issued a bull to the people of Europe.
(Music: Out)
CLEMENT. My children, hear me. This that you do is a crime not only against men but against God. I appeal to the Christian sense of justice and I appeal to you in the name of the imprescriptable rights of all mankind. I declare the innocence of the Jews regarding the charges against them. In districts where no Jew resides, men die of the plague. Do not the Jews themselves die of the plague? I admonish the clergy to take the Jews under their protection. I pronounce a ban against the false accusers and the murderers. Be just, my children, I entreat you in the name of God to be just and to be merciful.

THE BLACK DEATH

(*Music: Narrative theme and down*)

JUDAH. Perhaps they heard Clement the Sixth. But if they heard they gave no heed. In Zurich, in Basel, in Freiberg, in Speyer, in Worms, in Wurzberg, in Frankfort . . . God of Israel, in how many cities and villages were there murder and burning? And then it came to Mayence. The city where I was born, and my father's father. August, 1349 . . . it is not a month you should forget. Nor can I forget it. For then, in this month, it came to us in Mayence . . . it came to us.

(*Music: Out*)

(*Pounding on door*)

JACOB. (*Calling*) Judah, let me in. Judah, open the door.

(*Door opens*)

JUDAH. You'll break the door down, Jacob.

(*Door closes*)

JACOB. What's in your hand, Judah?

JUDAH. You say it as though it were an infamous thing.

JACOB. What's in your hand?

JUDAH. What should be in my hand on the Sabbath? It is the Book of the Law.

JACOB. You're out of your mind. The world is burning and you read the Law.

JUDAH. Why not? "The day is short and the work is great and the workmen are sluggish, and the reward is much."

JACOB. I've no time for that. They sent me for you.

JUDAH. They?

JACOB. The congregation. Do you think we're going to let ourselves be slaughtered? We're holding a meeting at the synagogue. Come, Judah, there's no time to lose.

(*Music: Bridge*)

(*Sound of crowd—not too large*)

JACOB. I think there's nothing more to say. There is no alternative but death for us. We must choose now whether we shall submit tamely to the assassin or whether we shall resist.

ONE. (*Off*) How can we resist, Jacob? We are six thousand; they are ten times six thousand.

JACOB. If they were a hundred times six thousand, we must still resist.

TWO. (*Off*) With what? We have no arms.

JACOB. Your naked fists then. The stick you use for walking, the knife that cuts the Sabbath bread. Those are your weapons. Judah!

JUDAH. Yes, Jacob.

JACOB. You came here with the Torah in your hand. Put it down and take up a club.

JUDAH. How can I, Jacob? The Torah begins with an act of love and it ends with an act of love. How can I put it down for a club, especially here—in the synagogue?

JACOB. Will you sing a psalm against your enemy, Judah? Are the Scriptures written with milk? Have you never heard of David and Joshua and Judah Maccabee? The only way is to resist.

ONE. (*Off*) Jacob is right.

JUDAH. There must be another way . . . a better way.

TWO. (*Off*) Tell us, Judah.

JUDAH. These people are not all evil.

JACOB. No?

JUDAH. No, Jacob. You have known them all your life. My friend Wilhelm is a good Christian. He will not join with the rabble to murder his own friends.

JACOB. Wilhelm is only one. There are sixty thousand against us.

JUDAH. No. The men who stand against us are those who have forsaken their own Christianity. You know Muller, and Sachs, the tanner, and Obermeyer, the smith? You have known them all your lives. Can you believe, can you believe that even in this time of madness, that they would turn against you? I can't believe it.

ONE. (*Off*) Jacob, he's right.

VOICES. *(Ad lib agreement)*

JACOB. You're fools all of you. Who burned the houses of the Jews in Erfurt? Were they not men like the men you speak of? Who murdered the 2,000 innocent Jews of Strasbourg? The same kind of men.

JUDAH. Then let us appeal to their humanity.

JACOB. Their humanity was appealed to in Strasbourg. Do not forget, Judah, that when you are killed, these men will take your house and whatever you own. They kill for hate but also for greed.

JUDAH. I will not believe it, Jacob.

JACOB. Then you have no eyes to see and no ears to hear. The Jews of Worms would not believe also. Where are the Jews of Worms? Where? Tell me where? They burned themselves in their own houses. Look among the ashes, Judah. Look and tell me if you still have faith in justice or mercy.

JUDAH. I do, Jacob. I am a Jew and I must have faith in the kindliness of men and in the righteousness of God. I appeal to you. I entreat you. Let me talk to our neighbors. Let me go among them and show them we are falsely accused. Let me speak against the bigotry and the superstition and the evil of this hour. Put up your barricades. Prepare to defend yourselves if you must. But first let me try the way of God.

(Pause)

TWO. *(Off)* We have nothing to lose.

ONE. *(Off)* All right, Judah. You talk, we'll arm ourselves.

CAST. *(Ad lib agreement)*

JACOB. Very well, Judah. You take the Torah. That's your way. Go to your house, give your son your blessing and then go out among them. Go, Judah. We'll stand in the synagogue and pray for you.

(Music: Bridge to narrative theme and down)

JUDAH. In the month of August, 1349, I went to my house and covered my books with rugs against the damp and the mice. Then when I saw that the house was in order, I spoke to Aaron, who was my son.

(*Music: Out*)

AARON. Yes, Father?

JUDAH. Aaron, you know where I'm going?

AARON. Yes, Father.

JUDAH. You know I may not return?

AARON. I know.

JUDAH. (*Very softly*) If you live, Aaron, and I die, do this for me.

AARON. Anything you ask.

JUDAH. Wash me clean, Aaron, comb my hair, trim my nails. I want to go clean to the grave as I went clean to the synagogue every Sabbath-Day. Will you do this for me?

AARON. If I am alive to do it, Father, I will.

JUDAH. You're a good boy. Ask them to put me in the ground at the right side of my father. Even if the space is a little narrow, he loves me well enough to make room by his side.

AARON. (*Very softly*) I . . . Father, I . . . God watch over you, Father.

JUDAH. Thank you, Aaron. Now do one more thing.

AARON. Whatever you say, Father.

JUDAH. I may not be home tonight. Will you say the night prayer now. I want to be sure you have said it.

AARON. It is day now.

JUDAH. The sun shines, Aaron, but it is night. Say it for me, please, Aaron.

AARON. Yes, Father. Blessed art Thou, O Lord our God, King of the universe, who makest the bands of sleep to fall upon mine eyes, and slumber upon mine eyelids. May it be Thy will, O Lord my God, and God of my fathers, to suffer me to lie down in peace, and to let me rise up again in peace. Hear, O Israel, the Lord our God, the Lord is One. (*Door shuts*) Father!

(*Music: Bridge*)

(*Footsteps running*)

WILHELM. (*Breathless*) Judah . . . Judah!

JUDAH. It's you, Wilhelm. I thought it was . . .

WILHELM. Where are you going . . . you can't go there.

JUDAH. It's very good of you, Wilhelm.

WILHELM. Turn back.

JUDAH. No, I must talk to them.

WILHELM. They are coming to the Ghetto with fire. You can't talk against fire.

JUDAH. You are a good man, Wilhelm, a good Christian.

WILHELM. I don't know what you are saying.

JUDAH. I'm grateful to you for the warning.

WILHELM. They'll kill you if you go into the city.

JUDAH. They'll kill me if I stay.

WILHELM. Please. The priest was arguing with them . . . they struck him down.

JUDAH. I don't want to die, Wilhelm. I'm afraid. There is a queasiness in my stomach and a nausea in my mouth. But I must try to do what should be done.

WILHELM. Let me go with you, then.

JUDAH. No. For their sake, no. Better one murder on their hands than two murders. But I thank you for it, Wilhelm.

(*Music: Closing theme and down*)

JUDAH. On the morning of August 24, 1349, they struck me down with a stone. The blood ran from my eyes and from my ears, yet I felt no pain. On the afternoon of August 24th they attacked the houses of the Jews and the Jews fought back. They fought with their fists and with their naked hands and with whatever weapons they could seize. Two hundred of the attackers fell. But what was the good of it? They fell with the same scream of hate. The Jews barricaded themselves in their houses and in the synagogue and then when defense was no longer possible, and when they were overpowered, they burned their houses down, and their synagogue. They perished in the flames. Six thousand perished. Old men, and infants in their mothers' arms, and Jacob, and Aaron, who was my son.

(*Music: Out*)

ONE. Bubonic plague: an acute infectious disease transmitted by the rat-flea—very fatal in the septicemic form, even more so in the pneumonic form.

TWO. A petechial eruption and hemorrhages from mucous membranes often occur.

THREE. In the middle of the Fourteenth Century, one-fourth of the population of Europe . . . twenty-five million people died.

JUDAH. I died also. Judah of Mayence. But I did not die of the plague, nor my son Aaron. I died of another plague. A plague of fear and hate. And this is the plague that you yourselves must now destroy. Trust not yourself against it until the day of your death. For while hate endures your synagogues and your churches rest on sand. Therefore, turn your love to the struggle and your understanding also. "For the day is short and the work is great and the workmen are sluggish, and the reward is much and the Master of the house is urgent."

(*Music: Curtain*)

THE MICROSCOPE AND THE PRAYER SHAWL

THE MICROSCOPE AND THE PRAYER SHAWL

The Microscope and the Prayer Shawl *follows* The Black Death *as logically as an autopsy follows a homicide. For in the Middle Ages panic and greed made the Jews "responsible" for plague and resulted in massacre, while in the last decade of the Nineteenth Century a scientist who carried a prayer shawl and a microscope found an answer to plague. This was Waldemar Haffkine's reply to the blood-libel against his people. It was a blood-libel echoed by the Czar's government which in a time of plague rejected an offer of aid with the words, "The Government of His Imperial Majesty prefers that the peasants should die with a prayer for the Czar on their lips rather than owe their lives to a Jew." As has been suggested, it takes a long time to forgive those you have wronged, even longer than five hundred years.*

The Microscope and the Prayer Shawl *had two performances. Ira Avery directed the first production on February 4, 1945 which featured Carl Swenson as Haffkine, Berry Kroeger as the Narrator, Roger De Koven as Pasteur, and Joseph Di Santis as Pierre. Others in the cast were Shepard Menken, Neil Fitzgerald and Bernard Lenrow. A second NBC production on April 28, 1946 featured Luis Van Rooten as Haffkine and Sidney Berry as the Narrator. Frank Papp directed.*

This script was approved by the War Department for transmission overseas to men and women in the fighting services and Armed Forces Radio made Haffkine's name known to troops from the Aleutians to New Zealand.

THE MICROSCOPE AND THE PRAYER SHAWL

VOICE. Thus it is written in the Book of Ben Sira . . . "Honor a physician with the honor due unto him . . . for the Lord hath created him . . . and the Lord hath given men skill that He might be honored in His marvellous works."
(*Cantor: Register with music and hold below*)
NARRATOR. What is more sacred than human life? And who more worthy of esteem than the healer? Thrice blessed are his fingers; "his vessels are full of healthy fluid and the marrow of his bones is well-moistened." (*Pause*) In the year 1888 there lived in the city of Odessa a physician called Waldemar Mordecai Haffkine. Mark his name well . . . Haffkine . . . for you may put his name beside Koch and Ehrlich and Katasato and Von Behring.
(*Cantor: Up briefly and fade out quickly under*)
NARRATOR. In the spring of 1888 the Rector of the Medical Faculty of the celebrated University of Odessa summoned to his office, Dr. Waldemar Haffkine; and, after permitting him to cool his heels for only an hour and a quarter, condescended to see him.
RECTOR. Haffkine, I'll come right to the point.
HAFFKINE. If you please, Excellency.
RECTOR. Professor Metchnikoff wants you for his staff.
HAFFKINE. Here?
RECTOR. Exactly. Here. I've known Metchnikoff to be wrong, but he thinks you have a future. Perhaps you have. We're willing to take a chance.
HAFFKINE. A chance on what, sir?
RECTOR. A chance on Assistant Professor Haffkine. That's the

offer, Haffkine, Assistant Professor of Bacteriology.
(*Pause*)

HAFFKINE. I'd be very glad to accept, sir.

RECTOR. Fine. That's what I like, Haffkine. No hemming and hawing; no false modesty. Congratulations, Professor.

HAFFKINE. Thank you, sir. I'm very happy.

RECTOR. Good. Now . . . just one thing, Haffkine. A necessary formality.

HAFFKINE. Yes?

RECTOR. Try to arrange your baptism ceremony for this week. We want you to begin teaching at once.

HAFFKINE. Did you say baptism, sir?

RECTOR. I believe that's what I said, and I believe you heard me. Baptism.
(*Pause*)

HAFFKINE. I beg your pardon, sir. I hadn't noticed it was nearly dusk. May I?

RECTOR. What are you talking about, Haffkine? May you what?

HAFFKINE. It's time for afternoon prayers. (*Pause*) Ahsh-ray yohsh-vay vay-seh-chaw, ohd y'hah-l-loo-chaw seh-law. Ahsh-ray haw-awm sheh-kaw-chaw loh. Ahsh-ray haw-awm sheh ah-doh-nawy eh-loh-hawv. T'hee-law l'daw-veed . . .

RECTOR. (*Breaking in*) Haffkine, what's this? How dare you?

HAFFKINE. I told you, sir . . . afternoon prayers.

RECTOR. I gather that's your answer.

HAFFKINE. I suppose it is, sir.
(*Footsteps briskly . . . door opens slightly off mike*)

RECTOR. (*Moving off slightly*) Nice to see you, my dear Haffkine.

HAFFKINE. (*Moving off slowly*) Yes, of course, sir. (*Pause*) Thank you very much.
(*Music: Bridge and take out with:*)
(*Escape of steam from R.R. engine*)
(*Crowd in background*)

PROFESSOR. Your microscope case, Haffkine.

HAFFKINE. Thank you, Professor Metchnikoff. (*Pause*) I'm very grateful.

PROFESSOR. What for?

HAFFKINE. For seeing me off.

PROFESSOR. I'm just selfish. I had hoped you might change your mind.

HAFFKINE. That's why I'm going to Geneva. They don't want me to change my mind about anything.

PROFESSOR. Yes, of course. Don't drop that case.

HAFFKINE. Let me open it, Professor Metchnikoff. (*Latch snaps*) Look in, Professor.

PROFESSOR. Well? It's a microscope, isn't it?

HAFFKINE. Yes, it's a microscope, Professor. And this velvet bag beside it holds a prayer shawl.

(*Pause*)

PROFESSOR. A microscope and a prayer shawl. Hmmph. Curious combination, Haffkine . . . but I suppose they're your convictions, and a man has a right to live by his convictions . . . but not in Odessa I'm afraid.

HAFFKINE. That's why I'm going to Geneva.

PROFESSOR. Haffkine, doesn't your science get in the way of your religion?

HAFFKINE. I don't think so. Both teach me to try to live decently. I haven't found any conflict. Should I?

PROFESSOR. I should think you'd be satisfied with the scientific method.

HAFFKINE. I don't know. Science tells me how . . . religion tells me why.

VOICE. (*Off*) Board. Board. All aboard!

(*Warning whistle toot*)

PROFESSOR. Good luck, Haffkine.

HAFFKINE. Thank you, Professor Metchnikoff. (*Pause*) Professor.

PROFESSOR. Yes?

HAFFKINE. His Excellency, the Rector of the Medical Faculty, is a fairly good scientist, isn't he?

PROFESSOR. Well?

HAFFKINE. Nothing. Only it occurs to me that he has a most unscientific interest in what religion he doesn't want me to practice.

VOICE. All aboard. Board! Board!

(*Train door slams . . . slow chug of engine . . . screech of wheels . . . build and move up . . . whistle into:*)

(*Music: Bridge and segue to narrative theme and down*)

NARRATOR. In the spring of 1888 a microscope and a prayer shawl journeyed from the city of Odessa to Geneva. And the life of Waldemar Haffkine recommenced in the West upon a symbol. For one year he labored in the laboratories of Geneva. (*Music fading*) And in the year 1890, a man called Louis Pasteur summoned him to Paris.

(*Rattle of knives, plates, etc. . . . hold under*)

PASTEUR. We're glad to have you, Haffkine. Professor Metchnikoff has recommended you very highly. (*Pause*) Don't you like food, Haffkine?

HAFFKINE. Why, the bread is fine, Monsieur.

PASTEUR. I'm sorry. Metchnikoff told me you observe the Jewish dietary laws. Let me get you some hard-boiled eggs.

HAFFKINE. Thank you, Monsieur.

(*Pause*)

PASTEUR. Haffkine, it's been my rule never to discuss a man's religion . . . but . . . uh . . . don't you as a scientist find these dietary restrictions . . . these injunctions against mixing milk and meat . . . well, don't you find them slightly incompatible with your profession?

HAFFKINE. Monsieur Pasteur, you're a bacteriologist, aren't you?

PASTEUR. I try to be. Why?

HAFFKINE. Under Hebrew dietary laws the blood is removed from the vascular system of all animals slaughtered for food. Would you call that bad bacteriology?

PASTEUR. No. I dare say I wouldn't. Mmm. It's quite true that after death the blood is invaded by microbial germs.

HAFFKINE. That's our dietary law, Monsieur. For three thousand years we have sterilized in boiling water all utensils contaminated by unclean objects. We have rejected animal carcasses tainted with infection. We have purified our meat with crystal salt. I find it very curious that these ancient rituals are now confirmed and blessed by the modern microscope.

PASTEUR. Perhaps so, Doctor Haffkine. But so *many* rituals.

HAFFKINE. You wonder that I observe them all, don't you?

PASTEUR. I'm afraid I do.

HAFFKINE. And I find myself wondering what life would be like without its ceremonials. No man can breathe pure oxygen.

PASTEUR. (*Laughs*) Metchnikoff warned me I was acquiring an excellent microscope and . . .

HAFFKINE. A prayer shawl?

PASTEUR. Yes.

(*They laugh*)
(*Music: Bridge*)
(*Voices briefly*)

PASTEUR. Gentlemen. (*Voices out*) Gentlemen, we have a problem. Asiatic cholera.

ONE. Is there another epidemic, Pasteur?

PASTEUR. Not in Europe, Monsieur. But once again in India. Inevitably it must reach us. Our problem is simple . . . that's why it is so difficult. Thanks to Herr Koch we know that the comma bacillus is responsible. Our simple little problem is to take the good Herr Koch's cultures and prepare a vaccine against cholera.

HAFFKINE. Monsieur Pasteur, I'd like to try.

ONE. All of us would, Haffkine.

HAFFKINE. I have a special reason.

PASTEUR. Have you, Haffkine?

HAFFKINE. Five hundred years ago people of my faith were massacred not many miles from this city because a pestilence came from the East. They were held responsible. I think I should like to work on a vaccine.

(*Pause*)

PASTEUR. Are there any objections, gentlemen? (*Pause*) It seems there are none. Very well, Haffkine. May I suggest you begin at once.

(*Music: Bridge*)
(*Sound of mice squeaking high on mike*)

PIERRE. These enough mice, Professor Haffkine?

HAFFKINE. They'll do, Pierre. Are they labeled?

PIERRE. Better than that. I've named them. This is Suzanne, This is Marie, Alouette, Jeanne, Sophie, Valerie, Marcelle, Antoinette, Yvonne . . .

HAFFKINE. All female?

PIERRE. Why not? All day long I see nothing but men. If some of these mice are not female, I am sure they will forgive me.

HAFFKINE. (*Chuckles*) All right, Pierre. Now be very careful. You know what we do first?

PIERRE. Shoot the micro-organisms into the mice . . . gradually increase the dosage, wait for antibodies to form, prepare a vaccine, inoculate the dying population of India, try to appear modest, and make speeches to all the stuffed-shirt societies explaining you are not a hero, only the saviour of half the world.

HAFFKINE. I see you have it all worked out, Pierre.

PIERRE. Naturally. I shall buy a villa at Cannes and eat snails in garlic sauce for the rest of my life.

HAFFKINE. Nothing else, Pierre?

PIERRE. Oh, yes. I shall become a patron of the arts. I am tone-deaf, I don't understand poetry, and I am color-blind. I feel I am qualified.

HAFFKINE. Pierre, you are wasting your talents in the laboratory. You should go in for dramatic criticism.
PIERRE. I will consider it.
HAFFKINE. Do that, Pierre. Now if you please, kindly consider the mice. Be careful as you inject. If some of that solution gets into your system . . . only God can help you. Please, Pierre, very careful.
(*Music: Bridge to narrative theme and down*)
NARRATOR. In the year 1890 Waldemar Haffkine working in the Paris laboratory of Louis Pasteur began the long vigil of science against death. He rose at dawn and put on his phylacteries and donned his prayer shawl, and glorified the God of Israel. And then he removed his prayer shawl and took up the microscope. He surrounded himself with death in test-tubes and he defended himself with the weapons of his profession and the armor of his faith. In the weeks that passed failure followed upon failure. The mice died. He prepared new cultures of the deadly cholera organism and began again. Still the mice died. (*Music out*) But defeat for the man of science is a better teacher than success. And Waldemar Haffkine tried again.
HAFFKINE. Pierre, the mice die because our injections are too deadly. We must attenuate the virus . . . weaken it so that the mice will not succumb after the first injection.
PIERRE. Poor Antoinette . . . I was very fond of her.
HAFFKINE. Pierre!
PIERRE. Sorry, sir.
HAFFKINE. Cook this solution.
PIERRE. Cook it?
HAFFKINE. Exactly.
PIERRE. You will kill the organisms.
HAFFKINE. Either kill or weaken them. And we inject with dead or dying bacilli. That may be our answer. Cook them, Pierre. Let's begin from the beginning.

(*Music: Montage theme and down*)
(*Mice squeaking*)

PIERRE. (*Happily*) Slight swelling at the point of injection, but no dead mice.

HAFFKINE. Increase the strength of the injection, Pierre, and repeat.

(*Music: Up and down*)

PIERRE. Yvonne No. 2 seems very happy, Dr. Haffkine.

HAFFKINE. Increase the dosage, Pierre.

(*Music: Up and down*)

PIERRE. All mice present and accounted for.

HAFFKINE. Continue building the dosage.

(*Music: Up and down*)

PIERRE. They've got enough cholera bugs in them to wipe out the population of Europe.

HAFFKINE. Step number two, Pierre. Our assumption is that their blood is loaded with anti-cholera bodies. Now . . . it's up to me to prepare a vaccine.

(*Music: Up and finish*)
(*Mice squeaking on mike*)

PASTEUR. These mice were inoculated with vaccine?

HAFFKINE. Yes, Pasteur.

PASTEUR. And these?

HAFFKINE. No vaccine. They're our control.

PASTEUR. I see. Then you are ready for your test.

HAFFKINE. I hope so. I've grown two cultures of cholera bugs on the peritoneum of guinea-pigs. It's the deadliest culture I've made. Now I'm going to shoot the stuff into both groups of mice.

PASTEUR. Good, Haffkine. If the vaccinated group survives, then . . .

HAFFKINE. I'm not going to hope. I'll just wait. Just wait and see. Pierre . . . all right, Pierre.

(*Music: Bridge*)

PIERRE. (*Breathless*) Dr. Haffkine. Step two . . . you're on the right track. Every control mouse is dead.

HAFFKINE. For Heaven's sake, Pierre, the vaccinated mice . . . how about them?

PIERRE. My friend Yvonne No. 2 . . . look.

(*Sound of mouse squeaking*)

HAFFKINE. Don't joke, Pierre . . . there are nineteen others.

PIERRE. Only three are dead. Seventeen out of twenty are alive. You've got an anti-cholera vaccine, Doctor. You've got it.

(*Music: Bridge to narrative theme and down*)

NARRATOR. But nothing is sure in life or in science and Waldemar Haffkine tried again. He repeated his experiment with new guinea-pigs, using new controls. The vaccine held. The mice who were not inoculated died; seventeen out of twenty, fifteen out of twenty, sixteen out of twenty of the vaccinated mice survived. Scientific proof. Now for Waldemar Haffkine . . . still another step. (*Music out*)

HAFFKINE. Pierre, is the vaccine sterile?

PIERRE. Sterile.

HAFFKINE. Good. Some antiseptic on my arm, please.

PIERRE. What are you going to do?

HAFFKINE. Prove the vaccine is non-toxic. I'm going to inoculate myself.

PIERRE. It's dangerous, Haffkine. Suppose you're wrong.

HAFFKINE. It's the only way to prove the vaccine is non-toxic. (*Pause*) I don't believe in story-book heroes. They're generally rather juvenile. But I've calculated the risks, Pierre. I know the odds. (*Chuckles*) And you see, I believe in God, Pierre. And even in Dr. Pasteur's laboratory, He helps, Pierre. He helps.

PIERRE. I hope so. Go ahead and inoculate yourself.

HAFFKINE. Where are you going?

PIERRE. Why, I thought I'd just go to the door and kiss that scroll you've tacked up . . . just for luck.

HAFFKINE. That's no good luck charm, Pierre. I'm religious

but not superstitious.

PIERRE. You kiss that doorpost scroll?

HAFFKINE. Not for luck, Pierre. There's a piece of parchment inside with a few passages from Deuteronomy. It's a reminder for me and for everyone of my faith that God is everywhere.

PIERRE. Well, I'm superstitious. You inoculate yourself. I'm going to kiss it for luck.

(*Music: Bridge*)

PASTEUR. Cramps?

HAFFKINE. None at all.

PASTEUR. Pain in the leg?

HAFFKINE. No pain.

PASTEUR. Put this thermometer under your tongue. All the way.

HAFFKINE. (*Talking with thermometer under his tongue*) I tell you I have no temperature.

PASTEUR. Shut up, I'm a scientist.

HAFFKINE. (*Mumbling*) Feel my head, Pasteur?

PASTEUR. With my lips, no doubt! Haffkine, stop talking. You'll break the thing.

HAFFKINE. All right.

PASTEUR. I said stop talking. Pierre, how is his pulse?

PIERRE. I don't know, I'm busy taking my own.

PASTEUR. What's that?

PIERRE. Well—if he could inoculate himself . . . well—so can I. I just took some of it. I'm scared stiff.

PASTEUR. You did, eh? My dear Pierre, the pathology of Asiatic cholera, after death in the stage of collapse, often is characterized by postmortem elevation of temperature, early and marked rigor mortis, sometimes preceded by muscular twitching. The skin is dusky . . .

HAFFKINE. (*No thermometer*) And shrunken, blood dark and concentrated. Serous membranes may be coated with fibrin. Small intestines may show . . .

THE MICROSCOPE AND THE PRAYER SHAWL

PASTEUR. What's your temperature, Haffkine?

HAFFKINE. Stop worrying, Pierre. My temperature is normal. (*Pause*)

PASTEUR. Congratulations, Haffkine. I think you've got it. The vaccine is potent, non-toxic and laboratory-tested.

HAFFKINE. That's just it. It works against a guinea pig infected with cholera; Pierre and I are going to prove it's not harmful to human beings . . . that's fine. But will it be effective against the cholera bug in a human being? That's the only test.

PASTEUR. Would you like to make that test?

HAFFKINE. Where? India?

PASTEUR. Not just yet. Haffkine, there's an outbreak of cholera in the city of Odessa. (*Pause*)

HAFFKINE. Pierre . . . a telegraph blank . . . I'm writing the Rector of the University right away.

(*Music: Bridge*)

PASTEUR. Here's your answer, Haffkine.

HAFFKINE. Wait until I dry my hands. (*Pause*) Thank you, Pasteur.

(*Sound of envelope torn open*)

PASTEUR. Well, Haffkine?

HAFFKINE. (*Slowly*) Yes, it's the Rector's answer. His Excellency has wasted no time. Read it for yourself, Pasteur.

PASTEUR. The Government of His Imperial Majesty prefers that the peasants should die with a prayer for the Czar on their lips rather than owe their lives to a Jew.

(*Music: Bridge to narrative theme and down*)

NARRATOR. In the year 1893 when the monsoons retreated from the Provinces of India, Asiatic cholera struck with dread force. In ten thousand cities and villages from Madras in the South to Rawalpindi in the North there was a shrivelling of the skin and a continental prostration. And a quiet man with a microscope and a prayer shawl, carrying gallons of an untried vaccine, disembarked at the port of Bombay. (*Music out*) And Waldemar Mordecai Haffkine began his work.

(*Crowd up and then hold in background*)

ENGLISHMAN. One at a time. Easy there. Hold them back. Back. One at a time. Dr. Haffkine, I think you can begin with the first one.

HAFFKINE. Thank you, sir. All right. Clerk.

CLERK. Name, Amtha Tribuhvan. Age 26. Wife's name. Rukhma. Caste, Mang. Birthplace, Karanja.

HAFFKINE. Clerk, you've explained that this is voluntary. I want it understood that these inoculations will be given without any compulsion.

VOICE. I speak English, Doctor. I understand.

HAFFKINE. Good. Please hold out your arm. Steady. It won't hurt very much. Steady. Good. Thank you, sir.

VOICE. No more?

HAFFKINE. That's all, sir.

CLERK. Sadoo Babaji next. Then Gulam Abdul Nahi, Govind Babaji, Tukaram Rama, Shamantar Ahmed, Babia Govind, (*Fading under*) Abdul Rahman Buda, Yasin Abdul, Dharma Mabadu, Alikhan Mogulkan . . .

ENGLISHMAN. In line, please. No crowding. Dr. Haffkine's here to stay. Please wait your turn. Dr. Haffkine's not leaving India.

(*Music: Bridge to narrative theme and down*)

NARRATOR. For fourteen years Dr. Waldemar Mordecai Haffkine did not leave India. Countless millions of lives were saved by his anti-cholera vaccine. And when the bubonic plague spread its black death in Mysore, in Hyderabad, in Hindustan, and in the Punjab, Haffkine discovered a serum against a second pestilence. Cholera and bubonic plague . . . scourges of mankind, most ancient of the death-riders . . . humble before the weapon of a man with a microscope . . . and a prayer shawl.

(*Music: With cantor in the clear and hold down*)

VOICE. It is written in the Book of Ben Sira . . . "Honor a physician with the honor due unto him . . . for the Lord hath created him."

HAFFKINE. If you will remember the name of Waldemar Haffkine, let it be for these things: that it was given me to add my small stone to the pyramid of history; that the banners I have held in my hand and pass on to you are the legacy of generations dead to generations still not born. Let it be for the glory of all men in the name of God.

(*Music: Curtain*)

(*Music. With cantor in the flies and bola down*)

voice. It is written in the Book of Ben Sira . . . "Honor a physician with the honor due unto him . . . for the Lord hath created him."

BERTRAND. If you will remember the name of Waldemar Halkin, let it be for these things that it was given me to add my small stone to the pyramid of history; that the lamp as I have held in my hand and pass on to you are the legacy of generations dead to generations still not born.

Let it be for the glory of all mankind the name of God.

(*Music. Curtain.*)

HOW THEY KNOCKED THE DEVIL OUT OF UNCLE EZRA

HOW THEY KNOCKED THE DEVIL OUT OF UNCLE EZRA

How They Knocked the Devil Out of Uncle Ezra *is an instance in which the title of the script was thought of first and the script itself written to justify the title. Uncle Ezra was done in virtual collaboration with Dr. Moshe Davis. It was Rabbi Davis who conceived the unblowable shofar, the unshakable lullab, the de-tasselled cantor, the sweet horseradish and the sour fish; suggestions which were promptly accepted. More important, however, Rabbi Davis kept the script away from outright farce by holding it to the central conflict of knowledge versus ignorance and superstition.*

At the close of the dramatization Rabbi Albert I. Gordon, Executive Director of the United Synagogue of America, brought Uncle Ezra home. He said: "There have always been large numbers of men and women in all civilizations who have assumed that amulets, incantations, charms, and magical formulas of one kind or another could solve all human problems.... Consider for a moment how frequently we have used the phrase 'One World' or how we have spoken of 'human freedom' as being inviolable." *And he added that when we attribute a magic quality to the utterance of a pious phrase about brotherhood we* "are guilty of the same error in thinking which in others we would call superstition."

How They Knocked the Devil Out of Uncle Ezra *was performed on November 24, 1946. Michael Artist was Uncle Ezra, Alexander Scourby was the Narrator, Roger De Koven was heard as Reb Isaac Aaron, and Adelaide Klein was the woman who tried to bake the untwistable twist. Other friends and relatives of Uncle Ezra were Guy Repp, Gene Leonard, Ronnie Liss, Billy Redfield, Charlotte Holland, Leon Janney, and Joseph Boland.*

HOW THEY KNOCKED THE DEVIL OUT OF UNCLE EZRA

NARRATOR. In the town of Dalid, which lies adjacent to the town of Gimel in the province of Aleph-Bes, there was born many years ago a rather unusual child. His facial features were quite ordinary, his body structure was average, and his family was altogether commonplace; and so wherein, you will ask, was he unusual? He was a seventh son. But you smile. There have been millions of seventh sons. Very true. But none like this boy Ezra; for each of his six older brothers, and for that matter each of his seven sisters, was at least twenty years his senior. (*Music out*)

In short, Ezra was a rather remarkable product of old age.

TWO. (*About thirty-five*) Father, do you think your grandchildren can see the baby?

FATHER. I see no objection. Let them all come in on tiptoe and take a look at their Uncle Ezra.

(*Music: Narrative theme and down*)

NARRATOR. This was Ezra's chief distinction. At birth he was already twenty-one times an uncle. And some years later visitors to the town of Dalid would rub their eyes when a grown man, passing a small boy, would stop for a moment and say . . .

ONE. Good morning, Uncle Ezra, here are some marbles for you. By the way, my wedding is this Sunday. It would be a personal favor, Uncle Ezra, if you washed your face for the occasion.

NARRATOR. Not long after, Uncle Ezra acquired two other distinctions. The first of these was an accumulation of superstitions, amulets and incantations incredible in a boy so young.

EZRA. Ny hory ny hory, ny buri ny kory. Say it twice and spit three times. It drives out bad luck.

NARRATOR. The second of these latter distinctions was a slyness that had something demonic in it.

(*Music: Out*)

ISAAC. Good morning. (*Door shuts*) Uncle Ezra didn't come for his lesson yesterday so I thought I'd stop by.

FATHER. Good morning, Reb Isaac Aaron. The boy says he's sick.

ISAAC. Boys are occasionally sick when they have to go to school. Do you think I could see him?

FATHER. It won't do any good. But you'll find him in there.

ISAAC. It never hurts to try.

(*Footsteps, door opens, shuts*)

EZRA. (*Groaning*) Oh, my stomach, oh, oh. (*Continue a bit*)

ISAAC. Try a little more tremolo. Like this. Oh-h-h-h.

(*Pause*)

EZRA. For a teacher, Reb Isaac Aaron, you have very little faith in human beings.

ISAAC. I have a good deal of faith in human beings but very little faith in your stomach-ache.

EZRA. (*Not pretending any longer*) It's a terrible stomach-ache.

ISAAC. Do you mind if I sit on your bed?

EZRA. Make yourself at home.

ISAAC. Thank you. (*Squeak of bedspring*) Uncle Ezra, just man to man. How do you manage to get away with it?

EZRA. Man to man?

ISAAC. You have my word.

EZRA. At the beginning I used to say I had a headache.

ISAAC. It worked, didn't it?

EZRA. Only the first ten times. Then they began to get suspicious. My sisters insisted on feeling my head to see if it was hot.

canopy and the Cantor sings, and the Rabbi is about to pronounce the benediction, she's going to try to step on your foot.

ONE. You're really crazy. Why should my future wife try to step on my foot just before the benediction?

EZRA. Because if she does, it will mean that she will rule you. But if you step on her foot first, it means that you will rule her.

ONE. Hmm! How do you know all this?

EZRA. Never mind how I know.

ONE. It's superstitious nonsense. I'll have no part of it. I'm not that gullible.

EZRA. Suit yourself, Nephew. Blood is thicker than water, and I thought I'd warn you. If she steps on your foot first, I'm not the one who is going to be dominated. (*Pause*) Well, you're probably right anyhow, it's just a lot of nonsense.

(*Music: Bridge*)

BRIDE. Uncle Ezra, he wouldn't do a thing like that.

EZRA. How do you know?

BRIDE. Because he loves me as much as I love him.

EZRA. You've very beautiful, Naomi, I'm sorry I spoke. Forget it.

BRIDE. Uncle Ezra, are you sure he plans to step on my foot while we stand under the bridal canopy?

EZRA. Forget it, Naomi. It isn't really important.

BRIDE. So he really thinks he can dominate me for the rest of my life?

EZRA. I shouldn't have brought it up, Naomi. Don't put any stock in these old wives' tales.

BRIDE. You believe in it, Uncle Ezra, don't you?

EZRA. I'm just a boy. I'll grow out of it.

BRIDE. You're sweet. Uncle Ezra, I want to give you a kiss.

EZRA. I don't deserve it, Naomi.

BRIDE. You do, Uncle Ezra. You really do. So he thinks he's

going to dominate me, does he? (*A quick laugh of scorn*)
(*Music: Bridge*)

THREE. The bridegroom will place the ring upon the forefingers of the bride's right hand. (*Pause*) Am I talking to myself? I said the bridegroom will now place the ring upon the forefinger of the . . .
(*Stamp of a foot*)

ONE. (*Exultant but sotto*) You missed, Naomi. It's my turn now.
(*Stamp of foot*)

NAOMI. (*Panting*) No you don't.
(*Stamping accelerates*)

THREE. (*Roaring*) What is this a wedding or a footrace? Children, stop before you cripple one another for life. Somebody stop them.

EZRA. (*Casually and close to mike*) Reb Isaac Aaron, they're silly, aren't they?

ISAAC. Of course. It's only a foolish superstition.

EZRA. That's exactly what I told them, Isaac Aaron, in exactly those words.
(*Music: Narrative theme and down*)

NARRATOR. It is not recorded what Reb Isaac Aaron replied, but the scholar and teacher of the town of Dalid had lost the second encounter to Uncle Ezra. For truth requires knowledge to nourish it, while ignorance feeds handsomely upon itself.
(*Music: Up and down*)

NARRATOR. From that moment on there was neither bride nor bridegroom in the town of Dalid who did not approach the marriage ceremony except with misgiving and trepidation. The first prerequisite for marriage became a limber ankle, a quick instep, and a determination to step first and to step hard. This was the beginning of the ascendancy of Uncle Ezra.
(*Music: Up to montage theme and down*)

EZRA. If you've had a bad dream during the night, spit three times when you wake up.

ISAAC. People of Dalid, stop spitting. Don't listen to the boy.

(*Music: Up and down*)

EZRA. Never step across a child or he won't grow.

ISAAC. You're not going to believe that, are you?

THREE. I don't exactly believe it, but there's no sense in taking chances, is there?

(*Music: Up and down*)

EZRA. If your right eye itches, you'll be happy; if your left eye itches, you'll cry before the day is out.

ISAAC. Nonsense. Pay no attention. If either eye itches, wash it with boric acid or go to the doctor.

(*Music: Up and down*)

EZRA. Knock on wood . . . thirteen's unlucky . . . never start a journey on a Monday. Spit three times . . . Ny hory ny hory, ny buri ny kori.

(*Music: Up and cut*)

ISAAC. Boy, you're a pagan.

EZRA. I believe in the same God you do, Isaac Aaron.

ISAAC. You believe in many gods. Gods of luck and misfortune. Uncle Ezra, you're an idolater.

EZRA. You've lost, Reb Isaac Aaron. If I had lost I'd call you no names.

ISAAC. "Thou shalt be wholehearted with the Lord thy God." That's a commandment. These people have listened to you. They are no longer wholehearted with the Lord.

EZRA. Yes, they are— they pray for luck.

ISAAC. That's infamous.

EZRA. What should they pray for?

ISAAC. For kindness, for justice, for peace. Uncle Ezra, do you worship luck or do you worship God?

(*Music: Sneak in and down*)

NARRATOR. He didn't answer. Uncle Ezra couldn't answer. He smiled. And his smile said nothing. Isaac Aaron studied him. And there was a look in the scholar's eye that had not been there before. (*Music very far in background*)

ISAAC. Uncle Ezra, I wouldn't be surprised if Satan himself is in you.

(*Music: Up and down*)

NARRATOR. A rather odd thing for a scholar to say. But the thing seemed to be confirmed by a new commercial enterprise entered into by Uncle Ezra.

EZRA. I cash sins. I buy sins. Little sins, medium sins, offenses, errors, faults, violations, small transgressions. I cash sins.

NARRATOR. It seems a peasant had told Uncle Ezra that it was possible for a boy to acquire another boy's sin without injury to his soul, while acquiring a little profit in the transaction.

(*Music: Out*)

BOY. I built a bonfire on the Sabbath. I didn't really mean to, but it's a sin. How much do you charge, Uncle Ezra?

EZRA. Seeing it's you, three apples and that watch your cousin Michael broke on Hannukah.

BOY. You're not afraid to buy my sin?

EZRA. I'll have the three apples, won't I? I'm not afraid.

(*Pause*)

BOY. Here. One, two, three apples and the watch. The sin is off my conscience.

EZRA. And it's on mine.

BOY. Uncle Ezra, why don't you shiver?

EZRA. What for?

BOY. Satan made me sin. And I've sold you the sin.

EZRA. What about it?

BOY. Uncle Ezra. (*Pause*) Uncle Ezra, how do you know that Satan himself isn't part of the bargain? How do you know that Satan himself is not in you at this moment?

(*Music: Chord*)

NARRATOR. Uncle Ezra pondered the idea and ate the apples.

(*Music: Full and down*)

NARRATOR. But somehow the commercial venture proceeded badly. The townspeople of Dalid seemed eager enough to sell their sins, but at the same time they seemed badly disposed to the buyer. And because he began to be troubled by heads that were lowered and eyes that were averted, Uncle Ezra began to reconsider matters. It was peculiar; dissatisfaction bred thought, and thought led to reflection, and reflection led him to Reb Isaac Aaron.

EZRA. I think I'd like to go back to school again.

(*Music: Up and down*)

NARRATOR. The only difficulty was that the townspeople of Dalid refused to unlearn the superstitions of Uncle Ezra.

ONE. Ny hory ny hory, ny buri ny kori. Say it twice and spit three times. It will keep away the Evil Eye.

EZRA. I'll tell you something. Maybe there isn't an Evil Eye. Not really.

BOY. He's a liar. He says that because Satan is in him. He's trying to trap us. Get away, Satan, get away.

(*Music: Out*)

NARRATOR. And Reb Isaac Aaron stood nearby and smiled bitterly. And it wasn't long after that things began to happen in the town of Dalid.

(*Music: Punctuation*)

BRIDE. May all the matriarchs of Israel blind my eyes.

ONE. Naomi, stop cursing yourself. What's wrong?

BRIDE. Taste this fish.

ONE. I'll have it for supper, I can wait.

BRIDE. Taste it now.

ONE. Don't raise your voice, I'll taste it. (*Pause*) Faugh. The fish is sour.

BRIDE. Now taste this horseradish I just made. Taste it. (*Pause*) Well?

ONE. It's impossible. Naomi, the fish is sour and the horseradish is sweet. It's impossible.

BRIDE. No, not impossible when Satan is around. Where is Uncle Ezra?

(*Music: Bridge*)

THREE. Quiet, everyone, quiet. Benjamin is going to blow the ram's horn and show us how it's going to sound on Rosh Hashanah. Are you ready, Benjamin? All right. Go on . . . blow it.

FOUR. (*He blows and blows but all that is heard is the expulsion of his breath*)

THREE. Benjamin, what's the matter?

FOUR. I don't know. This never happened before.

THREE. Are you the most celebrated virtuoso on the ram's horn or not?

FOUR. The best in the entire province of Aleph-Bes.

THREE. Even if you have to say so yourself. Then blow, Benjamin. Sound the shofar. Make room, everyone. There he blows.

FOUR. (*Wind and nothing else*)

THREE. Stop before your eyes pop out. Stop, Benjamin.

FOUR. (*Panting*) It can't happen to me. I'm disgraced.

THREE. No. You're not disgraced.

FOUR. No?

THREE. I know why you can't get any sound out of the ram's horn.

FOUR. You do?

THREE. Something's in it.

FOUR. What?

THREE. Satan, Benjamin. Satan is in the ram's horn, holding back the holy sound. Get a broomstick, we're going to find Uncle Ezra.

(*Music: Bridge*)

CANTOR. Blame it on Uncle Ezra, blame it on Satan, I don't care. This festival of Sukkos, I do not sing in the synagogue.

FATHER. But you can't refuse. You're the Cantor of Dalid.

CANTOR. I do not sing.

FATHER. People will demand an explanation.
CANTOR. I'll tell them. Who am I, I'll ask. The Cantor of Dalid, they'll answer. In what do I sing, I'll ask. In the tallest and the whitest skullcap in the entire province of Aleph-Bes, they'll answer. And what is on the tallest and whitest skullcap in the entire province of Aleph-Bes? A beautiful white tassel, they'll say. And where is the white tassel now? Uncle Ezra took it. Satan took it. No white tassel, no singing. I am not in competition with Satan. Not a single note.

(*Music: Bridge*)

ISAAC. What's puzzling you, boy?
BOY. Reb Isaac Aaron, is this the day before the Feast of Tabernacles or isn't it?
ISAAC. It is.
BOY. And am I supposed to bring home this citron and this palm branch?
ISAAC. You are. The esrog and the lullab. That's the tradition.
BOY. And tomorrow, do I shake this palm branch?
ISAAC. Just as your forefathers did.
BOY. No, I won't.
ISAAC. Why not, Mordecai?
BOY. (*Bursting into tears*) Because the lullab won't shake. I've shaken it and shaken it and shaken it. It won't shake. It's spoiled. Satan's gotten into it. Uncle Ezra, you're wicked, you're wicked. I want my three apples back.

(*Music: Bridge*)

WOMAN. Reb Isaac Aaron, this is the last straw.
ISAAC. What is, Sarah Leah?
WOMAN. Is this flour?
ISAAC. It looks like it.
WOMAN. Is this an egg?
ISAAC. A respectable egg from a respectable peace-loving hen.
WOMAN. And is this yeast, is this oil, is this salt, is this sugar?
ISAAC. Without a question. But calm yourself.

WOMAN. I'll have apoplexy before the day is over. I took ingredients just like this, I made this dough. The same dough to make the same twist that I bake each Sabbath and holiday except Passover. My mother baked her twist that way, my mother's mother baked her twist that way. It was a twist. Here's the dough . . . I twist it.
(*Music: A twisting little curl like a coiled spring*)
ISAAC. Sarah Leah, it's twisted very nicely.
WOMAN. Wait. May sixteen thousand black plagues never take Uncle Ezra between the eyes. Just wait.
ISAAC. It's still twisted.
WOMAN. May the cholera never loosen his back teeth. Keep looking.
ISAAC. I don't see a thing, Sarah Leah.
WOMAN. Look now.
(*Music: Uncurls*)
WOMAN. Matriarchs of Israel, did you see? The twist untwisted. Satan has crawled into my dough. Get Uncle Ezra.
(*Music: Bridge to marching theme and down*)
(*Shouting voices in background*)
NARRATOR. With pitchforks, broomhandles, sticks, kitchen knives, the townspeople of Dalid in the province of Aleph-Bes began to march.
ONE. Get the sweet horseradish, Naomi.
NARRATOR. Naomi marched with the sour fish and the sweet horseradish. The Cantor marched without his white tassel. Sarah Leah marched with the twistless twist. Benjamin, the virtuoso on the ram's horn, marched with the useless shofar to his lips. The boy Mordecai marched with the unshakable palm branch. They marched with grimness.
TWO. We're going to find him.
THREE. And when we find him, it's going to be just too bad.
ISAAC. (*Quietly*) Gentlemen, what do you propose to do?
FOUR. Nothing. Not a thing. All we're going to do is to knock the devil out of Uncle Ezra.

(*They yell into:*)
(*Music: Up and down*)

NARRATOR. They found Uncle Ezra cowering in a small tree beside a little stream.

(*Music: Out*)

ONE. Throw him in.

(*Sound of splash*)

TWO. Good. I know the way to get the devil out of him. Immerse him under water three times and take him out only twice.

(*Ad lib encouragement*)

ISAAC. Quiet, you fools. I said quiet. (*Pause*) Pull him out; do you want to drown the boy? I said pull him out.

WOMAN. Reb Isaac Aaron, Satan is in him.

BOY. He made a bargain. I was there.

ISAAC. Fools. Superstitious fools. Bring him here. (*Pause*) Here's my coat, Uncle Ezra. Throw it around you.

EZRA. Thank you, Reb Isaac Aaron.

(*Pause*)

ISAAC. Look at yourselves. All of you. There's hate in your eyes. Your lips are thin and bloodless. People of Dalid, look what's happened to you? You fools, you've sacrificed your own divinity through ignorance. What kind of a world is this where stupidity and superstition unite men more than knowledge and learning?

(*Pause*)

FOUR. Satan is in him.

ISAAC. You're an imbecile.

THREE. We've got to find a way to knock it out of him.

ISAAC. You're the chief imbecile. Be still all of you. (*Pause*) I'm a man of faith, do you hear. And I've tried to be a man of knowledge. I've tried to teach your children; but you let your children teach you. Listen to me: religion is not superstition. I deny that true religion can proceed from ignorance. Because life will not tolerate ignorance. When faith is born of ignorance, faith is superstition. Now go home and be ashamed of yourselves.

(*Pause*)

BRIDE. Reb Isaac, if what you say is true, then who made my fish sour and my horseradish sweet.

ISAAC. Not Satan, Naomi.

CANTOR. Then who took my tassel.

ISAAC. I did.

(*Pause*)

FATHER. Reb Isaac Aaron, do you realize what you're saying?

ISAAC. I realize it, do you? (*Pause*) All right, I'll tell you. Naomi, when sugar is put into horseradish, horseradish becomes sweet. I put the sugar in. And I substituted rotten fish for fresh fish.

BOY. Why didn't my lullab shake?

ISAAC. Because when glue is poured on a palm branch, no lullab will shake.

WOMAN. But my untwistable twist . . . that was Satan's work!

ISAAC. My work, Sarah Leah. Feel the dough. There's a fine steel rod in it. I put it there.

(*Pause*)

EZRA. Reb Isaac Aaron, you did all this because of me, didn't you?

ISAAC. Yes, Uncle Ezra. Because we're all men and women. Because we have eyes, we have minds. Our eyes are in front of us not behind us.

EZRA. Let's go home, Reb Isaac Aaron.

ISAAC. All right, Uncle Ezra, take my hand.

EZRA. No, Reb Isaac Aaron. You lead . . . I'll try to follow. I'll . . . I'll . . . (*He sneezes*)

WOMAN. God bless you, Uncle Ezra. You sneezed . . . that's a sign everything Reb Isaac Aaron has said is true.

EZRA. No, Sarah Leah. That's pure superstition. I sneezed because I thig I'b caud a cohd in my head frob beig throwd id the river.

(*Music: Closing narrative theme and down*)

NARRATOR. And, of course, that was true. It was true in the town of Dalid near the city of Gimel in the province of Aleph-Bes. It is true now. It will always be true. The conflict is perpetual . . . knowledge or ignorance, man or boy, Reb Isaac Aaron or Uncle Ezra. (*Pause*) Turn to the Book of Proverbs, the Second Chapter . . . "Then shalt thou understand righteousness and justice and equity . . . for wisdom shall enter into thy heart and knowledge shall be pleasant unto thy soul."

(*Music: Curtain*)

HUNGER

HUNGER

Hunger *is an example of the documentary technique in radio. In this form the narration extends like a clothesline between one pole marked "Famine" and another pole marked "American Relief." Pinned to the clothesline are statistics, medical data, actuarial reports, quotations, and dramatic vignettes. But it is the narrative clothesline upon which the data, quotations, and short scenes are suspended, and which gives the whole an emotional unity.*

The documentary radio script derives from the "Living Newspaper" experiments of the WPA Federal Theatre. A large cast is unnecessary; in fact, a large cast would clutter up a studio. What is needed are versatile professionals who can take many roles and impart to each an element of excitement and urgency. Better than any other radio form, the documentary is the technique for education.

Hunger *was first broadcast on June 2, 1946 with UNRRA Director Fiorello H. La Guardia as guest speaker. Roger De Koven was an extremely effective Narrator and others in the cast were Hester Sondergaard, Joseph Boland, Leon Janney, Gene Leonard, Gregory Morton, and Karl Malden. Recordings of the script were played at special rallies throughout the country and early in 1947 Rev. Everett C. Parker, Director of the Joint Religious Radio Committee representing the Congregational Christian Churches, the Methodist Church, Presbyterian U.S.A. Church, and the United Churches of Canada, transcribed a fifteen-minute version of the script. These transcriptions were broadcast over five hundred stations in the U.S. and Canada.*

HUNGER

NARRATOR. There is a guest at my table, and at yours also. Is his place prepared, and has a chair been put forward for him? He is invisible; yet he is there. He watches. His eyes are big, his belly is bloated, the odor of hunger is about him. And each spoonful that you carry to your lips measures the decay of his hope and covers the streets of your city with the footprints of his blood.

(*Music: Narrative theme and down*)

NARRATOR. We must come with emotion to the fact. The word is *fames,* a Latin word signifying hunger. And the subject is famine, for which your emotion must render the human equivalent. Translate hunger into a man, and for famine say instead five hundred million men, women, children. Five hundred million—one half a billion. One in every four upon the face of the earth. Do not be hasty. Speak no words, swear no promises, make no covenants. For the guest at your table is doomed to pursue but never to overtake. "He shall eat and not have enough." And unto you and unto me, and unto the ministers, the priests, the rabbis, the presidents, the kings, the dictators, the legislatures, the assemblies, and the parliaments—unto us all pertaineth the judgment.

(*Music: Up and finish*)

NARRATOR. We must begin with the fact and prove it. There are experts; they have gathered the testimony of the nations.

ONE. Of the population of Europe one hundred million people are now subsisting on a daily diet of fifteen hundred calories or less.

TWO. Of the population of Bulgaria, 9 per cent.

THREE. Czechoslovakia, sixteen per cent.
FOUR. Roumania, thirty per cent.
FIVE. Spain, forty percent.
ONE. Finland, forty-three per cent.
TWO. Hungary, fifty per cent.
THREE. Italy, fifty-nine per cent.
FOUR. Austria, seventy-four per cent.
FIVE. Germany, seventy-five per cent.
ONE. The total is one hundred million on a diet of fifteen hundred calories.
TWO. On this diet a man walks slowly. He cannot run. He is always exhausted.
THREE. On this diet a young boy or girl may possibly grow in height. But he will gain no weight.
FOUR. Those who receive less than fifteen hundred calories are not hungry. They are starving.
FIVE. A daily intake of fifteen hundred calories represents not enough food to die on, not enough to live on.
NARRATOR. Are you impatient with statistics? Perhaps you are wise in your impatience. The figures, the percentages, the multiplications, the numerical comparisons, they are all a trick. Nothing more or less than the device of the expert to shield the fact from your emotion. Yes, there is a great difference between actuarial death and actual death. One is merely a cipher, the other is flesh. Let us consider the flesh. The flesh of Asia.
ONE. Famine in China.
TWO. Already dead of starvation . . . four million.
THREE. Unless help is quickly forthcoming, you may write off thirty to forty million Chinese by the end of the year.
ONE. Famine in India.
FOUR. In 1943, a famine year, five hundred thousand died.
FIVE. It is variously estimated that an additional ten to twenty millions will die.
NARRATOR. Be careful. This is still another trick. The word

"million." Beware of it. You are not expected to comprehend it. One man is your brother. One man who knows wetness, cold, pain, "the affection of youth, the love of his espousals," the first fruit of marriage. This you know and understand. But one million is nothing or less than nothing. I understand one man. I do not understand one million men. One man is a Moslem, Buddhist, a Christian, a Jew. He is a mystic, an agnostic, an atheist. His skin is black, yellow, white. He was conceived in the womb as I was conceived. He breathes the air I breathe. He dies as I will die. I understand one man; I do not understand one million men. And not understanding one million, how shall you and I understand five hundred million?

(*Music: Narrative theme and down*)

NARRATOR. Allow the expert his conclusion.

VOICE. The famine emergency will not pass this summer; it will not even pass next summer. We face five years of famine. These are the dry and barren statistics of catastrophe.

NARRATOR. "The dry and barren statistics of catastrophe." But he is not finished.

VOICE. I have read the reports of the investigating commissions. They are founded on a deplorable error. The food quotas proposed are too low. The famine countries need more than food for minimum life; they need food for work. That's the problem facing us.

NARRATOR. Why? How? When? Ask the questions. Why? *Why* is war? How? *How* is the missing farmer buried in a soldier's uniform; *how* is rainless skies and parched fields; *how* is sterile soil lacking fertilizer, lacking seed, lacking the plough and the tractor. (*Pause*) When? *When* is now.

(*Music: Up and down*)

NARRATOR. Why, and how, and when? Oh, there are many questions, and many entrances, and only one door to go out. And how does a child or a woman or a man go through that door? The gnawing sensation of the upper abdomen, the tissue wasted, the fat consumed of itself, the restlessness of the mind, the languor, the lassitude, the numbing faintness and the blessed end of all sensation in the land of thick darkness.

(*Music: Up and finish*)

NARRATOR. Yet it takes a long time to starve to death. And there is still a guest at the table. And he, too, asks a question.

ONE. We were promised food with victory.

TWO. I remember.

ONE. Why aren't you prepared?

TWO. We didn't expect the war to last so long.

ONE. Why wasn't the food accumulated and saved?

TWO. We didn't expect the war to be over so soon.

NARRATOR. The question is true, the answer is true. The true and lunatic answer for the lunatic time in which the nations were prepared neither for death nor for life.

(*Music: Narrative theme and down*)

NARRATOR. Do not search for villains. There are no villains, there are only five hundred million hungry. And for them our feasts, our new moons, our sabbaths, and our seasons are a steady time appointed for the contractions of the stomach.

(*Music: Up and quickly out*)

NARRATOR. For all this there is an explanation. The first is war and the payment of war. The second is drought. The worst drought in modern history. And the drought came with the war. Drought in . . .

ONE. Australia.

TWO. China.

THREE. North Africa.

FOUR. The Danube Basin.

FIVE. South Africa.

ONE. The Ukraine.

HUNGER

NARRATOR. While Winston Churchill was saying that war "dragged a hot rake up Italy," fields were parched in the grainlands of the world. And with drought came hurricane, and typhoon and tidal wave . . . the doom of the rice harvests in Burma, in India, in Indo-China, in Siam. Explain this to the guest at the table, but he will not hear. He is no longer a reasonable man. Cause and effect have no logic for him. He is a man obsessed, fanatic, perverted by the fantasy of food. Explain other causes, other effects. Explain to him the tragedy of Holland. A farmer standing in a desolate field . . .

THREE. Feel this soil.

NARRATOR. This?

THREE. Take it in your hand.

(*Pause*)

NARRATOR. It doesn't feel like soil. It's more like dough.

THREE. Yes. Spongy like dough. (*Pause*) Out there . . . beyond. There are the dikes. When the Nazi invaded, we broke the dikes. Two hundred years to reclaim this land from the sea. Two minutes to explode the dikes and let the sea come back.

NARRATOR. The salt sea. The salt sea which transformed the fertile lowlands of Holland into sterile, viscous muck.

THREE. (*Slowly*) It'll take years before the salt will wash out. The land can't feed us now.

(*Music: Narrative theme and down*)

NARRATOR. Agricultural consequence of war. Repeat this in China, in Hupeh Province, in Kwangsi, Kwang-tung, Kweichow. Two million acres of rich soil flooding from the Yellow River to keep the Japanese back. Two million acres which fed three million people. And three million people now in the valley of the Yellow River who eat *clay*.

(*Music: Up and down*)

NARRATOR. Leave China. Return to Europe. Poland. (*Music Out*) Poland is a good example.

(Sound of thunder)
NARRATOR. Looks like rain.
TWO. Yes.
NARRATOR. Good for the land.
TWO. Sure.
NARRATOR. Your potatoes in the ground?
TWO. No potatoes. We eat the seed potatoes.
NARRATOR. How can you do that? That's agricultural suicide.
TWO. Yes.
NARRATOR. You're a farmer, aren't you?
TWO. I am a farmer. Also a father. We eat the seed potatoes. The children have nothing else.

(Music: Narrative theme and down)

NARRATOR. In one month, in two months, he will also be a guest at your table. He and his wife and his children. They are not alone. *(Pause)* Seed potatoes in Poland, seed wheat in France, seed rice in India . . . and a winter harvest of famine! This is the biological consequence of war. This is the erosion of human life. This is the Book of Jeremiah. It is a land of deserts and drought where none passes through and no man dwells. These are the men and women left with nothing but their eyes to weep with. *(Music out)* Listen, this is the Mayor of the Yugoslav city of Vlasencia.
FIVE. Our children eat every other day.
NARRATOR. He has nothing else to say. Ask him a question. For example, ask how old this child is.
FIVE. He's fourteen years old.
NARRATOR. You must be mistaken. This boy is hardly eight or nine.
FIVE. He is my own son. He is fourteen years old.
NARRATOR. There are no more questions. He is a guest at the table. Also ask no questions of the teacher in this French schoolhouse.
FOUR. *(Slowly)* Mes enfants, ecoutez. J'ai faim. Avez vous du pain? *(Pause)* Alors, continuons.

NARRATOR. He is too weak to teach. They are too weak to learn.
WOMAN. Doctor, my little girl does not see.
ONE. How many fingers, little girl?
NARRATOR. An incident in Greece. Any city.
ONE. How many fingers, little girl?
(*Pause*)
WOMAN. Doctor, she does not see.
ONE. Don't worry. It's not permanent blindness. Merely a deficiency of Vitamin A. Feed her milk. (*Pause—exploding*) Well, for heaven's sake, stop looking at me. What do you want me to do?
NARRATOR. If he were not so hungry, he might apologize later. But he does not apologize. He knows his own symptoms. The physiological irritation of hunger. Let us proceed. At least here in this place there are no emaciated scarecrows.
TWO. They look rather plump and well-fed, don't they? It's dropsy. Famine dropsy. Hunger edema if you want to be fancy. The body fluid escapes through the blood vessels into the tissues. And don't be taken in by the rosy cheeks. That's tuberculosis.
(*Music: Narrative theme and down*)
NARRATOR. Biological consequence of war. And for those who have transgressed the covenants of biology there are new synonyms. The synonym for Roumania is pellagra. The synonym for many districts in Italy is a garbage can scraped clean. There are few pleasant recitals in the Europe of 1946. If this is hard listening for you, believe that it is hard telling for me . . . but for them it is harder still. And for the mothers in civilized Europe it is hardest of all. (*Music out*) In Poland of every thousand births this happens two hundred and fifty times.
MAN. I want to see my wife.
THREE. Not now, please.
MAN. Let me in . . . please.

THREE. She doesn't want to see you.

MAN. She's my wife, isn't she? (*Pause*) Anna.

THREE. She doesn't want to talk to you.

MAN. Anna, in God's name, is it my fault that the baby was born dead?

(*Pause*)

WOMAN. Better that there should be no birth and none with child and no conception.

MAN. Anna, you don't know what you are saying. I will go and pray for you.

WOMAN. The altar is covered with thorns and with thistles. Say to the mountains, "Cover us," and to the hills, "Fall upon us."

(*Music: Narrative theme and down*)

NARRATOR. In Poland, of every thousand babies born, two hundred and fifty babies die. And those who do not die make the peculiar sound of children who are hungry. They shall say to the mountains, "Cover us," and to the hills, "Fall upon us." (*Music out*) These are the facts. These are the partial facts of catastrophe. Only the partial facts. But the answer must be full and complete. Are there answers to give?

(*Music: Up and down*)

NARRATOR. Yes, there are answers. There is the statement and the action of the Director General of UNRRA, Fiorello H. LaGuardia.

VOICE. From this point on the protocol is off. It is food that we need. People are crying for bread, not advice. I want plows, not typewriters. The people need relief, not sympathy. I want fast-moving ships, not slow-moving resolutions. The people in our country learned during the depression that ticker tape ain't spaghetti.

(*Music: Bridge*)

NARRATOR. The guest is at the table. Has a place been prepared for him? And what shall be prepared?

THREE. Bread, fats, milk for the people.
TWO. Fertilizer, seed, draft animals, farm machinery for the land.
NARRATOR. The land and the people ... five hundred million hungry people. One half a billion. One of every four on the face of the earth. The guest at the table.
(Music: Narrative theme and down)
NARRATOR. Yes, the guest is at the table. He is invisible and he has no voice for speech. But he is there. And his silence is a warning. *(Music fading)* His silence is a prophecy. It takes a long time to starve to death; but death from disease is swift. And there will be disease. There is always disease. First rides war, and then famine rides. And after famine the pestilence follows.
ONE. Pellagra.
TWO. Beri-beri.
THREE. Diphtheria.
FOUR. Scarlet fever.
FIVE. Tuberculosis.
ONE. Influenza.
TWO. Typhus.
THREE. Cholera.
FOUR. Plague.
FIVE. Epidemic dysentery.
NARRATOR. The pestilence is come. And it will not be content to stay where it is. It will move. It will not ask your permission, nor stop at the consulates for entry visas or tourist permits. Disease carries no passports. You cannot exorcise it with an immigration quota.
(Music: Narrative theme and down)
NARRATOR. We return now to the fact of our emotion. The word is *fames,* a Latin word signifying hunger. And the subject is famine. And the subject is also the Biblical verse: "Sow to yourselves according to righteousness, reap according to mercy." You and I cannot reject that text. It is writ-

ten upon our eyes. But eyes can only see and hands must do. The time is now. And now is very late. They faint in the streets, they walk with the tread of mourners at their own funerals, they suspend on the margin of life. One more season of drought, another succession of bad harvests and they are dead. Dead in the tens of millions. It is a race, and for better or for worse, rightly or wrongly, we in America are the runners. They cannot come to meet us; we must go to them and our hands dare not be empty. *(Pause)* "Sow to yourselves according to righteousness; reap according to mercy."
(Music: Curtain)

A CHASSIDIC TALE

A CHASSIDIC TALE

Chassid means "Pious One" and Chassidism was a religious folk movement which began in the middle of the Eighteenth Century with Israel of Podolia, called by his desciples, Baal Shem Tov or "Master of the Good Name." The Chassidim, finding God everywhere, worshipped with joy, with dancing and with song. The Eliezer of A Chassidic Tale *has his prototype in a hundred "Rebbes" and belongs to the legends and melodies which brought to Judaism new lyricism and vitality.*

Some of the Chassidic improvisations were to the synagogue chants what melody is to recitative. Their folk composers were probably innocent of musical notation but that in no way inhibited them from creating a literature of musical laughter and ecstatic piety.

A Chassidic Tale *assembles a few of the better-known parables and anecdotes of the movement and sews them together with a thread of narration. It is greatly in debt to* A Hasidic Anthology *edited by Louis I. Newman in collaboration with Samuel Spitz.*

Richard Keith was featured as Avrum and Will Geer as Eliezer. The other Chassidim were Harold Huber, Daniel Ocko, Joseph Boland, Eleanor Audley, and Don Appell. Cantor David Putterman was the soloist, Milton Katims conducted a score composed by Morris Mamorsky and Frank Papp directed. The broadcast was on December 16, 1945.

A CHASSIDIC TALE

AVRUM. This whole thing happened to me, Avrum Isaacson, one hundred and thirty-five years ago. If you ask me how it is that a man does not stop talking after one hundred and thirty-five years, I will give you a proper answer: It's none of your business. If you want to argue, I can argue. But if you want to be reasonable, please sit where you are and be quiet while I, Avrum Isaacson, will tell you.

(*Music: Register a Chassidic air and fade to background*)

AVRUM. Myself, I'm not a fool, you understand. When I was younger, the old Rabbi, may he rest in peace, said to me, "Avrum," he said, "you are a person of what I might describe as the middle measure. Neither a very great scholar ... nor a very small ignoramus." So instead of becoming a student of the Talmud, I became a wagon driver. You understand, I'm not altogether a fool. Still, this has nothing to do with my story. Well, to make matters short, ours was a small town in the Ukraine on the Polish frontier. Not a rich town, not a poor town ... a town of middle measure.

(*Music: Fading*)

Well, one day there came to the town a Rabbi—one of those who called themselves Chassidim. Myself, I did not know much of the Chassidim. But I learned. As I was saying, this Rabbi came to our town ... a total stranger he was.

ONE. We've already got one Rabbi, tell him, Avrum.

AVRUM. You—tell him we've already got a Rabbi.

TWO. My friend, they say we already have a Rabbi.

AVRUM. May he live to be a hundred and twenty years.

TWO. We already have a Rabbi, may he live to be a hundred and twenty years.

ELIEZER. Tell him my name is Eliezer.

TWO. Avrum, he says his name is Eliezer.

AVRUM. All right, so his name is Eliezer.

TWO. He says, "All right."

ELIEZER. Tell him I am a Chassidic Rabbi.

TWO. What is a Chassidic Rabbi?

ELIEZER. I believe in the love of God and the love of man.

TWO. He says he believes in the love of God and the love of man.

ELIEZER. I believe that it is sinful to be melancholy. Men must approach God through prayer, but the prayer must be full of joy and ecstasy.

TWO. You heard what he said?

AVRUM. I heard. Tell him we already have one Rabbi in this town.

ELIEZER. Nevertheless, I shall settle in this town.

AVRUM. But we barely support our own Rabbi; how in the name of Heaven can we support another? How can we . . .

ELIEZER. Sssh. Listen. Once there was a goose. Not a very large goose. Not a very small goose.

AVRUM. A goose of middle measure.

ELIEZER. Exactly. And this goose was owned by a thoughtless master who sometimes forgot to feed her.

ONE. Well?

ELIEZER. The goose suffered.

TWO. Naturally.

ELIEZER. One day the master bought a rooster and placed it in the same coop with the goose.

AVRUM. But the goose was already hungry?

ELIEZER. That's what the goose said.

AVRUM. Oh.

ELIEZER. "Now I shall surely starve," said the goose. "There are two of us to eat from my small portion." But the rooster said, "Don't worry. I can crow when I feel hungry. This will be a reminder to our master and then we'll both be fed." *(Pause)* I shall settle in this town.

(Music: Theme and down)

AVRUM. That is how Rabbi Eliezer came to our town with roosters and geese! Almost immediately there was trouble. I, Avrum Isaacson, I had nothing to do with him. He was an instrument of Satan. I told him so. Myself, I'm not a scholar, you understand. But I know that scholars should be busy with the study of the Talmud instead of . . . instead of playing checkers. *(Music out)* Can you imagine what I'm saying? He found scholars playing checkers, and even I know that checkers are not an especially holy pastime. Yet he refused to scold them!

(Sound of two moves cued with:)

ONE. Aha . . . Aha . . . two for one.

(Sound of checkers clicking)

AVRUM. What a shame. What a waste. Rabbi Eliezer, why don't you drive them to the House of Study?

ELIEZER. Why should I?

AVRUM. Because, Rabbi Eliezer, because I am only a wagon driver, but I know that it is written, "He who does not increase his knowledge decreases it."

ELIEZER. Avrum, you may learn much wisdom from the rules of this game.

AVRUM. From checkers? A likely story!

ELIEZER. Yes, Avrum, you may learn from playing a game of checkers. See. You surrender one in order to capture two. You may not make two moves at one time. You must move up but not down. But when you reach the top, you may move as you like. Yes, even in the rules of the game of checkers there is much wisdom.

AVRUM. Hmmph! And you call yourself a Rabbi. You're a

fraud. If they want to remain here, it's all right with me, I'm leaving.

(*Door opens and slams shut*)

ONE. Rabbi Eliezer.

ELIEZER. Yes?

ONE. Avrum insulted you.

ELIEZER. Perhaps.

ONE. I'm sorry. (*Pause*) You should have answered him.

ELIEZER. No. My own teacher, may God bless his memory, never expressed his displeasure on the day a person offended him. He would wait for the next day. Then he would say, "Yesterday I was displeased with you. But today is today and a new day." (*Pause*) Go on with your game. I find pleasure in watching you.

(*Music: Narrative theme and down*)

AVRUM. You see, he won them over with deceit and with trickery. But he couldn't win me over, not Avrum Isaacson. In the House of Study, we read, we sang. When we carried the Holy Scroll from the Ark, we walked soberly as befits the House of Worship. Did he walk? He danced. Is that a way to commune with God? Dancing and singing? It was a black day when he came.

(*Music: Fading*)

And it wasn't enough for him to do this. He made the others dance and sing. I tell you, it was a revolution. Nothing was sacred. The cantor would be rehearsing for the Sabbath.

(*Cantor: "Oo-v'yohm hah-shah-baws . . ."*)

AVRUM. (*After ten to fifteen seconds*) Now that's a proper Sabbath welcome. But what would he do? This Eliezer?

(*Cantor: Continues . . . but he stops after he is drowned out by:*)

(*Soloist: Fading in with choir in a sprightly Chassidic version . . . Continue in the clear for twenty seconds then fade under narration*)

AVRUM. A scandal. Is this the way to worship God? Laughing and, God forbid, almost making jokes? "Avrum," he said to me, "God does not like a sour face." Well, I like a sour face. It's my face. The sight of him was enough to make my mouth fill with live coals . . . in a manner of speaking. You would think the people would catch on to him, discover him to be what he really was?

(*Soloist and choir out*)

AVRUM. But no. They used to come to him with their problems. Would I come to him? Not Avrum Isaacson. But they came . . . including Feivel, the farmer, who was as poor as a synagogue mouse.

FEIVEL. Rabbi Eliezer.

ELIEZER. Yes, Feivel.

FEIVEL. It's impossible, Rabbi Eliezer.

ELIEZER. What is impossible?

FEIVEL. My house.

ELIEZER. What about your house?

FEIVEL. I have one room. We can't turn around. Me; my wife; six sons; four daughters; my wife's uncle, may his name not be erased; my nephew, Naftali; Naftali's wife . . . and she's expecting . . . fourteen people—all in one room. Rabbi Eliezer, we can't turn around in our house. Is there anyone worse off than me. (*Pause*)

ELIEZER. Hmm, I see your problem. Feivel, do you own a cow?

FEIVEL. Naturally, Rabbi Eliezer. What Jew doesn't own a cow?

ELIEZER. Listen to me. (*Pause*) Take the cow into your house.

FEIVEL. But, Rabbi Eliezer . . .

ELIEZER. Do as I say, take the cow into your house.

(*Choir: "Oo-tzoo Ay-tzaw"—One line and response*)
(*Cow mooing loudly*)

WIFE. (*Shouting*) You're going crazy. Who ever heard of bringing a cow into a house? And such a house.

FEIVEL. Be still. The Rabbi told me to do it.

(*Thud of hoofs. Mooing*)

WIFE. You go back to your fine Rabbi and ask him what you're to do now that a cow is in the house? Go ahead, ask him.

(*Mooing, cover with:*)
(*Choir: Very briefly—"Oo-tzoo-Ay-tzaw"*)
(*Sound of goat bleating*)

WIFE. Take that goat out! Take him right out of the house!

FEIVEL. Now be reasonable. I told the Rabbi about the cow, so he said take the goat into the house also.

(*Goat up combine with mooing*)

WIFE. You go right back to him, Feivel. Look what he's done to us.

(*Ad libs with:*)
(*Goat and cow up . . . add a few voices*)
(*Choir: Very briefly—"Oo-tzoo-Ay-tzaw"*)
(*Clucking of chickens*)

WIFE. (*Desperately*) No chickens . . . the children yes, your relatives, yes. A cow all right. Even a goat.

(*Chickens clucking—cow mooing—goats bleating—voices building under*)

Feivel . . . no chickens. Do you hear? No chickens. Six sons; four daughters; my uncle; your nephew, Naftali; Naftali's wife, who is expecting, God bless her; one cow; one goat . . . but no chickens. I draw the line at chickens!

FEIVEL. It's what Rabbi Eliezer said. He said, "Take the chickens into the house."

(*Cut all sounds and voices*)
(*Soloist: "Oo-tzoo Ay-tzaw" . . . choir for one response*)

FEIVEL. Rabbi Eliezer, they're in the pots; they're under the beds; the goat is eating my phylacteries; my wife's relatives are sitting on the rafters . . . Rabbi Eliezer, what have you done to me?

ELIEZER. Sssh. So it's bad, Feivel, is it?

FEIVEL. Bad? Did you say bad? It's Gehenna, that's what it is.
ELIEZER. Calm yourself.
FEIVEL. How can I be calm? It's the end of the world.
ELIEZER. Sssh. Sssh. Be calm. Listen.
FEIVEL. No—I won't bring the pigeons in.
ELIEZER. No more, I promise. (*Pause*) Go home, Feivel. Go home and turn the cow out of the house.
 (*Pause*)
FEIVEL. What? Turn *out?*
ELIEZER. Yes, then turn out the goat.
FEIVEL. Bless you, Rabbi Eliezer.
ELIEZER. Turn out all the chickens.
FEIVEL. How can I thank you?
ELIEZER. Come back tomorrow. Turn all the animals out and come back tomorrow.
 (*Choir: With soloist for short bridge—"Oo-tzoo Ay-tzaw"*)
 (*Door slams*)
FEIVEL. Rabbi Eliezer . . . behold me, Feivel. Look, I want to dance. I'm a radiant man.
ELIEZER. You turned the animals out, did you?
FEIVEL. Out . . . every last one.
ELIEZER. And is your house too small now?
FEIVEL. Oh, no. Oh, no, no. Too small? What a question? A fine house like that too small for fourteen people! A thousand blessings, Rabbi Eliezer. My house is a palace now. Ten thousand blessings, Rabbi Eliezer.
 (*Music: Narrative theme and down*)
AVRUM. Tricks. Magician's tricks. "Laugh," he said. "Rejoice in your God," he said. Be merry. Not me. Not Avrum Isaacson. I may be only a wagon driver, but I can recognize an impostor when I see one.
 (*Music: Cross fade with Cantor and choir*)
 (*Cantor: Singing "Sheer Hah-mah-ah-lohs" with choir . . . up and down*)

AVRUM. Do you hear? He won over the Cantor, too. Even our own Cantor! I ask you, will you ever trust a tenor? The whole town was mad. Songs on the Sabbath. Songs after the Sabbath. Songs before the Sabbath. Songs in the middle of the week.

(*Cantor and choir building*)

ELIEZER. Never stop singing. Sing, all ye children of men. Approach your God with a song on your lips. Let him see the grace of your countenance. Affirm in your melody the joy of life. Affirm the compassion, and the charity, and the love among men. Let your gloom be dissipated. Put away the dryness of your book-lore and the stiffness of your piety. Make it warm, make it rich, make it fervent. Listen, all of you, listen as you sing. In the lowliest of men there dwells a soul, a sacred mystery, the garment of the living God. Keep this garment spotless with your joy. And when you are bidden, return this garment without blemish . . . with your song.

(*Cantor: Up with choir and finish— "Sheer Hah-mah-ah-lohs"*)

AVRUM. Listen, do you think this Eliezer was all piety and good works? Don't believe it! I myself saw him insult a fine young man. Perhaps he wasn't so fine, perhaps he was even a fool, for he came to Rabbi Eliezer and (*Fading*) he said, I actually overheard it because I was exercising my horse in the snow, and I overheard him say . . .

YOUNG MAN. Rabbi Eliezer, I wish to be ordained as a Rabbi.

ELIEZER. Do you?

YOUNG MAN. With all my heart, Rabbi Eliezer.

ELIEZER. Why do you want to become a Rabbi?

YOUNG MAN. I don't know exactly. But it's what I want more than anything else.

ELIEZER. Hmm. Tell me something of yourself. Tell me something of your daily conduct.

YOUNG MAN. Well, every morning, I always dress in white.

ELIEZER. Do you now?

YOUNG MAN. Yes. I drink only water.

ELIEZER. Only water? Hmm.

YOUNG MAN. Every day I place tacks . . . sharp tacks in my shoes.

ELIEZER. In Heaven's name, why do you do that?

YOUNG MAN. For self-mortification. I also roll naked in the snow. And when I'm finished, I order the synagogue caretaker to give me forty stripes with a lash on my bare back. Each day, Rabbi.

(*Pause*)

ELIEZER. And you think all this entitles you to become a Rabbi?

YOUNG MAN. (*Virtuously*) Yes, Rabbi Eliezer.

(*Footsteps plodding in snow coming on*)

(*Fade in horse ditto . . . whinny*)

ELIEZER. Young man . . . that is Avrum Isaacson's horse. What color is he?

YOUNG MAN. White.

ELIEZER. Yes, the creature is white, it drinks only water, it has nails in its shoes, it rolls in the snow, and I suppose that our friend, Avrum, gives him even more than forty stripes a day with his whip.

(*Hoofbeats fading off—whinny*)

ELIEZER. Still, as you doubtless see, it is only a horse.

(*Music: Bridge and segue to:*)

(*Cantor: With choir in "Die Alte Kashe" . . . and hold under*)

AVRUM. Yes, after Rabbi Eliezer came nothing was the same. He had respect for no one. No one at all. After all, a man should know the difference between a beggar and let us say, Asher Horowitz, who was the wealthiest man in the town. But Rabbi Eliezer, did he know the difference? Not at all. He pretended that there was no difference between Asher Horowitz and his hundreds of roubles, and a beggar like Nachum Fishman, who didn't have a broken zloty to his name. "Gut Shabbas," he would say to Asher Horowitz. "Gut Shabbas," he would say to Nachum Fishman. Just like that. As though they were the same.

(*Cantor and choir fading*)

AVRUM. It happened once that Asher Horowitz lost a wallet and Nachum Fishman found it. Immediately, Rabbi Eliezer had to meddle.

(*Footsteps ascending short flight of stairs*)

ELIEZER. I'm very glad for you, Nachum. Asher Horowitz has promised a reward of ten roubles to the one who finds the wallet.

NACHUM. Ten roubles? It's a fortune. Rabbi Eliezer, two loaves of bread for Sabbath and wine for the Kiddush. My wife is going to be happy.

(*Knock on door*)

ASHER. (*Off*) Come in.

(*Door opens . . . shuts*)

ELIEZER. Asher Horowitz, your wallet has been found.

ASHER. (*On*) Wonderful. Quick, let me have it.

ELIEZER. Hold on, Nachum. Asher, haven't you forgotten something?

NACHUM. Yes . . . the reward.

ASHER. Of course, of course. Hand the wallet over. I've got to make sure that the money is all there, don't I?

(*Pause*)

NACHUM. It must be there. I didn't even open it because it wasn't mine. Just as I found it, that's how I'm returning it.

ASHER. I'll see in a moment. (*Counting*) One hundred, two hundred, two fifty, seventy-five, three hundred, twenty-five, fifty, seventy, eighty, ninety . . . four hundred. Only four hundred roubles. I don't give any reward. I lost five hundred roubles.

NACHUM. Rabbi Eliezer, he can't be telling the truth. I swear, I haven't even looked inside the wallet.

ASHER. (*Unctuously*) No reward. Good day, Rabbi. Good day, Nachum.

(*Pause*)

ELIEZER. Asher Horowitz, you will please give the wallet to Nachum.

ASHER. What's that?

ELIEZER. Give it to him, I say. Take it, Nachum.

ASHER. But, what . . . what are you doing? Here, give me back my wallet.

ELIEZER. Oh, no, Asher. This is not your wallet. You are an honest man. You lost a wallet containing five hundred roubles. But Nachum is also an honest man. He found a wallet containing only four hundred roubles. Clearly, the wallet is not yours. Nachum will keep it until its rightful owner claims it.

ASHER. (*Laughing*) It's a joke, heh? Sure, a joke. Nachum, you're a good fellow. Of course. Everyone says so. Here's your reward of ten roubles, now give me my wallet.

ELIEZER. Oh, no, Asher. That would be a crime. As you say, the wallet you lost contained five hundred roubles. (*Pause*) Come, Nachum. The Almighty has blessed you today. Good day, Asher.

(*Music: Bridge to narrative theme and down*)

AVRUM. This meddling was bad enough . . . but it was more painful to have to listen to Rabbi Eliezer preach. Why did I listen, you might ask? Did anybody make me? I'll tell you. First, it's none of your business, and second, I, Avrum Isaacson, listen to anyone I want to listen to. So I developed the very bad habit of listening to Rabbi Eliezer.

(*Music: Out*)

Make no mistake, he was a meddler all right; yet, I must confess, some of the things he had to say were good enough, after a fashion, that is.

(*Cantor: With choir in "Hi-nehy Mah Tohv . . ." and down for:*)

ELIEZER. One who thinks that anything can be accomplished by money is likely to do anything for money.
(Cantor: Up with choir and down)
ELIEZER. One who thinks he can live without others is mistaken. One who thinks that others cannot live without him, is even more mistaken.
(Cantor: Up with choir and down)
ELIEZER. I have greater love for the wicked man who knows he is wicked than for the righteous man who knows he is righteous. The first one is truthful and the Lord loves truth. The second one falsifies, since no human being is exempt from sin, and the Lord hates untruth.
(Cantor: Up with choir and down)
ELIEZER. To sin against a fellow man is worse than to sin against God. The man you have harmed may have gone to an unknown place, and you may lose the opportunity to beg his forgiveness. God, however, is everywhere, and you can always find Him when you seek Him.
(Cantor: Up with choir and take out with:)
(Music: Theme and down)
AVRUM. Myself, I'm not a fool, you understand. I know a good thing when I see it, and I know a bad thing when I see it. But, Rabbi Eliezer . . . well, for a hundred and thirty-five years, I've been thinking of him. Mind you, I haven't changed my opinion . . . only as Rabbi Eliezer says, to sin against your fellow man is worse than to sin against God. So, Rabbi Eliezer, can you hear me? It's me . . . Avrum Isaacson. If I have . . . well, mind you, Rabbi Eliezer. I haven't changed my mind. But, well, you know how it is. Besides, I liked the singing.
(Music: Up and segue to Cantor and choir)
(Cantor: With choir in "A Dudele" . . . and finish)

A SECOND EXODUS

A SECOND EXODUS

The year 1492 marked the discovery of America by Columbus. It was also the year when the Jews were expelled from Spain by the Inquisition.

Bigotry, like virus diseases, is highly infectious and it is not surprising that Portugal should have succumbed to the Spanish infection. So, while A Second Exodus *is a story of Portugal it is also a story of Spain.* Jews who had settled on the Iberian Peninsula many years before the establishment of a Christian Church were forced from their homes and from an intellectual climate that had nourished their great mathematicians, physicians, astronomers, poets, and philosophers. Maimonides had been born in Cordoba; Solomon Ibn Gabirol, the poet who wrote, "How shall I repay mine enemy if not by increasing mine own good works?" was born in Valencia; Judah Halevy, the greatest Hebrew poet since Biblical times, was born in Toledo. The things these men stood for was virtually the only baggage that the refugees took with them out of the land.

This script was first heard under the auspices of the NBC University of the Air as part of a historical series called Lands of the Free. *In its present form it was broadcast on March 25, 1945. Bernard Lenrow was the Narrator, Roger De Koven was the Father, the boy was Michael Artist and others in the cast were Richard Keith, Richard Sanders, Guy Sorel and Joseph Boland. The director was Ira Avery.*

A SECOND EXODUS

(*Cantor: A Passover chant . . . register with orchestra and down*)

NARRATOR. It was a song they sang when the Passover came round. Slaves were we in Egypt, they sang . . . and the words were only words and the melody was only a melody. For we lived in Portugal and the year was a welcome year . . . for it was 1497. Portugal in the year 1497, the Portugal of King Manuel and Queen Isabella, and yes, the Portugal of my father . . . Baruch Halevy, the son of Abraham.

(*Music: Up with Cantor and down*)

NARRATOR. It was a good place . . . this place of my boyhood. We lived in a pleasant valley and the vineyards were fruitful. (*Cantor fading*) From our house to the synagogue it was only a thousand and twenty steps and on the Sabbath I would scrub my face and put on clean linen and hug the prayer shawl to my breast and walk with my father.

FATHER. (*Laughing*) Careful you don't drop the shawl, Benjamin!

BOY. Six hundred and seventy-two, seventy-three, seventy-four, sev . . .

FATHER. Benjamin!—

BOY. Yes, Papa. I'm holding it tight. (*Quickly*) Seventy-seven, seventy-eight, seventy-nine.

NARRATOR. My father would laugh and I would count a thousand and twenty well-remembered steps as we walked together through the narrow little street which was also clean and scrubbed for the Sabbath and where the sun smelled of grapes and the shadows were cool. And always we would meet the baker, who was a disputatious man, and who would say to my father . . .

BAKER. Baruch, look to your son.

FATHER. Good Sabbath.

BAKER. Good Sabbath. The boy is a mumbler.

FATHER. Benjamin, the baker says you are a mumbler.

BOY. Yes, Papa. (*Continues softly*) Seven hundred and ten, eleven, twelve.

BAKER. It is a desecration of the Sabbath.

FATHER. Leave him alone. Baker. He is only a boy. It amuses him to count the steps. Besides, it does you no harm.

BAKER. He should be memorizing the Talmud.

FATHER. All in its proper place, Reb Baker.

BAKER. And what is more proper than the Talmud on the Sabbath day?

FATHER. A smile, perhaps.

BAKER. Oh, no, oh, no. Hillel says, "He who does not increase his knowledge decreases it; and he who does not study deserves to die."

FATHER. Benjamin is studying numbers, eh, Benjamin?

BOY. Thirty-two, thirty-three, seven hundred and thirty-four . . .

(*Continues under*)

FATHER. (*Laughing*) You see, Reb Baker! Come on, man, smile.

BAKER. Hmmph! And why should I smile? Tell me why I should smile, hah, Baruch?

FATHER. Because the sun is shining, and the Sabbath is meant for joy and, Reb Baker, it's good to be alive.

(*Music: Establishes narrative theme with Cantor and hold under*)

NARRATOR. Yes, it was good to be alive and to be a Jew and to live in Portugal. And good to have a father like my father, to play chess with him, to listen to him speak and watch his nose wrinkle when he smiled. And once when

I was playing with a stone, and throwing it in the air, the way a boy throws a stone in the air, I threw it too far and it fell and killed the baker's chicken. I did not mean to do it and my father knew that. (*Music out*)

FATHER. Come here, Benjamin.

BOY. I'm sorry, Papa . . . it slipped. (*Pause*) The baker wouldn't have known it was me, except the other boys told him.

FATHER. (*Chuckling*) Wouldn't you have confessed yourself, Benjamin?

BOY. Well . . .

FATHER. Tell the truth, son.

BOY. No, I wouldn't. That's wrong, Papa, isn't it?

FATHER. Very wrong. You have destroyed another man's property.

BOY. It was only a chicken . . . the one that wouldn't lay eggs.

FATHER. Even a chicken that gives no eggs. It's another man's property.

BOY. Are you angry with me, Papa?

FATHER. No, I am not angry. But I want you to do something for me.

BOY. Of course, Papa.

FATHER. Find other friends. I do not like you to play with boys who tattle. I don't like informers, Benjamin. In this world, Benjamin, justice is always the most important thing, but there is also something else.

BOY. What else, Papa?

FATHER. Mercy. Remember that, son. In this world people ask for justice, but sometimes they ask also for mercy. Yes, that is always wise to remember.

(*Music: Bridge softly to Cantorial theme and down*)

NARRATOR. That was Baruch Halevy, my father. Everything that was good in this world he taught me. To read, to play chess, to press grapes and make wine, to be modest and, best of all, to be silent.

(Music: Fading)

FATHER. It is as Simon, the son of Rabbi Gamaliel said: "All my days I have grown up among the wise, and I have found nothing better for a man than silence."

BAKER. Nonsense, Baruch. It is a foolish thing to tell the boy. If a man is learned let him speak up. How else will others profit by his words?

FATHER. Reb Baker, is learning so important? Not learning but doing is the chief thing. Remember, it is also said, "Whoso multiplies words, occasions sins."

BAKER. Aah. A man with a stutter must have written that.

FATHER. Reb Baker, Reb Baker, perversity is your Torah. I say day, you say night. I say milk, you say meat. I say smile, you say . . .

BAKER. What's there to smile about? Truly, what is there to smile about?

FATHER. We're alive.

BAKER. But we live in a ghetto.

FATHER. There is no ghetto for a man's mind. If the mind is free the body is free.

BAKER. Piffle. I am a baker . . . and because I'm a Jewish baker I have to pay a special tax.

FATHER. What difference? You're not starving.

BAKER. Pretty soon I will be. A Jew in Portugal has to pay a tax to walk on a road. Imagine, for thirteen hundred years Jews have lived in Portugal and now along comes a King who tells us we have to pay a tax to see our own country!

FATHER. You're quite right about that, Reb Baker.

BAKER. Oh, so I am right about something?

FATHER. About this, yes. Portugal is our country. We Jews came here before there was a Christian Church.

BAKER. Yes, and now they say—do you know what the Queen says? We defile the purity of the national bloodstream.

FATHER. What?

BAKER. I'm not making it up. So help me.

FATHER. That's preposterous. What purity? What bloodstream? Is Portugal pure? What is the Portuguese bloodstream?

BAKER. Don't ask me.

FATHER. It's Phoenician, Iberian and Celt, Carthaginian, Greek, Visigothic, Roman, Vandal, Moorish. What is she talking about? Portugal is half the world. A mixture of races.

BAKER. And religions, Baruch. Christian, Mohammedan, and Jewish.

FATHER. I haven't forgotten. Defile the purity? What impossible nonsense!

BAKER. That's why I don't smile, Baruch. The times are not for smiling.

FATHER. You may be right, Reb Baker. Whenever I hear this talk of racial purification, I know it's time to worry ... not only for ourselves but for the sanity of the whole world.

BAKER. Baruch, there's danger.

FATHER. Yes, Reb Baker. Real danger.

(*Music: Ominous, cut sharply on:*)

(*Pounding on door*)

FATHER. (*Fading in*) I'm coming, I'm coming, you'll beat the door down.

(*Door opens*)

SOLDIER I. Baruch Halevy?

FATHER. Yes, Baruch Halevy is my name.

SOLDIER I. Sir!

FATHER. I don't understand.

SOLDIER II. Shall I teach him?

SOLDIER I. Hold your fist. (*To Father*) Say sir next time you address us.

FATHER. Very well.

SOLDIER I. Sir!

FATHER. Sir.

SOLDIER II. Say it all, Jew.
FATHER. Very well, sir!
SOLDIER II. I don't like the way he says it.
SOLDIER I. Let him be. Baruch Halevy, I ask you for thirty denarii.
FATHER. You ask me, sir?
SOLDIER I. You're quite right. I should say I demand. In the name of the King I demand thirty denarii.
FATHER. Surely, I'm entitled to some explanation.
SOLDIER I. With pleasure.
SOLDIER II. We demand you pay—that's the explanation.
SOLDIER I. Don't interrupt; I'll do the explaining. (*Pause*) Their blessed Majesties King Manuel and Queen Isabella are in need of funds. That's simple. Thirty denarii, Jew. That's your tax.
FATHER. I see.
SOLDIER I. Hand it over. Thirty pieces of silver.
FATHER. It's nearly all I have. It's a very large sum, sir.
SOLDIER II. Don't argue, Jew.
FATHER. Oh, I'm not arguing, sir. It doesn't escape me that the gun you carry is a most superior argument.
SOLDIER I. (*Almost sweetly*) Then hand it over and be quick or we'll bash your head in.
(*Music: Bridge to Cantorial theme and down*)
NARRATOR. And the sins of the fathers shall be visited on the sons even unto the ten thousandth generation. Yes, the more history changes, the more it stays the same. Nothing changes. Persecution is a pattern, fixed, sour, immutable. Yes, Baruch Halevy, Baruch my father, Baruch the son of Abraham, the good man and the generous man stood in the synagogue like a rock and spoke to the dwellers of the ghetto.
(*Music: Out*)
(*Voices briefly*)
FATHER. People, this is the beginning. Israel is in Egypt.

Egypt, not Portugal. Portugal is the land we have loved and this no longer is that land. Here is where our ancestors have lived and died and brought their books and now the books are closed. There is a tax on conscience, and respect is extorted with a gun. And it is clear now there will be more guns. Baker . . .

BAKER. (*Slightly off*) Yes, Baruch.

FATHER. You may no longer follow your trade. Jews are forbidden to deal in flour. Butcher!

VOICE. (*Further off*) Yes, Baruch?

FATHER. You also. No Jew may deal in meat. Also you, vintner. And apothecary, you also. People, the doors are closing. The Ghetto is surrounded by laws.

BAKER. More than laws, Baruch. The son of Gamaliel is dead in his father's house. He refused to pay the tax.

VOICE. Let us stand together and go to him. Let us go to Gamaliel.

FATHER. No. Let Gamaliel be. Do not appease thy fellow in the hour of his anger, and comfort him not in the hour when his dead lies before him. We have greater things for decision.

BAKER. You're right, Baruch.

FATHER. Hear me, all of you. These taxes are a beginning. There will be more. They will fall on all alike. Let all be responsible for each. Let us give our money, rich and poor, to a central treasury, so that none may be taken from us or harmed for want of a single coin. Let us all stand together —and if need be—let the Ghetto perish together.

(*Music: Bridge*)

(*Pounding on door*)

FATHER. (*Fading in*) Yes, my friends, I'm coming. I expected you, my friends. (*Door opening*) Welcome, sirs.

SOLDIER II. I still don't like the way he says it.

ONE. Oh, be quiet, you fool. Baruch, we come again on King's business.

FATHER. Naturally, sir. A new tax?
ONE. Oh, no. Business, I said.
FATHER. The Jews have no business. It is the King's command, sir.
ONE. There is money in the Ghetto treasury, yes?
TWO. You see, we know everything.
FATHER. Very astute, sir.
TWO. Shall I give it to him?
ONE. Why don't you shut up? Baruch, the King wishes *a loan*.
FATHER. A loan from us?
ONE. Exactly. Wars are expensive. How much do you have in your treasury?
FATHER. I see.
ONE. We'll be gentle. We'll take two-thirds.
TWO. As a loan.
FATHER. I understand. And the King will pay us back, of course.
ONE. Of course. Don't you trust the King?
FATHER. It would be foolish for us not to, wouldn't it?
ONE. Very foolish. But the King is generous. Here, take this paper. It won't bite. That paper is the King's authorization.
TWO. It gives you power to be the King's tax-collector.
ONE. Yes, to the amount of your debt.
FATHER. Most generous. And from whom do we collect?
ONE. From all the good Christians in this province. They pay taxes, you will collect them.
FATHER. I see, sir. It is not enough to strip us, not enough to bar us from our trades, but now you force us into usury. Now you make it certain that the name of Jew will be an abomination throughout the land, and that when we come for our taxes, we will collect the King's debt and the enmity of every citizen.
ONE. Exactly, Baruch. That is exactly what we intend. And

you must admit, Baruch, the plan is not a bad one . . . is it, Baruch?

FATHER. No.

TWO. No what?

FATHER. You must excuse me. No, sir. I seem to have lost my manners. The plan is not a bad one. No . . . sir!

(*Music: Bridge to narrative theme and down*)

NARRATOR. No, not a bad plan. For it was a plan that worked. The Jews became the tax collectors of Portugal, and there was hatred of the Jew. And it was not a difficult thing to fan this hatred. And where there is hatred there is rumor —rumor that has the bite of a fox and the sting of a scorpion, and the hiss of a venomous serpent. And all this was for the Jew. And for the Jew there were two roads now.

(*Music: Out*)

EZRA. Baruch, I cannot stand it any longer. There is only death for us or . . .

FATHER. Or what, Ezra?

EZRA. I cannot say it, Baruch.

FATHER. Or what, Ezra?

EZRA. It is not for myself. Believe me, it is not for myself. I have three little children. They must not die.

FATHER. Ezra, or what, or what?

EZRA. You know what the alternative is.

FATHER. I do not know that there is an alternative for a Jew.

EZRA. Conversion.

FATHER. So!

EZRA. I swear to you it will be the conversion of the lip. In our hearts we will remain loyal. Don't you hear me?

FATHER. What do you want me to say?

EZRA. Say that what I'm doing is not terribly wrong.

FATHER. But it is wrong. Terribly wrong. You will be both an apostate and a liar. You will wrong two religions instead of one.

EZRA. I can't help it, I tell you. I have three little ones, do you hear? The youngest is six weeks old. Why should she suffer? I won't let it happen. She mustn't die. And if we don't allow ourselves to be converted we will all be dead, all be dead, Baruch . . . dead.
FATHER. Stop trembling, Ezra. Do whatever you think is right.
EZRA. Baruch, will you be my friend?
FATHER. Someone will have to be your friend, Ezra. Yes, I'll be your friend, and may God have mercy on you.
(*Music: Bridge to narrative theme and down*)
NARRATOR. Conversos. Thousands were converted in the mounting terror. You could touch the fear over the ghettos. You could feel it and smell it, sharp and acid, like a secretion from the skin. And it did not help. For while some were converted in good faith, many more secretly retained the faith of their fathers . . . and this became a poison and a scandal and an infection. And to meet the poison and the scandal and the infection—there was a remedy . . .
(*Music: Out*)
BAKER. (*Whispering*) They burned him.
FATHER. Yes, Reb Baker, they burned Ezra.
BAKER. Poor Ezra. Burned at the stake. And what was his crime?
FATHER. He changed his linen on the Jewish Sabbath, and put on his cleanest suit. Judaizing, they called it.
BAKER. How many conversos have been killed?
FATHER. I don't know, Reb Baker. They sought to find life by escaping their faith—and all that they found was the pit.
BAKER. And what will become of us, Baruch? What will become of those who stand firm?
FATHER. Don't you know, Reb Baker? Look in the book of Exodus. We have lived in the land for thirteen hundred years. We have given it the store of our learning, the fruit of our wisdom, our science, our astronomy, our medicine.

Now it is time for us to depart. The year is 1497, Reb Baker, it is the season of Passover. Let us go to our homes and read of the exodus from Egypt.
(Music: Bridge and Cantor in "V'hee sheh-awm-daw" and down)

NARRATOR. Yes, it was the season of the Passover. And the song he sang was "V'hee sheh-awm-daw lah-ah-voh-say-noo . . ." And Baruch Halevy, my father, sat at the table which was covered with a white cloth, and before him was the dish filled with marah and in his mouth there was the bitterness of the thing, and we covered the matzoth and raised the wine glass and he read to us from the book . . .

FATHER. V'hee sheh-awm-daw lah-ah-voh-say-noo . . . "This is the promise which has stood by our forefathers and stands by us. For neither once, nor twice, nor three times was our destruction planned; in every generation they rise against us, and in every generation God delivers us from their hands."
(Cantor: Up for fifteen to twenty seconds and down)

FATHER. My family, it is happening again. Once it was their turn . . . now it is ours. Soon there will come a proclamation from the King. It will be soon. It is a thing that does not fail.
(Cantor: Briefly in the clear and fade out quickly with music)

NARRATOR. And what my father spoke came to pass. Even as we broke the unleavened bread of the holy day and sat at our table . . . His Majesty, King Manuel of Portugal issued his proclamation, and affixed his royal seal.

MANUEL. All Israelites will depart this land forever under penalty of death. Any Christian found concealing a member of the Jewish faith will be summarily deprived of his property. None who leave may be permitted to take coins of any description, neither gold nor silver, nor precious stones. This is our royal command.

(*Music: Narrative theme and down*)

NARRATOR. It is a sad thing to give your possessions away and to empty the house where you have lived and your grandfather has lived and his grandfather before him. It is sad to turn one final time and see the pleasant valley and the fruitful vineyards of your childhood taken by the despoiler. In the year 1497, we turned this last time. And some wept, and some walked on the roads to the seaports with bowed heads. And many fell by the side and did not rise. And there were Christians who stood in their doorways and wept also and when my father, Baruch, the son of Abraham, fell sick of the fever, they gave him water to drink. I shall not forget that. And when he fell for the last time, they stood by my side and helped me wash him with warm water as is fitting, and wrap him in his prayer shawl and cover him with the earth of Portugal. And this was good. We came to the seaport and waited for a ship to take us away and when we sailed, we overtook a vessel with square sails, and the Baker, who stood by my side, said to me:

(*Music: Fading out below . . . sound of wind very softly in background*)

BAKER. (*Softly*) What are you staring at, boy?

BOY. Look, Baker, look at the sails. They are flung out by the wind and seem to want to embrace the whole world.

BAKER. But not us. All humanity, Benjamin, but not us.

BOY. Do you know what ship that is?

BAKER. Yes. It is the ship of a man called Columbus, a man who has found a new land and sails again.

BOY. Do we sail together, Reb Baker?

BAKER. No, Benjamin. He sails west to begin a new world, we sail east to make the most of an old one.

BOY. I hope he finds it, Reb Baker.

BAKER. For what, Benjamin? To bring it the intolerance and the inhumanity of the Old World . . .

BOY. No, not that. But perhaps it will give him something to take back to the Old World.

BAKER. What, Benjamin . . . a sense of justice?

BOY. Perhaps, Reb Baker, perhaps that—or something my father once said was nearly as good—a sense of mercy.

BAKER. Come away, boy, lie down on the deck and cover yourself with your rags—it is only a dream.

(*Sound of wind up, creak of ship's rigging*)

(*Music: Curtain*)

THE DEATH OF AKIBA

THE DEATH OF AKIBA

The Death of Akiba *presented a problem. Rabbi Akiba was scourged and flayed to death. With his last breath he uttered the* Shemah, *"Hear O Israel, the Lord is Our God, the Lord is One." And since the time of Akiba those have been the daily words of prayer of the Jewish people. It was historically and dramatically important to show why Akiba uttered the* Shemah. *But only the most masochistic listener would demand that the sound of his flaying be heard. It was necessary to find an alternative to sound. Music suggested itself. But music is a sound, and violins and woodwinds in rhythmic dissonance would sound many times more terrible than a whip. The solution was simple. The alternative to sound is no sound. The final scene was begun against a background of silence. Silence became a character in the play. It was the executioner and the instruments of the executioner. And silence justified the anguished* Shemah *of the Cantor which closed the script.*

Louis Finkelstein's book Akiba *supplied the background material for this script.*

The Death of Akiba *was performed on April 30, 1945. Edgar Stehli was Akiba and Kermit Murdock was Tineius Rufus. Others in an excellent cast were Berry Kroeger, Bernard Lenrow, Alexander Scourby, William Adams, Paul Conrad, Joseph Boland, and Rod Hendrickson. Ira Avery directed.*

THE DEATH OF AKIBA

(*Rapping of gavel*)
RUFUS. Let the prisoner rise.
VOICE. The prisoner will rise and face the court.
RUFUS. I, Tineius Rufus, Governor of Judea, by the power vested in me by Hadrian, Caesar of the Roman Empire, do pronounce sentence on you, Rabbi Akiba ben Joseph, Elder of the Sanhedrin of Israel.
VOICE. Prisoner, are you ready to hear the sentence?
AKIBA. I am.
RUFUS. It is my sentence, Akiba ben Joseph, that you be flayed and that you be scourged until you are dead.
(*Rap of gavel*)
VOICE. Does the prisoner know any reason why the sentence of this court should not be executed?
AKIBA. I do not question the sentence of the court.
RUFUS. Have you anything you wish to say, Akiba, some final word?
AKIBA. Thank you, Tincius Rufus. Yes, I have a final word I wish to say.
RUFUS. You may proceed.
(*Pause*)
AKIBA. An old man with the sound of eternity in his ears, speaking a final word. It is strange. On my lips there is praise of God . . . in your hands there is a sword. My lips and your hands.
(*Music: Sneaking in and under*)
AKIBA. Why do you slay me? It is a question not an entreaty. Is it for what I have done? I have done nothing except to

study the Law of God. Is it for what I have taught? I have taught that the worship of God is an expression of love and justice. Did that offend you, Tineius Rufus? Yet you were offended. We sat at the Academy of Yabneh, the elders of Judea, studying, handing down the Oral Law of Israel . . . and we were content . . . despite the presence of the Roman legions in our land. But you were not content. No. I remember when it began. (*Beginning to fade . . . music fading*) That night we slumbered, we were at peace . . . then the horsemen came. (*Horses in rapidly*) And the sleepers were wakened.

(*Pounding on door on mike*)
(*Door pounded simultaneously off mike*)

(*Mike I*)

SIMEON. (*On*) Master, wake up. Everyone . . . the time for sleeping is done, awaken.

AKIBA. What is it, Simeon?

SIMEON. Hurry, Master. Summon the elders, the disciples.

AKIBA. What's wrong?

SIMEON. Judah and I . . . we come from Caesaria.

AKIBA. Wait. I will come.

SIMEON. Hurry, Rabbi Akiba.

AKIBA. Joshua ha Garsi, quickly a candle. Rouse the Academy.

(*Mike II*)

ONE. (*Off*) Rabbi Joshua, Rabbi Gamaliel, Rabbi Tarfon. Wake up.

JOSHUA. (*Off*) Is it you, Judah?

ONE. Yes. Rabbi Joshua. Rouse the others. Simeon and I bring news from Caesaria. (*Pounding off mike*) Rabbi Tarfon, Rabbi Gamaliel, wake up, wake up. (*Move further off and ad lib*)

(*Voices up strenuously*)

SIMEON. (*Projecting*) Elders of Israel, awaken. Evil tidings from Caesaria. We meet now by moonlight.

(*Music: Bridge*)

AKIBA. We are all gathered. Simeon ben Yohai, what is the news from Caesaria?
(*Voices down . . . crickets sounding during pauses*)
SIMEON. Master, instruct us.
AKIBA. It is for you to instruct us, Simeon. We are listening.
(*Pause*)
SIMEON. Sages of Israel . . . yesterday in Caesaria, Tineius Rufus issued a new proclamation. (*Pause*) From this day the covenant of Abraham is denied to our newborn sons. Circumcision is forbidden. (*Pause*)
JOSHUA. (*Slightly off*) Tineius Rufus will be made to see that he wrongs us.
SIMEON. Wait. That is not all. (*Pause*) Observance of the Sabbath is forbidden. And all the festivals. (*Pause*)
ONE. Masters, instruct us. What shall be done?
AKIBA. Rabbi Ishmael, do you wish to speak?
ISHMAEL. (*Off*) Yes, Rabbi Akiba. (*Coming on*) How long? How much longer? Is this the first affront? Is this the tenth affront? How long do we abide in the land and remain slaves to the Caesars?
JOSHUA. (*Slightly off*) The commandment is for peace, Ishmael. Your counsel is for war.
ISHMAEL. And why not?
JOSHUA. (*Off mike*) No, Ishmael. I am ready to die for the Torah. But do not ask us to kill for the Torah.
ISHMAEL. Joshua, will you transgress the law of the Sabbath?
JOSHUA. (*Off*) You know I will not. I will keep the Sabbath.
ISHMAEL. They will kill you for it.
JOSHUA. (*Off*) If God so wills, I shall be killed.
ISHMAEL. Before God, are you craven? Have you courage only to endure? Only to submit? Only to yield? Is there no courage to defend? Judaism no longer needs martyrs . . . it needs soldiers.
(*Pause*)

AKIBA. Ishmael, you are overwrought. It is for us to love peace and to pursue peace. What hope is there for the world when scholars plead for war? We are men of learning. The last stronghold of reason and intellect. Shall we confess our lives a failure?

ISHMAEL. If we vanquish the enemy, we are not a failure.

AKIBA. Ishmael, when the dead lie unburied in the open pit, who is the victor and who is the vanquished?

ISHMAEL. It does not matter. If we die, we shall not die alone.

AKIBA. Ishmael, you forget so soon. "Thou shalt not take vengeance, nor bear any grudge against the children of thy people, but thou shalt love thy neighbor as thyself: I am the Lord and ye shall keep My Statutes."

ISHMAEL. I will not listen, Akiba. Do what you wish. I go to the hills . . . I join Simeon bar Kochba.

JOSHUA. (*Off*) To make rebellion, Rabbi Ishmael?

ISHMAEL. To make war, Joshua. (*Pause*) Akiba, do you come?

(*Pause*)

AKIBA. No.

ISHMAEL. Then you will stay and rot here.

AKIBA. No, not that either. I must go to Tineius Rufus. I will explain that we are of peaceful intent. He will understand. And he will alter his attitude toward us and treat us with reason.

(*Music: Bridge to narrative theme and down*)

AKIBA. I came to you, Tineius Rufus? Do you remember? Yes, I came to you and I said that the world was ruled by kindness and that the merit of man consisted in the multitude of good deeds. You nodded your head, Tineius Rufus. Why did you nod your head? I believed you then to be a man like other men. It was wrong of you to deceive me. You spoke so gently and so honorably. Was it to mock me, Tineius Rufus? Your smile was amiable.

(*Music: Fading*)

(*Akiba fading*) You took my hand ... we spoke, you asked a question. Do you remember, Tineius Rufus, do you remember the question you asked?
RUFUS. (*Fading in laughing*) A very apt reply, Rabbi Akiba. Tell me, why does your people place so much emphasis on charity?
AKIBA. What are the gifts we can make to God? Charity to the poor.
RUFUS. Ah, but you are not giving to your God ... you give to the poor.
AKIBA. He that is gracious to the poor lendeth to the Lord.
RUFUS. I don't understand your God. I like a God I can see. Like this one. (*Rapping on wood*) Now, that's a handsome god.
AKIBA. I see only an idol made of wood.
RUFUS. He is good enough. If your God is so powerful, why doesn't he come down and smash these idols?
AKIBA. Tineius Rufus, what other gods do you worship?
RUFUS. You evade my question.
AKIBA. No—what other gods do you worship?
RUFUS. The sun, the moon, the planets, the stars. Why do you ask, Akiba?
AKIBA. Don't you see? If the only idols worshipped were things of clay or wood ... God might destroy them. But you worship the sun and the stars. Shall God destroy His entire world because some men are foolish?
RUFUS. (*Chuckles*) Rabbi Akiba, I have met many sages of Israel but you are the most learned and the most humble. Be proud, Rabbi Akiba. I don't believe in false modesty.
AKIBA. Tineius Rufus.
RUFUS. Yes?
AKIBA. Out there ... lying in the road ... what do you see?
RUFUS. Nothing but a dead cat. Run over by a chariot, no doubt. I'll see that the carcass is removed.
AKIBA. Tineius Rufus, he who glories in the knowledge of

the Law is like to the carcass of an animal which lies in the road. It attracts the attention of all, it is true . . . but whoever passes by puts his hand to his nose and turns away.

RUFUS. (*Chuckling*) And are you a live cat, Rabbi Akiba? And I a mouse? (*Sharply*) Let us stop playing. What do you want?

(*Pause*)

AKIBA. I see I have misjudged you, Tineius Rufus.

RUFUS. (*Nastily*) I have not misjudged you. What do you want?

AKIBA. I have not dissimulated. I want what I told you I want. I had believed that you understood.

RUFUS. Power is the only thing I understand. My laws remain, do you hear?

AKIBA. You will force our people into rebellion.

RUFUS. Exactly. And we will know how to take care of them. Especially this rebel, Bar Kochba.

(*Pause*)

AKIBA. It was stupid of me not to see that, wasn't it?

RUFUS. Very stupid. Do you still want to talk to me about the law of kindness and charity and your God?

AKIBA. No, Tineius Rufus. Not to you. The Emperor Hadrian has come to Antioch. Perhaps he will listen.

RUFUS. (*Laughs*)

(*Music: Bridge*)

HADRIAN. My dear Rabbi Akiba, there is nothing I detest quite so much as a fool. I shall have to admonish Tineius Rufus.

AKIBA. Thank you, Caesar.

HADRIAN. Oh, don't misunderstand my motives. I am not concerned with what you call justice. I want to maintain the Roman Empire. You don't maintain an empire by antagonizing your subjects.

AKIBA. You are very wise, Caesar.

HADRIAN. Thank you, Rabbi. My friend, I noticed on my tour

THE DEATH OF AKIBA

of inspection that Jerusalem is completely laid waste. I shall have it rebuilt.

AKIBA. *Caesar!* He who gives delight to his fellow creatures also gives delight to God.

HADRIAN. Very nice. My respects to your God. Oh yes, your Temple. The one Titus destroyed . . . the simpleton. We shall rebuild it for you.

AKIBA. Blessed are Thou O Lord who hast brought me to this day.

HADRIAN. Come come, Rabbi Akiba, don't anticipate. I shall have the Temple rebuilt. To Jupiter naturally.

AKIBA. Caesar, you do not know what you are saying.

HADRIAN. You will get used to it. It's a fine gift.

AKIBA. A poisoned gift, Caesar.

HADRIAN. What a curious people. I promise to rebuild Jerusalem, isn't that enough.

AKIBA. Do not defile our holy sanctuary.

HADRIAN. Curious. You are more concerned about your theology than your bread.

AKIBA. I plead with you, Caesar, if Jupiter is placed on Mount Moriah, blood will be shed.

HADRIAN. Let's not discuss it, Rabbi. I like the idea.

AKIBA. Caesar, I entreat you. Do not desecrate our holiest symbol. Blood will be shed over it.

HADRIAN. Whose blood, my friend? Isn't that the question?

(*Music: Bridge*)
(*Trumpet call*)
(*Sound of cavalry moving off mike*)
(*Single horse . . . fading up . . . whinny*)

BAR KOCHBA. Rabbi Ishmael, do you ride to the hills with me?

ISHMAEL. I am ready, Bar Kochba.

BAR KOCHBA. Here is your mount. (*Whinny*) There is no time to lose.

ISHMAEL. (*Softly*) Akiba ben Joseph, bless me before I go.
  (*Pause*)

AKIBA. You bless me by your going, Rabbi Ishmael.

ISHMAEL. I hope so. It is not easy for me to take up arms. All my life I have studied and preached for peace. Now there is an end of scholarship.

AKIBA. No, Ishmael. There is no end. What is a scholar of Israel but a warrior armed with the law of justice? God go with you, Ishmael.

BAR KOCHBA. Master, do you have a blessing for me?

AKIBA. I am dry with age, Bar Kochba, and my hands are infirm . . . but let me touch your standard. (*Pause*) There shall step forth a star out of Jacob, and a sceptre shall rise out of Israel, and shall smite through the corners of Moab, and break down all the corners of Seth.

BAR KOCHBA. Thank you, Akiba ben Joseph.

(*Trumpet off mike*)

ISHMAEL. Good-bye, Akiba. (*Pause*) Bar Kochba, I am ready.

(*Horses up, hold, and take out with:*)

(*Music: Bridge and segue to narrative theme and down*)

AKIBA. That was your victory, Tineius Rufus. They rode forth to battle and they did not return. "The righteous perisheth, and no man layeth it to heart, and godly men are taken away, none considering that the righteous is taken away from the evil to come." Yes, Tineius Rufus, they died before the evil to come. How many did your legions slaughter in three years, O Governor of Judea? How many women and how many children? How many thousands did you enslave? "How doth the city sit solitary that was full of people! How is she become as a widow!" (*Fading*) And even this was not enough for you.

(*Music: Out*)

RUFUS. Summon Rabbi Akiba.

(*Footsteps . . . door opens*)

VOICE. (*Projecting*) Rabbi Akiba ben Joseph.

(*Footsteps coming on*)

(*Door shuts . . . slightly off*)

AKIBA. You summoned me, Governor of Judea. I am here.
RUFUS. No greeting, Rabbi?
AKIBA. What do you want?
RUFUS. I expect a greeting, my friend.
AKIBA. Tineius Rufus, what do you want of me?
RUFUS. I respect your age. I shall overlook this discourtesy.
AKIBA. I ask you once more. What do you want?
RUFUS. Not too much discourtesy, Rabbi. I am an impatient man. (*Pause*) This is what I want. Read it.
AKIBA. You cannot do anything more to us. What is there to read?
RUFUS. Still stubborn? I shall read this to you. My proclamation.
AKIBA. Don't read it. Tell me what's in it.
RUFUS. Very well, a rebellious people must be punished. What have you left, Rabbi?
AKIBA. Nothing. Our festivals are prohibited, the Sabbath observance is forbidden. Our ceremonials are proscribed. Our warriors are dead. All we have left is the study of the Law.
RUFUS. Rabbi, now you have nothing left. I forbid the study of the law of Moses. Your Torah is shut. Tight. Not to be opened. Be sure you understand me, Akiba ben Joseph. The penalty for violation of this order is death.
(*Music: Bridge*)
(*Voices subdued . . . establish and cut on:*)
AKIBA. What are you waiting for? We are scholars. Let us study the Law.
JOSHUA. Will you instruct us, Master?
AKIBA. Yes, Joshua Ha-garsi, will you begin?
(*Pause*)
ONE. The penalty for study is death.
AKIBA. Scholars of Israel, I ask you to begin.
(*Pause*)
TWO. Akiba ben Joseph, we do not fear for ourselves.

AKIBA. Do you fear for me? *(Pause)* I answer you with a parable. The fox came to the river bank and said to the fishes, "The fishermen are spreading their nets. Come to the dry land and you will be safe?" But the fishes replied: "If in the water, which is our element, we are in danger, what will happen to us on the dry land which is not our element?" Scholars, if there is no safety for us in the Torah which is our home, how can we find safety elsewhere? Let us disdain secrecy. It is unworthy of us. Joshua Ha-garsi, I ask you to begin.

(Music: Bridge)
(Voices ad lib)
(Long whistle off mike . . . cut voices)

AKIBA. Why do you stop, my sons?

JOSHUA. It is the signal, Akiba.

AKIBA. Continue with the text, Joshua Ha-garsi. The Romans are coming. And they will find us in study. It is proper that they should find us this way.

JOSHUA. Master.

AKIBA. Yes, my son?

JOSHUA. Whatever befalls us, whatever happens to me . . . I want to tell you now that . . .

AKIBA. Hush, my son.

JOSHUA. At least let me tell you how much you have given to us.

AKIBA. I have given nothing. I have given you the fragrance that comes sweet from the citron, the light taken by one candle from another, the water drawn from a brook. I have lost nothing and you have been sweetened by the odor of citron and refreshed by the water, and increased by the light. And I am augmented and not diminished. *(Pause)* Now read on, Joshua Ha-garsi.

JOSHUA. Akiba! *(Long whistle off mike)* Akiba!

AKIBA. Read on, my son.

JOSHUA. And Balaam lifted up his eyes, and he saw Israel

dwelling tribe by tribe; and the spirit of God came upon him. And he took up his parable, and said: How goodly are thy tents O Jacob, Thy dwellings O Israel! As valleys stretched out . . .

(*Music: Sneak in above and up for bridge*)
(*Sound of marching men coming on mike*)

AKIBA. Be composed, my sons.

ONE. Akiba ben Joseph, there is still time for you to flee.

AKIBA. It is better to die at once than to flee from study.

(*Marching men closer*)

JOSHUA. Instruct us, Master.

AKIBA. Hear me closely . . . The world is judged with mercy. The shop is open; the hand writes. (*Marching closer*) (*Akiba building*) Whosoever desires may come and borrow; but the collectors make their appointed rounds, and the payment cannot be evaded. The warrant is there. The judgment is correct, and everything is prepared for the feast.

(*Marching men on mike . . . and cut*)

VOICE. Akiba ben Joseph.

AKIBA. Yes, Captain.

VOICE. I place you under arrest.

(*Music: Bridge and take out with:*)
(*Rapping of gavel*)

AKIBA. I am done, Tineius Rufus.

RUFUS. Once again, Akiba ben Joseph. I pronounce sentence. You will be taken to your dungeon. At dawn tomorrow you will be led forth and flayed and scourged until you are dead. (*Rap of gavel*) Let the prisoner be removed.

(*Music: Bridge*)
(*Echo throughout*)
(*Footsteps moving on*)
(*Heavy door opens*)

RUFUS. Akiba ben Joseph?

AKIBA. (*Slightly off*) Is it time, Tineius Rufus?

RUFUS. Not yet.

AKIBA. (*Moving on*) Then why have you come?

RUFUS. I cannot sleep.

AKIBA. Strange. I was asleep

RUFUS. Perhaps it is not strange. Old man, if you had been born in Rome, you could have been my father. (*Pause*) I would have been proud of such a father.

AKIBA. Thank you, my son.

RUFUS. You call me that?

AKIBA. If you were my age, I should call you brother. Did not He that made me in the womb make you? And did not One fashion us in the womb?

RUFUS. Akiba ben Joseph, I come to offer you a pardon, if you recant.

AKIBA. Pardon is for criminals, Tineius Rufus. It is I who should pardon you. (*Pause*) I pardon you now.

RUFUS. Save your life, Akiba ben Joseph.

AKIBA. I cannot, my son.

(*Pause*)

RUFUS. You are accursed, Akiba ben Joseph . . . your people is accursed.

AKIBA. Then let me be the cursed, not he who curses. Let me be of them that are persecuted not of them that persecute.

(*Pause*)

RUFUS. You will not change your mind?

AKIBA. No, Tineius Rufus. (*Pause*) You have come in kindness. I shall ask you then for one small thing.

RUFUS. Whatever it is, Akiba ben Joseph. Ask it.

AKIBA. Let Joshua Ha-garsi stand by my side tomorrow.

RUFUS. Nothing more?

AKIBA. No. Nothing more.

RUFUS. Very well . . . he shall stand by your side . . . tomorrow.

(*Music: Bridge*)

RUFUS. (*Muttering*) Is it done yet?

VOICE. No.
RUFUS. He is so old, why does it take so long?
VOICE. I don't know.
RUFUS. Do you feel a pulse?
VOICE. Yes.
RUFUS. (*Starting to fade*) Call me when the end comes.
AKIBA. (*Softly—but no quaver*) And thou shalt love the Lord thy God with all thy heart, and with all thy soul, and with all thy might.
RUFUS. (*Coming on*) Akiba. Do you hear me, Akiba ben Joseph?
AKIBA. I hear you.
RUFUS. Give it up. Are you insensible to pain? Why don't you die?
AKIBA. All my life, Tinieus Rufus, I have been waiting for the moment when I might truly fulfill the commandment. I have always loved the Lord with all my might, and with all my heart; now I know that I love Him with all my life. Hear, O Israel, the Lord is our God, the Lord is One. (*Pause*)
VOICE. Tineius Rufus!
RUFUS. Yes.
VOICE. Come away.
RUFUS. No, not yet, I must wait.
VOICE. You have your victory. Can't you see? Akiba ben Joseph is dead.
   (*Cantor: Shemah yis-raw-ayl ah-dow-nawy eh-loh-hay-noo ah-dow-nawy eh-chawd.*)
   (*Music: Curtain*)

THE DAY OF THE SHADOW

THE DAY OF THE SHADOW

This is still The Day of the Shadow. *While human fat is no longer rendered into soap, the fires kindled by the Nazis are not extinguished. Human beings are called Displaced Persons. Men and women made stateless by Hitler are denied visas by Hitler's conquerors because they are stateless.*

In the fall of 1945, when The Day of the Shadow *was written, it was possible to speak of these things without incurring resentment. But eighteen months later the same words breed uneasiness and irritation. For the events of 1945 continue to hold true in 1947 and that is much too long a time to ask decent men to remind themselves of a Buchenwald charnel house or to remain suspended in a state of horror. Men possess nerve-endings and nerve-endings cry out for relief and forgetfulness. Yet, two years after the European war there are still Jacob Dworetzkys whose nerve-endings are also frayed and cry out for appeasement; but they rot in the DP camps of Germany.*

The Day of the Shadow *was originally presented at the Waldorf-Astoria in the form of a simulated radio broadcast. It received an NBC production on November 18, 1945. Roger De Koven was featured as the Chaplain and Peter Capell was Jacob Dworetzky. Others in the cast were Norman Rose, Gregory Morton, Joseph Boland, Mitzi Gould, Ronnie Liss, and Joseph Di Santis.*

Late in 1946 The Day of the Shadow *and* A Lantern in the Inferno *(see the facsimile script at the end of the volume) were presented by a group of DP's at the Yiddish Theatre in Munich. The translation into Yiddish was made by Israel Blumenfeld, Editor of the* Judische Rundschau, *organ of the liberated Jews of Germany.*

THE DAY OF THE SHADOW

CHAPLAIN. Listen. Listen to the silence. I have come from the land of the day of the shadow. I have seen the naked cities and the dead lips. Someone must speak of this. Someone must speak of the memory of things destroyed. O Lord, my God, God of my Fathers, break open a shaft in the darkness, and let me speak, for I have a right to speak.
(*Music: Narrative theme and fade down*)
CHAPLAIN. I am the Chaplain who stood before the crematorium of Belsen. I buried 23,000 Jews. I have a right to speak. I stood last month in Cracow when "Liberated" Jews were murdered. I have no pretty things to tell you. But I must tell you. God of Israel, forgotten things are not forgotten and blood does not wash clean from the hands. Someone must speak for the anguish; someone must speak of the day of the shadow; someone must bring you the terrible wonder of their hope. This is what I saw with my eyes. But first I must tell you the things I did not see, but things nevertheless that are plain, and written down, and true.
(*Music: Up and take out with:*)
(*Sound of adding machines*)
CHAPLAIN. Listen . . . the adding machines of the statistician.
(*Pause*) The Jews of Poland . . . before and after.
ONE. Nineteen thirty-eight . . . Jewish population of Poland.
TWO. Three million, three hundred thousand.
ONE. Nineteen forty-five.
TWO. Four hundred and seventy-five thousand.
ONE. Survivors . . . fifteen per cent.
TWO. Dead . . . eighty-five per cent.

CHAPLAIN. Czechoslovakia . . . before and after.
THREE. Nineteen thirty-eight . . . Jewish population of Czechoslovakia.
FOUR. Three hundred and fifty-four thousand.
THREE. Nineteen forty-five.
FOUR. Sixty thousand.
ONE. Dead . . . ninety-five per cent.
  (*Adding machine*)
CHAPLAIN. Lithuania . . . before and after.
ONE. Nineteen thirty-nine . . . Jewish population of Lithuania.
TWO. One hundred and fifty thousand.
ONE. Jewish population of Lithuania . . . Nineteen forty-five.
TWO. Seven thousand.
ONE. Dead . . . ninety-five per cent.
  (*Adding machine*)
CHAPLAIN. Germany . . . before and after.
THREE. Nineteen thirty-nine . . . Remaining Jewish population of Germany.
FOUR. Two hundred and seventy-five thousand.
THREE. Nineteen forty-five.
FOUR. Less than five thousand.
  (*Pause*)
THREE. There were some promises Hitler kept.
ONE. Roumania . . . four hundred and fifteen thousand dead.
TWO. Hungary . . . one hundred and ten thousand and one hundred dead.
FOUR. Austria . . . eighty-six thousand dead.
ONE. France . . . eighty thousand dead.
TWO. Occupied Russia . . . one million two hundred and fifty thousand dead.
THREE. Let us say the prayer for the dead—
FOUR. Holland . . .
  (*Music: Sneak in*)
THREE. Yis-gah-dahl . . .
ONE. Belgium—

FOUR. V'yis-kah-dahsh . . .
TWO. Italy—
THREE. Shmay rah-baw . . .
FOUR. Denmark—
THREE. B'awl-maw dee v'raw chir-oo-say . . .
ONE. Yugoslavia—
THREE. V'yam-leech mahl-choo-say . . .
TWO. Estonia—
THREE. B'chah-yay-chohn . . .
FOUR. Luxembourg—
THREE. Oo-v'yoh-may-chon . . .
ONE. Norway—
THREE. Oo-v'chah-yay . . .
TWO. Greece—
THREE. Dee chawl bays yis-raw-ayl . . .
FOUR. Latvia—
THREE. Bah-ah-gaw-law oo-veez-mahn kaw-reev . . .
ONE. Bulgaria—
THREE. V'im-roo aw-mayn.

(*Music: Chord*)

(*Sound of adding machine*)

STATISTICIAN I. My totals show that of a pre-war Jewish population in Europe, eighty per cent are dead, twenty per cent survive.

STATISTICIAN II. For the twenty per cent who survive, malnutrition, tuberculosis, secondary anemia, diseases of the cardio-vascular system, etc., must all reduce the life expectancy of the survivors.

STATISTICIAN III. Inasmuch as the survivors are predominantly males, with, in some areas, a negligible percentage of females capable of procreation, the birth-rate may be expected to reveal a profound imbalance.

STATISTICIAN IV. In brief, it would appear that the biological prognosis for the remaining Jews of Europe is not favorable.

(*Music: Narrative theme and down*)

CHAPLAIN. Prognosis, etceteras, statistics. What good are the figures? Can you comprehend a ghastliness so vast? I cannot. Let the adding machines be still. The cup is empty, the light has gone out. A single child in a single bed . . . a child dying of fever . . . that is comprehensible. But four million seven hundred and fifty thousand dead of six million who once lived, that is beyond comprehension. God is merciful and men do not weep over statistics. Let the numbers and the percentages be for the cost accountant who has no flesh.

(*Music: Up and down*)

CHAPLAIN. Let us speak now of the living. The living who are few in number and therefore comprehensible. Let us speak of the man and the child I saw in the American Zone of Occupation.

JACOB. They tell me I have to go back to Poland.

CHAPLAIN. Please believe me, Jacob—I tried to stop it.

JACOB. I understand, Chaplain, here we are not admitted and in Poland once again—there are pogroms. (*Pause*) Chaplain, at least admit this boy.

CHAPLAIN. I'll try. But, Jacob—perhaps in Poland he can find his parents.

JACOB. He does not want to go to Poland. Moshe, speak to the American Rabbi. Tell him what you want.

BOY. I want to stay here.

CHAPLAIN. But this is a concentration camp.

BOY. I want to stay here.

JACOB. Chaplain, we mustn't make him cry again. Last night we found a place to sleep. But he cried all night. Do you know why he cried? Tell the Chaplain, Moshe.

BOY. It was different. I was afraid. I want to stay here.

JACOB. A woman gave us a bed in her house. He was frightened of the bed.

BOY. I want to stay here.

JACOB. He cried for three hours. Chaplain, do you know what I did? I let him sleep on the floor. That was better but he still cried. So I left the light burning.

BOY. I want to stay here.

JACOB. Then I found some barbed wire and I put it over the window. Just like in the concentration camp. But he cried. So, I walked up and down like a sentry. And then he stopped crying and he slept on the floor.

BOY. I want to stay here.

JACOB. He wants to go back in the concentration camp, Chaplain, he wants to be restored to his normal existence. For him it is not enough to bring light . . . first you must teach him to see. Come, Moshe, come with me to Poland, perhaps we shall find a concentration camp.

CHAPLAIN. Jacob Dworetzky, wait . . . wait for me.

JACOB. Do you come because you pity us?

CHAPLAIN. No, there is no progress through pity.

JACOB. I am glad you said that! We do not pity ourselves. We do not beat our breasts. Moshe, tell the Chaplain how your father died.

BOY. There is nothing to tell. My father was not the only one. They took a thousand Jews that day.

JACOB. Tell him . . . you saw it . . . you were there.

BOY. Those who had faith . . . they were not afraid. They stood on line waiting to go into the crematorium. Then my father found a piece of broken glass.

CHAPLAIN. To kill himself.

BOY. No . . . not to kill himself.

CHAPLAIN. But the broken glass . . . what was that for?

BOY. To cut his garment . . . when someone dies, he told me, you stand up and cut your garment. First he did it . . . then they all did it. A thousand men stood on line and cut their garments before they died.

CHAPLAIN. Moshe, were they mourning for themselves? Is that why they did it?

BOY. They mourned for those who died without faith. Father said it is a terrible thing to be a martyr and not have a cause. Father was a Jew . . . he believed he had a cause.

CHAPLAIN. Thank you. I understand. Now let me go with you.

(*Music: Bridge*)

OFFICIAL. You there . . . come off the line.

CHAPLAIN. They're waiting for food and clothing. This is an UNRRA depot. They have a right to stand on line.

OFFICIAL. Please come here. I think you shouldn't wait on line.

CHAPLAIN. But you have no right to say that.

OFFICIAL. Believe me, sir, I'm trying to be their friend. You're Jews. You've suffered a great deal. But—if some of these people see you on line, they'll get angry. It's for your own good.

CHAPLAIN. You mean it's for their own best interest that they be treated badly?

OFFICIAL. Yes. Treat them decently . . . you'll have another pogrom. It's for their own interest.

JACOB. He means well, Chaplain. Come, Moshe. I think you will sleep in Poland. If you just close your eyes a little, I think you will be able to see the barbed wire.

(*Music: Briefly*)

OFFICIAL II. Why come to me, Chaplain? There's nothing I can do for these people. There's no discrimination now.

JACOB. No. The Germans treated us as Jews, the Russians say you must treat us as Poles, and the man in charge of the line says if he treats us as Poles, there will be another pogrom.

CHAPLAIN. Sir, isn't there anything you can do for this man?

OFFICIAL II. To be frank, while there is no discrimination now in Poland . . . nothing.

JACOB. Once I had a little business . . . before the Germans invaded Poland.

OFFICIAL II. I wouldn't pursue that if I were you. Take my

advice. Some man probably bought it in good faith. If he has to give it up there will be . . .

CHAPLAIN. More pogroms?

OFFICIAL II. Don't blame me. That's how it is. Look. Jacob, take my advice . . . leave Poland.

JACOB. Where shall I go?

OFFICIAL II. Wherever you want to. You're liberated.

JACOB. Then I should like to go to Palestine. Palestine is home. They say that home is a place where they've got to take you in.

CHAPLAIN. Jacob, I'm afraid that right now, Palestine is impossible.

JACOB. Then, Chaplain, perhaps you will let me come to America?

CHAPLAIN. It's not up to me. I'm afraid that's impossible.

OFFICIAL II. There are other places, you're still free to emigrate.

JACOB. Very well, I shall go to England.

OFFICIAL II. Oh, no. That's out of the question, of course.

(*Pause*)

JACOB. I understand. There are two kinds of countries . . . countries where Jews cannot live and countries where Jews cannot enter.

(*Pause*)

OFFICIAL II. Well?

JACOB. You have a suggestion?

OFFICIAL II. I don't know. Why don't you see, uh, see my superior. Sure, go to see him. You can't lose anything more, can you?

(*Music: Bridge*)

OFFICIAL III. I'm a very busy man.

CHAPLAIN. He's a hungry man.

OFFICIAL III. I was hungry, too. I'm a Pole. In Poland you get used to hunger.

JACOB. And homelessness.

OFFICIAL III. Yes. You get used to homelessness.

CHAPLAIN. This man suffered a great deal; can't something special be done for him?

OFFICIAL III. Well, if we could establish his political reliability.

CHAPLAIN. He spent six years in a concentration camp.

OFFICIAL III. What was your offense?

JACOB. I refused to stop being a Jew.

OFFICIAL III. Not good enough. We need to prove his *political* reliability—only political prisoners receive special treatment. (*Moving off*) Excuse me, gentlemen, I'm rather busy.

(*Door closed*)

CHAPLAIN. I don't know what to tell you now. I'll cable America if they'll let me.

JACOB. Perhaps. But I know what I have to do. Come with me. A woman has just given birth to a child. Things are never so bad but that there isn't someone worse off than you are. Come, Chaplain.

(*Music: Bridge*)

(*Sound of baby crying*)

JACOB. (*Wondering*) Chaplain, she gave birth to a baby. Her man is dead and she has consumption . . . but here is a baby.

CHAPLAIN. Leave this chocolate bar for her, Jacob. It's all I have now, we'll get her something else later.

(*Baby again*)

JACOB. Do you hear? They think Israel has died, but Israel dies in childbirth.

(*Baby cries and out*)

CHAPLAIN. What a time to be born in!

JACOB. Is there a better time or another time? "What is my strength that I should wait and what is my end that I should be patient?" You see, I remember the words of Job.

CHAPLAIN. "Why died I not from the womb?

Why did I not perish at birth?
Why did the knees receive me,
And wherefore the breasts that I should suck?
For now should I have lain still and been quiet;
I should have slept; then had I been at rest."
(Baby cries again)
JACOB. "As a hidden untimely birth
As infants that never saw light."
(Baby's cry)
(Music: Bridge)
CHAPLAIN. You shouldn't have done that, Jacob. I saw you leave a piece of bread.
JACOB. Why not? You gave me two pieces. Chaplain, let the pauper help the pauper.
CHAPLAIN. But, Jacob, you can't afford it. You need food.
JACOB. That's the trouble. Every day the body needs food, but doesn't the conscience also require something?
(Pause)
CHAPLAIN. To lie in the gutter and not to forsake dignity.
JACOB. Do you marvel at it? There can be cleanliness in the gutter.
(Pause)
CHAPLAIN. Jacob, what's going to become of you?
JACOB. I don't know. The pretexts change but the hatred remains the same.
(Music: Briefly)
GIRL. *(A long burst of coughing)* Chaplain?
CHAPLAIN. Yes.
GIRL. Jacob told me . . . thank you for the chocolate.
CHAPLAIN. How is your baby?
GIRL. He lives.
CHAPLAIN. Is there something . . . anything I can do for you?
GIRL. Maybe . . . Maybe you can find a woman who will nurse him for me. I have no milk.
CHAPLAIN. I'll try.

GIRL. I shouldn't have had the baby, should I? But my husband... he wanted... (*Coughs*)
CHAPLAIN. Don't try to speak.
GIRL. It's all right. Jacob, you knew my husband?
JACOB. Yes. Yes, I knew him.
GIRL. I think he was a good man... I'm not sure. He wasn't a soldier. He wasn't shot on the battlefield. They didn't even kill him in hot blood. He stood on a line and waited his turn... They *processed* him. (*Coughs*) Chaplain, if my baby lives... His father died a Jew... he must live a Jew.

(*Music: Bridge*)

JACOB. Chaplain, you will go back and tell them that there is still a remnant.
CHAPLAIN. Yes, Jacob. I'll go back and tell them.
JACOB. Tell them we hold fast. Tell them... that the normalcy of the Jew in the European Diaspora is not the inferior category of the tolerated Jew, but the Jew who holds his faith like a Torah.
CHAPLAIN. I wish you could tell them yourself.
JACOB. It can't be. I stay here and I wait. It's hard to wait. The synagogues down, the yeshivahs broken, the books torn. Tell them not to forget the books.
CHAPLAIN. But the food comes first, Jacob. And you must not give away your own food.
JACOB. I'll try not to do it again. But that is how I pay for the grave of Moshe's father. The good deed to pay for blood.
CHAPLAIN. You mean that, Jacob, don't you?
JACOB. Yes, sometimes in the middle of the night I wake up screaming and I am ashamed. I think to myself, I think, Jacob Dworetzky, there is a Judaism to build, and Jacob Dworetzky, you are only a liberated Jew without a home. But that's foolish. One man can't build a whole world. But one man can give away a piece of bread. I know what

has to be done now. (*Accelerating*) The small things are what count. You teach a little boy how to study and you build a world. When a man falls down, you take his hand and you help him up, and you build a world. You stay honest and you don't sell your heart, and you build a world. Such small ways, Chaplain. And that's all there is to it. I must have been a fool not to have known it before.
(*Music: Up for bridge to narrative theme*)

CHAPLAIN. Jacob Dworetzky—I put Job's question to you. (*Passionately*) "Dost thou still hold fast to thine integrity? Blaspheme God and die." (*Pauses*) The miracle of Poland . . . they held fast to their integrity. They waited for life and there came darkness; in the fields they found thistles upon the wheat and weeds among the barley; for them there was no green thing; for them an extermination was determined; the words of solace they received were from the tongue of the stammerer . . . and yet they held fast. Jacob Dworetzky, teach me! There is a stubbornness of cowardice and a stubbornness of faith, and one is true to the surface and one is true to the depths. God of Israel, let me speak in the anguish of my spirit of the day of the shadow . . . they held fast.

(*Music: Up and out*)

CHAPLAIN. Last month I stood where the day was a shadow. Last month I stood amid the obscenity of annihilation. Between Poland and America how many miles is it? How many miles between the pity that does not heal the bruise and the terrible harvest of the red fruit? How many miles between the normalcy of starvation, and the dreadful normalcy of the guilt-obsession? Now I am home and I know neither the distance nor the dimension, nor the answer. I know only this.

(*Music: Sneak in*)

CHAPLAIN. I have seen the naked cities. I have listened to the silence of the dead lips. Where is the shaft of light to break open the day of the shadow? And I know. The surface must be true to the depths. Jacob Dworetzky, the tree which is cut down must be planted again. Jacob Dworetzky, stand fast where Israel has died in childbirth. For the seed is in the ground. "Yea, thou shalt be steadfast and thou shalt not fear. For thou shalt forget thy misery. Thou shalt remember it as waters that are passed away; and thy life shall be clearer than the noonday . . . Though there be darkness, it shall be as the morning."

(*Music: Curtain*)

THE BROKEN SABBATH OF RABBI ASHER

THE BROKEN SABBATH OF RABBI ASHER

There is a story that many years ago there lived an actual Rabbi of Yanov who, under circumstances resembling those set forth in the script, went into a deep woods, confused north and south, lost his way and before he was done, mislaid a day in the week, kept Friday as the Sabbath and threatened the sanity of his congregation, to say nothing of the purity of his own soul.

To those unfamiliar with Jewish tradition the humorous crisis of The Broken Sabbath of Rabbi Asher *may seem either incomprehensible or overdrawn. But it was neither to the townspeople of Yanov where Sabbath customs were observed with deep fervor and where Sabbath desecration was tantamount to a denial of the physical laws of the universe. The most savory dishes were for the Sabbath, the cleanest clothes, the sweetest songs, the most ardent prayers. Six profane days of the week were made sacred by the crown of the seventh. Therefore, how could you tell a man of more than sabbatical goodness, like Rabbi Asher, that he had violated his law and his birthright?*

The Broken Sabbath of Rabbi Asher *was broadcast on November 3, 1946. Gregory Morton was the Narrator and Rod Hendrickson was Rabbi Asher. Roc Rogers was the Teamster, Guy Repp was the Miller, Joan Lazer was Tamar, and Hester Sondergaard was Hannah. Others in the cast were Norman Rose, Marvin Marx, and Ralph Locke. Frank Papp was the director; Morris Mamorsky composed the musical score conducted by Milton Katims; and Cantor David Putterman was the soloist.*

THE BROKEN SABBATH OF RABBI ASHER

NARRATOR. Many, many years ago—I believe it was on a Wednesday afternoon when the world had not entirely lost its innocence—Rabbi Asher of Yanov forgot the day of the week. The consequences were altogether remarkable.
(*Music: In and down*)
NARRATOR. It began with the utmost simplicity. Rabbi Asher merely said ...
ASHER. Teamster, are you able to take me to Lizensk and back?
NARRATOR. A perfectly straightforward question. And the Teamster gave a perfectly straightforward answer.
TEAMSTER. I am, Rabbi Asher, but can you afford it?
NARRATOR. By a rare coincidence Rabbi Asher happened to have the necessary four roubles and so he was driven from Yanov to Lizensk. Now what was his business in Lizensk? It was to be present at the wedding of his youngest sister's grandchild. So he attended the wedding, which was a good deed.
ONE. We see you so rarely, Rabbi Asher. Won't you remain in Lizensk over the Sabbath?
ASHER. Thank you very much, but I promised my congregation that I would be with them at services as usual. I'm afraid we must be going.
NARRATOR. And so many, many years ago, in fact on a Thursday, Rabbi Asher and the Teamster turned about and headed home for Yanov.
(*Music: Up and segue to:*)
(*Sound of wagon wheels and hoofbeats*)

(*Fade sound behind*)

ASHER. I wonder if you would mind stopping for a moment?

TEAMSTER. Do you want to stretch your legs?

ASHER. Thank you, Teamster. It's just that it's time for afternoon prayers.

TEAMSTER. Don't let me stop you. Go right ahead.

ASHER. You don't understand. I have to wash my hands.

TEAMSTER. I thought you said you have to recite your prayers?

ASHER. Certainly, but I can't until I wash my hands first.

TEAMSTER. You can't?

ASHER. That's the commandment. The hands must be washed before prayers and before eating.

TEAMSTER. Well, all I can say is that it's a pretty peculiar commandment. (*Projecting*) Whoa! (*Cut sounds*) Go through the forest, right past the rock there. Head due west for about a hundred and fifty yards. You'll find a little brook. You can wash your hands there.

ASHER. That's very kind of you, Teamster.

TEAMSTER. Don't mention it.

ASHER. I'll be right back. Thank you.

(*Music: Bridge to narrative theme and down*)

NARRATOR. Past the rock, due west through the forest went Rabbi Asher. After all he was a man accustomed to forests—the great forest of the Talmud and the massive growth of decisions, opinions, prohibitions, injunctions, admonitions, maxims, parables, commentaries and super-commentaries. Unfortunately, this was a forest made of trees and without too much difficulty Rabbi Asher succeeded in getting himself hopelessly lost.

(*Music: Out*)

ASHER. (*Projecting*) Teamster! Oo-oo-oo. Teamster!

NARRATOR. There was no answer.

ASHER. Oo-oo-oo-oo. Where are you?

NARRATOR. Naturally, the Teamster was exactly where the Rabbi had left him. On the road—a quarter of a mile away.

TEAMSTER. How long does it take a man to wash his hands anyway?

ASHER. Oo-oo-oo-oo. Teamster, can you hear me?

NARRATOR. Obviously he couldn't. For by very skillful blundering Rabbi Asher had increased the distance to a good half-mile. Being a thoughtful man, Rabbi Asher came to a thoughtful conclusion.

ASHER. I believe I'm lost.

NARRATOR. And you could say Amen to it and not be guilty of an exaggeration.

(*Music: A forest theme and down*)

NARRATOR. He was alone in the dense forest ... a lonely place of dark silence and the smell of dead leaves. And the night descended and an old man in a white beard and a black skullcap put his finger to the ancient earth.

(*Music: Out*)

ASHER. I have no cause for complaint. Does the earth complain? We tread upon her, we dig her, we spit on her, but the earth accepts our abuse without murmur. Earth, earth, thou art of better make than I, and yet here am I treading thee underfoot. But be patient for a little while. Soon I will lie below thee, thy humble servant.

NARRATOR. He lay himself down on the floor of the forest and near his face a fern bent softly. The incense of bark, the bark of a hundred thousand trees, suddenly mounted to nostrils familiar only with the musty smell of old books, and Rabbi Asher felt a swelling in his throat, and he remembered the words of the blessings.

ASHER. Blessed art Thou Who has kept us in life, and preserved us, and has enabled us to reach this season.

(*Music: Forest theme in and down*)

NARRATOR. He whispered the night prayer and an owl overhead did not complain. A bear padded out of a thicket and sat on black haunches and watched him. And then when Rabbi Asher finished his prayer, the bear departed. And it was night, and Rabbi Asher slept peacefully upon the earth, secure in the Lord.

(*Music: Up and down*)

NARRATOR. And then it was day. He found a nut under a tree, he found a berry on a bush, and he was no longer hungry. He went on this way, lost and yet not lost. How many days and how many nights? He was old and feebler than he thought, and his mind lost hold of its tight grasp of time. Rabbi Asher of Yanov forgot the day of the week. He was not aware that he had forgotten. But he had forgotten, he had confused the Sabbath day with an ordinary week day.

(*Music: Cut sharply*)

NARRATOR. It was nearly a week later when the searching party found him. And it was not a minute too soon.

(*Sound of wind*)

For a cold wind had suddenly come down from the northwest.

(*Sound of brush breaking under following*)

ASHER. You really don't have to carry me. I tell you I am not sick.

ONE. (*Softly*) The pulse is very irregular. We must get him back quickly.

ASHER. Yes, of course. I should save my strength for tomorrow evening.

TWO. What's tomorrow evening?

ASHER. The inauguration of the Sabbath, of course.

ONE. Tomorrow evening?

ASHER. Of course.

TWO. (*Heartily insincere ... like a radio announcer*) Why, of course, of course. Tomorrow evening. The inauguration of the Sabbath.

(*Music: Bridge and cover with:*)
(*Voices ad lib*)
(*Door shuts off mike*)

TWO. (*Projecting slightly*) Baruch, any improvement?

ONE. (*Off*) Yes, the fever has left him. (*Coming on*) The doctor says he'll be as good as new.

THREE. That's fine. Then we can tell Rabbi Asher that he's mixed up the days of the week. After all, if it's Thursday night, it can't be Friday night. And if it isn't Friday night, it's ridiculous for a man to begin the Sabbath. It's more than ridiculous—it's illegal!

TWO. You know, Nathan, that's something we can't tell Rabbi Asher, not now.

THREE. Why not? It's perfectly simple. Knock on the door. Then open it, then say—Oh, by the way, Rabbi Asher, today happens to be Thursday, not Friday. That's all there is to it.

TWO. Fine, there's the door. Go ahead, Nathan, knock on it.

THREE. I'll do it right now.

TWO. Don't be an idiot. You can't disturb him.

THREE. Why not?

ONE. Because in the first place, he's asleep. The doctor gave him a sleeping powder.

THREE. I can wait, Baruch. I'll tell him when he wakes up.

TWO. No one is going to tell him. You understand me, Nathan.

THREE. What black plague has come over everyone? What's all this fuss and mystery and whispering? Why can't you tell him? A pious old man gets lost in the woods, period. He mixes up north and south, period. He mixes up the week day and the Sabbath, it's understandable. He was confused, he was feverish, now let's tell him he was confused.

ONE. We can't. If he kept last Friday as the Sabbath, then he didn't keep the Sabbath. He committed a transgression.

THREE. It was unintentional—God will forgive him.

ONE. I'm sure He will, but Rabbi Asher will not see it that way. All he's going to see is that he transgressed the Sabbath. Think of it, Nathan, Rabbi Asher, a Tsaddik, one of the holiest men ever born. He, Rabbi Asher, in the

eightieth year of his life, has violated the Sabbath. You're a very brave man, Nathan. Go ahead, knock on the door.
(*Pause*)

THREE. Excuse me, I think I have a headache.

TWO. I think we all have.

ONE. There's only one thing to do—Rabbi Asher must think that the Sabbath actually begins tonight.

THREE. What are we going to do—pretend that it is the Sabbath? (*Long pause*) Why doesn't somebody answer?

TWO. Something tells me we're cooking ourselves a very fancy kettle of fish.

ONE. Something tells me you're right. Let's call a meeting in the synagogue while Rabbi Asher is asleep.

(*Music: Bridge*)

TWO. Hannah, what do the women think?

HANNAH. The women leave the thinking to the men. The women are already doing.

TWO. Doing what?

HANNAH. Making provision for the Sabbath evening meal. If Rabbi Asher thinks the Sabbath begins tonight, it's going to begin tonight.

(*Music: Chord*)

NARRATOR. And, of course, there was no alternative.

(*Music: Narrative theme and down*)

NARRATOR. What alternative could there be? He was an old man. For eighty years the Sabbath had been his delight. Could he be told in his eightieth year, that he, Rabbi Asher, even through a pardonable error, had broken the Sabbath? Could Hannah tell him?

HANNAH. The shock might kill him.

NARRATOR. And they couldn't kill Rabbi Asher. He was their guide, their lantern, their teacher, their father. And, beyond this, he was their friend. The congregation of Yanov made its decision, which Baruch stated rather concisely.

ONE. From now on there will be two Sabbaths.

TWO. Rabbi Asher's Sabbath on Friday and the Lord's Sabbath on Saturday.
NARRATOR. It was practically the beginning of the five-day week.
(*Music: Up and out*)
NARRATOR. Some extraordinary things immediately began to happen.
(*Pounding on door*)
TWO. Who is it?
TEAMSTER. It's me, the Teamster.
TWO. What do you want?
TEAMSTER. I brought you the load of hay you ordered.
TWO. I can't accept it now.
TEAMSTER. Why not?
TWO. It's Rabbi Asher's Sabbath. His window faces here.
TEAMSTER. All right, I'll bring it tomorrow.
TWO. Oh, no. Tomorrow is my Sabbath. Bring it on Sunday.
TEAMSTER. How can I do that? Sunday is my Sabbath.
NARRATOR. It was practically the beginning of the four-day week.
(*Music: Into "Gute Voch"*)
(*Cantor: Singing with orchestra and then down*)
NARRATOR. But the trouble was only beginning. The men and the women and the children put on their best clothes on Friday and went to the Synagogue to pretend to celebrate Rabbi Asher's Sabbath. And what was more natural, at the conclusion of the Sabbath than to express the wish for a good week.
THREE. Ah gute voch, Hannah.
HANNAH. Ah gute voch, Rabbi Asher.
ASHER. The best week in the whole world, Hannah, to you and to all of us.
NARRATOR. And then they all raced to their homes, all that is except Rabbi Asher, and secretly they began to usher in the Lord's Sabbath.

(*Music: A quick segue to "Sholom Aleichem" . . . very softly*)
(*Cantor: "Sholom Aleichem" softly and down*)
NARRATOR. And they didn't dare raise their voices.
HANNAH. Gut shabbas, Baruch.
ONE. Gut shabbas, Samuel.
TWO. Gut shabbas, Nathan.
THREE. (*Natural voice*) How much longer is this going to continue?
CAST. Ssh!
THREE. (*Whispering*) Well, all I can say is that it's a lucky thing he is eighty years old.
HANNAH. (*Natural voice*) What a wicked thing to say! May Rabbi Asher live to be a hundred and twenty.
CAST. Amen!
HANNAH. Well, Nathan!
THREE. All right, Amen, if you insist on it. But the way we're going a hundred and twenty years can seem like a lifetime.
(*Cantor: Finish in the clear*)
(*Music: Segue briefly to narrative theme and drop out quickly*)
NARRATOR. Trade was at a standstill three days each week, the liturgy was increasingly complicated. Sabbath clothes were beginning to wear out because of the additional use. Something had to snap. It snapped.
HANNAH. Tamar, what did Rabbi Asher teach you in school today?
TAMAR. (*She is about six*) The Ninth Commandment. "Thou shalt not bear false witness against thy neighbor."
HANNAH. Hmm. (*Pause*) Have your soup, it's getting cold.
TAMAR. Mama, don't you want to hear what else he said? He told us that truth is the funniest thing in the world. It's just as it is. If you made it bigger or if you try to make it less, it stops being the truth.
HANNAH. You talk too much. Eat your soup.

TAMAR. And do you know what he also said? The Sabbath without honesty and truth isn't the Sabbath.

HANNAH. All right, Tamar, all right. Have your supper.

(*Sound of spoon against plate, repeat*)

HANNAH. Well, what are you stopping for? If it needs salt, add salt.

TAMAR. (*Quietly*) It doesn't need salt.

HANNAH. What is it, Tamar?

TAMAR. I was thinking. (*Soberly*) Mama, are you a liar?

(*Music: Bridge*)

HANNAH. Understand me, Baruch. She asked the question without anger or disrespect. But she's going to ask it again. She's going to think about it. I'm her mother. I can't have her thinking things like that about me.

ONE. Hannah, what do you propose we do?

HANNAH. Before worse things happen, we have to go to Rabbi Asher and tell him the truth.

TWO. It's too late for that now. It was a harmless lie at first. But it's grown too big. It seems lies generally do.

HANNAH. Then the lie will grow bigger. It's already poisoned our Sabbaths, it will poison the whole week, and the month, and the year . . . all our years. We have to go to him and ask him to forgive us our deception.

TWO. Will you go?

(*Pause*)

HANNAH. All right, I'll tell him.

(*Pause*)

ONE. Hannah, the doctor says that he doesn't have much longer to live. Any little shock might do it. Not to tell him, Hannah, is like sparing his life.

TWO. Hannah, if what we have done so far is wicked, then for the sake of his life, let us be wicked a little longer.

(*Pause*)

HANNAH. No. No, it can't be. I can't accept that. I was once a child in his classroom. He taught me that you can never bury falsehood but that truth springs up out of the ground. He's going to find out anyway. Let him find out from someone who loves him.

ONE. Then you're going now?

HANNAH. Yes, I am.

TWO. Wait until tomorrow. It's a cold night. He's warm in his bed now. His mind is untroubled. Do him a kindness, Hannah. Wait until tomorrow.

HANNAH. I see what we've done. We've been good, kindly, compassionate and our goodness and our compassion have been at the expense of a lie. A lie we have forced on Rabbi Asher. Don't you see that's why I've got to tell him tomorrow?

(*Music: Narrative theme and down*)

NARRATOR. It was a cold night and the wind was now from the northwest, carrying frost on its breath and a promise of early snow. Tomorrow Hannah would tell Rabbi Asher the truth about the Sabbath . . . but now she slept in her warm bed. All Yanov slept. All Yanov, so it seemed, except Rabbi Asher. (*Music fading*) Rabbi Asher stood in his nightshirt, his coat wrapped hastily around him, and he was pounding on the door of Reb Miller's house, Reb Miller, the wealthy merchant.

(*Pounding has come in above*)

MILLER. (*Off*) Who is it? What lunatic is out in the cold on such a night like this?

(*Door opens*)

(*Gust of wind*)

MILLER. Rabbi Asher!

ASHER. Yes, Reb Miller, may I speak with you?

MILLER. Of course. Come in.

ASHER. No. I want you to come out here.

MILLER. I'm in my nightshirt. I'll catch my death of cold.

ASHER. Put a coat on, and come out here.

MILLER. Why can't we talk in the house where it's warm?

ASHER. I'm an old man. Please humor me. Throw your coat around your shoulders and come out here. I'll wait for you.
MILLER. I don't understand it. Wait one second.
(*Door shuts*)
(*Bring up wind slightly*)
NARRATOR. (*Close*) Rabbi Asher shivered in the cold and waited for Reb Miller.
(*Door opens and shuts*)
MILLER. Here I am, Rabbi. What is it? Brr, it's cold.
ASHER. You don't like the shoemaker, do you?
MILLER. Is that why you called me out?
ASHER. Answer my question. You don't like him, do you?
MILLER. The shoemaker is a disgrace to the community. He keeps his family starving because he gambles away whatever he earns on dice-playing and cards. Now may I go back into the house?
ASHER. Not yet. The shoemaker's wife has just had another baby.
MILLER. Congratulations.
ASHER. There isn't a stick of firewood left in that house. They've already burned all the wood I gave them. Reb Miller, are your teeth chattering?
MILLER. I must say, Rabbi Asher, this is a fine time to ask me if my teeth are chattering. I'm freezing.
ASHER. They're freezing too. They are suffering from this same cold that chatters your teeth.
(*Pause*)
MILLER. That's why you made me come into the cold.
ASHER. Forgive me for doing it. But it was the only way to make you appreciate their situation.
MILLER. It's all right, Rabbi Asher. I'll bring the wood to the shoemaker's house. I'll bring it myself. (*Pause*) God bless you, Rabbi Asher. God bless you for reminding me that I am a man. Now go home quickly before you catch pneumonia.

(*Music: Narrative theme and down*)
NARRATOR. Hannah did not go to Rabbi Asher the next morning. For Reb Miller's story had awakened the householders at dawn. And when they heard it, they said . . .
ONE. He is holy and he makes us holy.
TWO. Hannah, can you tell a man like Rabbi Asher he has desecrated the Sabbath? Hannah, tell me the truth, can you?
NARRATOR. So they continued with their pretense and there were two Sabbaths in Yanov and a Sunday in Yanov.
TEAMSTER. Listen, it's Sunday . . . listen good. What don't you hear?
THREE. Teamster, what are you drivelling about? What do you mean what don't I hear?
TEAMSTER. Bells, you fool. You don't hear the churchbells. They're not ringing the churchbells so that old Rabbi Asher will think yesterday was Sunday. And the bells rang yesterday because there was a wedding.
NARRATOR. And so the plot against the Sabbath became the custom in Yanov . . . through the winter, into the spring, during the summer heat . . . and then . . . catastrophe.
(*Music: Out*)
HANNAH. Yom Kippur. We're fools. This year Yom Kippur falls on a Sabbath day.
ONE. No. No, there must be a mistake. She's wrong, isn't she? Samuel, tell her she's wrong.
TWO. She isn't wrong. And Baruch, we can't conceal it. Because he himself will discover it.
(*Voices ad lib panic*)
MILLER. Wait a minute. Don't get into a panic. We still have time.
HANNAH. You can't play tricks with time, Reb Miller.
MILLER. (*Significantly*) Can't you, Hannah? (*Pause*) Rabbi Asher played a trick with time. Why can't I?
ONE. Say what you mean.

MILLER. It all began when he lost a day in the week. And Saturday became Friday. Suppose we added a day to the week and changed his Friday to Saturday?
(*Pause*)
HANNAH. It isn't possible.
MILLER. That's because you are a woman of small faith. (*Laughs*) I invite you all to my house for Rabbi Asher's Sabbath. And Hannah, will you please be good enough to tell the doctor I should like to speak with him.
(*Music: Bridge to "Gute Voch" and down*)
NARRATOR. It was perfectly obvious. On Friday, which was Rabbi Asher's Sabbath, he came home from the synagogue as usual, and then he went to Reb Miller's house, which was not usual. And the cantor of the synagogue sang the song of Sabbath departure, which, of course, was part of the pretense. And Rabbi Asher hummed the melody, which he always did.
ASHER. (*Close—humming with cantor*)
NARRATOR. And then he stopped humming, because it was time to sip the usual glass of wine. However, there was a powder which the doctor had given Reb Miller, and now the powder was dissolved in Rabbi Asher's glass.
ASHER. (*Humming noisily*)
(*Cantor: Has faded out*)
ASHER. (*Hums more and more drowsily and then stops*)
(*Music: Simultaneously out*)
HANNAH. (*A nervous laugh*) Reb Miller, it worked. He's asleep.
(*Music: With gusto into "Sholom Aleichem" ... segue to other Sabbath melodies under following*)
NARRATOR. They lifted him very tenderly and carried him to his bed. Then the doctor came in and chuckled ...
VOICE. (*Chuckle*) His pulse-rate is fine. Sleeping like a baby.
NARRATOR. And the townspeople of Yanov rushed to the synagogue and openly welcomed the true Sabbath. Never in

the whole history of Yanov had the portion of the Law been read with such fervor as it was read on the following day. It was a Sabbath to remember. And Rabbi Asher lay in his bed and slept the sleep of the very old and the very good.

(*Music: Fading*)

ONE. The Sabbath is nearly over.
TWO. Lift him carefully.
THREE. I've got him.
HANNAH. Now seat him in the chair.
MILLER. Carefully, carefully. Good!
HANNAH. Tamar, come here.
TAMAR. Yes, Mama.
HANNAH. I want you to wake Rabbi Asher. If he asks you anything, just say the Sabbath is over.
TAMAR. I'll be telling the truth, won't I?
HANNAH. Yes, Tamar.
MILLER. Wait a minute. Cantor, go ahead.

(*Cantor: "Ah Gute Voch"*)
(*Music: Sneaks behind him*)

TAMAR. Rabbi Asher, Rabbi Asher, wake up . . . your Sabbath is over.
NARRATOR. And Rabbi Asher awoke, and seeing all the familiar faces about him, and hearing the Cantor sing the familiar melody, sensibly concluded that he had dozed for a few seconds. And so a day that had been lost from the calendar of the week was found again.
TAMAR. Wake up, the Sabbath of Rabbi Asher is over.
ASHER. That's a peculiar way to put it, child. You mustn't say Rabbi Asher's Sabbath. It's the Lord's Sabbath.
TAMAR. It's the same thing, Rabbi.

(*Cantor: In the clear with orchestra to curtain*)

BRANDEIS

BRANDEIS

During his lifetime Louis Dembitz Brandeis came to be regarded as the outstanding Jew in America. There was irony in the fact because this moralist, idealist, and liberal jurist of democracy did not discover Judaism until middle age. But discovery brought with it instant allegiance. He was not a man who only expounded ideas. He believed in putting them into action. When it was necessary to raise money for the causes with which he identified himself, he said that he believed that "it is wise to spend a thousand dollars on gathering one thousand individual dollars." When he was cautioned to go slow and to allow others to share the burden of sacrifice, he answered quietly, "I know nothing about sacrifice, I know only duty." In 1916, while the Senate was debating his nomination to the Supreme Court and the Bilbos and the McKellars of the day seemed strong enough to block confirmation, Brandeis sat in his office trying to think of new ways to relieve the suffering of poverty-stricken Jews in Galicia.

Brandeis *was given two performances on* The Eternal Light. *The first performance on January 7, 1945 featured Roger De Koven as Brandeis and Alexander Scourby as the Narrator. Ira Avery directed a cast which included Martin Wolfson, Sidney Slon, Richard Keith, Bernard Lenrow, Joseph Boland, Maurice Franklin, Toni Merrill, and Louis Whiteman. The second performance was directed by Ed King.*

BRANDEIS

NARRATOR. I have a story to tell you. But you cannot understand my story unless you understand this fact. And the fact is this. Every step you take toward the future leaves behind a footprint . . . a footprint of the past. And there is no escape from the past. Nor should there be. For a man cannot escape his heritage. If it is good, he may redeem it, but no more. I know this. You must know it. In the year 1910, in the fifty-fourth year of his life, Louis Dembitz Brandeis knew it also.

(*Music: Narrative theme and down*)

NARRATOR. What are the things a man may not forget? I say to you that I may not forget that I am pursued by the Middle Ages, like a neurotic haunted by a phantom dream. My days are warm with the memory of three thousand years of civilization, but my sleep is fitful with the cry of two thousand years of persecution. And both by day and by night, I am a Jew; and this is a fact sealed in my flesh like the covenant of Abraham. (*Pause*) Now I shall tell you the story. On a day more than thirty-five years ago, in the city of Boston, I sat in the offices of the firm of Brandeis, Dunbar & Nutter and listened to a man with blue eyes talk to two visitors.

(*Music: Out*)

BRANDEIS. Mr. Kelly, what is your grievance, why do the shoe workers threaten this strike against my client, Mr. Williams?

KELLY. It's pretty simple, Mr. Brandeis. The men can't live on what they get.

BRANDEIS. Williams, is this true?

WILLIAMS. You're my lawyer, Mr. Brandeis. You know I pay my men eighteen dollars a week. For these times it's not a bad wage.

KELLY. We ain't denyin' that, Mr. Williams. It ain't a bad wage.

BRANDEIS. You do admit that, don't you?

KELLY. We admit it, sure.

BRANDEIS. Then why do you want to strike?

KELLY. We want more money, that's why.

WILLIAMS. Brandeis, I told you there was no point in asking him here. The workers are unreasonable. Absolutely unreasonable.

BRANDEIS. Mr. Kelly, let's be clear about this. You admit that Mr. Williams pays a decent wage.

KELLY. Highest in the business, sure.

BRANDEIS. Yet you want more? Aren't you being a little unfair?

KELLY. No, sir. Ask him about the two long slack seasons when the men are laid off?

BRANDEIS. Are there slack seasons, Mr. Williams?

WILLIAMS. Naturally, it's a seasonal industry.

KELLY. But we don't live seasonal. We live fifty-two weeks same as you. Average our fancy pay over the year and what do we get? I'll tell you A gripe in the belly and no coal in the stove.

BRANDEIS. Mr. Williams, I'd like your figures on seasonal lay-off.

WILLIAMS. Look here, Brandeis. I'm a manufacturer not a settlement-house worker. What do they want me to do, give 'em champagne for breakfast and caviar for supper? I pay good wages, and I'm not raising them for nobody.

BRANDEIS. Don't you think Mr. Kelly has a point to what he's saying?

WILLIAMS. Then you tell him my point. You're my lawyer.

I pay you, not him. Don't forget that little thing.

BRANDEIS. I haven't forgotten it, sir. But wouldn't it be a rather unfortunate thing for a lawyer to advocate something which he can't approve as a citizen?

WILLIAMS. Listen, I hired a lawyer, not a citizen.

BRANDEIS. Perhaps, Mr. Williams, when you hired me, you hired both.

WILLIAMS. Did I, though?

BRANDEIS. Mr. Williams, I think perhaps you did.

WILLIAMS. All right, Mr. Citizen, you just go right ahead and sit behind this desk. Me . . . I'm going out to get me a lawyer.

(*Music: Bridge*)

KELLY. Well, Mr. Brandeis, you talk mighty funny for a conservative.

BRANDEIS. Funny? I don't think so. There was a time when the working relationship was between a master and servant. Today, it's between employer and employee. All I want is to make both employer and employee partners—partners to a contract.

KELLY. That's still pretty radical for Mr. Williams.

BRANDEIS. So are Isaiah and Amos, Mr. Kelly. (*Pause*) That gives me an idea. Excuse me, Mr. Kelly.

KELLY. Go right ahead.

(*Telephone receiver off*)
(*Sound of hook being jiggled*)

WOMAN. (*Filtered*) Yes, Mr. Brandeis?

BRANDEIS. Have you finished my holiday list?

WOMAN. Yes, I have, sir.

BRANDEIS. Please add another item, will you? A book.

WOMAN. Of course, sir. For the children?

BRANDEIS. No, for Mr. Williams.

WOMAN. Yes, sir.

BRANDEIS. Inscribe my compliments and please send him a copy of the Bible.

(*Music: Bridge*)
(*Voices briefly*)

ABBOT. Whitman, suppose you do the talking.

WHITMAN. All right, Abbot. Mr. Brandeis, a number of Boston businessmen have organized a committee—a committee that needs some legal advice in a hurry.

BRANDEIS. Yes.

WHITMAN. I believe your firm represents the Great American Assurance Society.

BRANDEIS. Yes, we handle their local matters.

WHITMAN. Do you know much about them, Mr. Brandeis?

BRANDEIS. A good deal, why?

WHITMAN. Abbot and I are policyholders—pretty big policyholders. Abbot, tell Mr. Brandeis what you found.

ABBOT. Something pretty dirty. A few of the vice presidents have formed a syndicate. They're buying securities with treasury funds.

BRANDEIS. If the securities are sound, I don't see what's wrong.

ABBOT. Oh, the securities are sound enough. What's wrong though is that they're buying the securities for themselves.

BRANDEIS. Can you prove that?

ABBOT. Look at this. (*Sound of paper rustling*) Sworn affidavits.

(*Pause*)

BRANDEIS. Hmm. They're using other people's money, aren't they?

WHITMAN. Brandeis, we know you represent the company; we're asking now if you want to represent us *against* the company.

ABBOT. Mr. Brandeis, if this embarrasses you as a lawyer, why tell us.

BRANDEIS. It's embarrassing, all right. I'm embarrassed to be the company's lawyer.

WHITMAN. Then you'll take this case?

BRANDEIS. I'll be glad to, Mr. Whitman.

WHITMAN. Fine. We're prepared to give you a retainer of ten thousand dollars.

BRANDEIS. No, Mr. Whitman.

WHITMAN. *(Laughs)* Well, they told us you were a good businessman. We'll make it fifteen thousand.

BRANDEIS. You don't understand. I'll take the case, but without fee. This isn't a private matter and I don't think I have a right to charge the public for my services.

WHITMAN. We can afford to pay, Mr. Brandeis.

BRANDEIS. All right, Whitman, I'll take half of what you're getting from this.

WHITMAN. Why . . . I'm . . . I'm getting nothing.

BRANDEIS. Good, I'll take half of that.

(Laughter)

ABBOT. Mr. Brandeis, I think I know now why your friends call you a liberal.

BRANDEIS. Thank you, sir. *(Pause)* Mr. Abbot, what . . . what do my enemies call me?

(Pause)

ABBOT. What do you suppose, Mr. Brandeis?

BRANDEIS. You tell me.

ABBOT. Why, Mr. Brandeis, they call you a Jew.

(Music: Bridge to narrative theme and down)

NARRATOR. Louis Dembitz Brandeis smiled. To be called a Jew! It was amusing. Had not Uncle Louis Dembitz been one of the three men in 1860 to nominate Abraham Lincoln for President? Had he not himself as a young man sat at the feet of Emerson and Lowell? He was the man consulted by presidents . . . the friend of Oliver Wendell Holmes and William Allen White and a college president called Woodrow Wilson. Yes, it was amusing to call this tall, slender, blue-eyed man a Jew. His synagogue was the court of law, his Scriptures were legal precedents, his altar was social justice. Louis Brandeis smiled a puzzled smile and then dismissed the incident. But it kept recurring.

(*Music: Out*)

WHITMAN. Congratulations, Mr. Brandeis. You certainly made them crawl back into the woodwork.

BRANDEIS. I believe I did, Mr. Whitman. There's a good deal of fun in being a public servant, isn't there?

WHITMAN. Maybe. Well, anyhow, you got yourself some free publicity in the *Tribune*. (*Chuckles*) Listen to this. (*Reading*) "Brandeis possesses the rare knowledge of knowing when to stop. When he has exasperated his opponents to the limit of their endurance, he grows gentler than a suckling dove and . . ." (*Pause*) Say . . . I'm sorry, Mr. Brandeis.

BRADEIS. (*Gently*) It's quite all right, Mr. Whitman . . . read on.

WHITMAN. (*Troubled*) Let's forget it.

BRANDEIS. Please . . . read the rest of it.

WHITMAN. All right. (*Reading unhappily*) "Gentler than a suckling dove and more persuasive than a second-hand clothes-dealer trying to sacrifice himself to give you a bargain." That's pretty low, Mr. Brandeis.

BRANDEIS. Mr. Abbot was quite veracious, it seems. My friends call me a liberal and, apparently, those who aren't my friends call me a Jew. If you'll excuse me, Mr. Whitman, I think I'll have to talk to my friend Filene about this.

(*Music: Bridge*)

BRANDEIS. Filene, have you got a ready definition of a Jew?

FILENE. Hmmh?

BRANDEIS. Yes, I seem to be in need of a definition.

FILENE. Well, I don't know who the philosopher was, but someone is alleged to have said that a Jew is like everybody else—only more so.

(*They chuckle*)

BRANDEIS. Filene, I think I ought to meet some Jews.

FILENE. That's a real coincidence, Brandeis. How would you like to go to New York and arbitrate a labor dispute?

BRANDEIS. I wouldn't, I've got my hands full fighting the railroad trust. (*Pause*) What's the coincidence about the New York thing?

FILENE. You've heard of the I.L.G.W.U.—that's quite a mouthful.... It stands for the International Ladies' Garment Workers' Union.

BRANDEIS. What about them?

FILENE. The New York cloakmakers are on strike. It happens that many of the workers and employers are Jewish.

BRANDEIS. Well?

FILENE. That's your chance to find out something about the Jews. The situation shrieks for an arbitrator.

(*Pause*)

BRANDEIS. It might be interesting at that.

(*Receiver off ... hook jiggled*)

WOMAN. (*Filtered*) You called, Mr. Brandeis?

BRANDEIS. Yes. Please ask Mr. Dunbar if he wouldn't mind taking my notes and dictating the rest of my Ballinger-Glavis brief. I'm going to New York.

(*Music: Bridge*)

(*Voices ad lib trying to talk at once*)

VOICE. You see, Mr. Brandeis... (*Voices down*) In the union it's a real democracy—everybody wants to talk—nobody wants to listen.

(*Laughter*)

BRANDEIS. Mr. Dyche, if you have no objection, I'd like one of the shop chairmen to present the case.

VOICE. Moskowitz, tell Mr. Brandeis.

MOSKOWITZ. It's very simple, Mr. Brandeis. All we want is a contract and union recognition.

BRANDEIS. I thought you were striking for higher wages and the elimination of sweatshop conditions?

MOSKOWITZ. Naturally, but the union comes first.

BRANDEIS. But suppose I were able to get an increase for you, would you turn that down?

MOSKOWITZ. Look, Mr. Brandeis, my own boss isn't a bad fellow. He came to America on the same boat with me. But that doesn't make him Santa Claus. Today he feels generous, so he gives us a raise. Tomorrow his wife burns the coffee, and he gives us a cut. Excuse me, Mr. Brandeis, we don't want favors, we want a union.

(*Ad lib agreement*)

VOICE. That's the consensus, Mr. Brandeis. You can tell that to the employers.

(*Music: Bridge*)

MANUFACTURER. Mr. Brandeis, what the workers want is absolutely out of the question.

BRANDEIS. Then you refuse to sign a contract.

MANUFACTURER. We refuse to recognize the union, period.

BRANDEIS. That's too bad. I'm afraid the strike will continue.

MANUFACTURER. (*Confidential*) Between me and you, Mr. Brandeis—I don't want the others to hear this—maybe if I were a worker, I'd continue with the strike.

BRANDEIS. You?

MANUFACTURER. Don't you think I was once a worker? Why do you think I became an employer? Conditions in this industry are terrible.

BRANDEIS. I'm really amazed. I thought I had heard all the answers, but this one is absolutely new.

MANUFACTURER. (*Chuckling*) The trouble with you, Mr. Brandeis, is that you were born in Kentucky. (*Pause*) Go back and tell those idiots they can strike until they're blue in the face. In Yiddish there's another way to say it—but you tell it to them in English.

(*Music: Bridge*)

MOSKOWITZ. We'll stay out, Mr. Brandeis.

BRANDEIS. Look here, you can't. Some of your people are literally starving.

MOSKOWITZ. If it was just for hours and wages, we'd go back tomorrow; but this is a principle. When I was a young fellow in Kishinev, I used to study the Talmud. When I came to America, I found the word I studied. They call it democracy.

BRANDEIS. Is that what the Talmud is about, Mr. Moskowitz?

MOSKOWITZ. They call it something else . . . but that's what it's about. You know, Mr. Brandeis, it's a shame. A smart man like you should learn a little Hebrew.

BRANDEIS. I think it is a shame. (*Pause*) Someday, perhaps someone like you should teach me.

MOSKOWITZ. Free of charge. If you want a small lesson, here it is. Look . . . I'm writing . . . that's Hebrew.

BRANDEIS. It looks like a dentist's chart.

MOSKOWITZ. It spells a word. I'll say it for you. Tzeh-dehk.

BRANDEIS. Tzeh-dehk. What does it mean?

MOSKOWITZ. Justice and righteousness. Now here's another word. Tz'daw-kaw. It comes from the word for justice.

BRANDEIS. Tz'daw-kaw. I see.

MOSKOWITZ. And it means charity. That's a wonderful thing, Mr. Brandeis. In the Hebrew language the word for charity comes from the word that means justice and righteousness. Now, please go back to those fine bosses of ours and tell them for us a little less Tz'daw-kaw and a little more Tzeh-dehk.

(*Music: Bridge*)

MANUFACTURER. (*Laughing*) Mr. Brandeis, don't believe anything Moskowitz tells you. At night, he's studying to be a lawyer.

BRANDEIS. What is Mr. Moskowitz during the day?

MANUFACTURER. He thinks he's an operator. Between you and me, he's a botcher. It will be a fine day for my business when he gets his diploma.

BRANDEIS. What I can't understand is why your association refuses to negotiate. There's such an extraordinary amount of hostility on both sides and yet there seems to be much kinship and understanding.

MANUFACTURER. You know something, Mr. Brandeis, when two people are enemies it's not such a terrible tragedy. But when they're enemies because they both want the same thing, then it is a tragedy. Please ... go back and see if you can talk some sense into those crazy lunatics.
(*Music: Bridge*)
BRANDEIS. Mr. Moskowitz, a wise man knows when to yield.
MOSKOWITZ. With the greatest satisfaction, Mr. Brandeis. Tell him Moskowitz says he can be a wise man. I give him the honor. Let him yield.
BRANDEIS. This is the most extraordinary strike I've ever known. It's like a passage from the Talmud with both sides trying to write a commentary. (*He laughs*)
MOSKOWITZ. Yes. Mr. Brandeis, I have a little boy. Papa, he says, what's democracy? Sonny, I tell him, democracy's in the classroom, in the store where Mama buys tomatoes, in the Board of Aldermen, in the polling place—but for ten hours a day it's not in the shop. The boss doesn't have time for it. Please, Mr. Brandeis, tell him the shop is on East Broadway. East Broadway is in New York, and New York is still in America.
(*Music: Bridge*)
BRANDEIS. And so you see, I'm a little tired of being an intermediary. I've brought you both together.
MANUFACTURER. Like old times, eh, Moskowitz?
BRANDEIS. The association has approved an increase, hours will be cut, shop-sanitation will be improved. Mr. Moskowitz, I think these are generous concessions.
MANUFACTURER. They are, Moskowitz. We're willing to do whatever we can.
MOSKOWITZ. What's the catch?
MANUFACTURER. See, one year in law school and he wants to know what's the catch. That's what they teach in law school.

MOSKOWITZ. Mister, I know you from the old country, what's the catch?
BRANDEIS. The association will yield on all demands except union recognition.
MOSKOWITZ. Of course, they want to build a fine house for us. The only thing they don't want is that the house should have a foundation.
MANUFACTURER. Moskowitz, don't be a stubborn mule.
MOSKOWITZ. Mr. Brandeis, he goes to the synagogue. Let him tell me if the words are only for Saturday or if he's supposed to practice them every day.
BRANDEIS. But he does see these things. I think he's making substantial concessions.
MANUFACTURER. Of course.
MOSKOWITZ. It's a regular merry-go-round. We want a union, we want a contract. That comes first.
BRANDEIS. Mr. Moskowitz, I think you're right about this. I recognize it as a lawyer and as an American.
MANUFACTURER. You can say also as a Jew.
BRANDEIS. On whose side are you arguing?
MANUFACTURER. Since it's going to cost me money, I'll argue on both sides.
BRANDEIS. Then . . . you . . . you're willing to come to terms?
MANUFACTURER. Maybe. But I'll have to talk to the other employers.
MOSKOWITZ. Good. It's not a pleasure to be on strike.
MANUFACTURER. Listen, you Talmudist, you . . . you've said enough. Mr. Brandeis, look at him. Do you think he's the only one who can speak a little Hebrew? Maybe I can quote a little too. Tzee-yohn b'mish-pawt tee-paw-deh.
BRANDEIS. (*Slowly*) Tzee-yohn b'mish-pawt tee-paw-deh.
MOSKOWITZ. Don't break your teeth, Mr. Brandeis . . . Tzee-yohn b'mish-pawt tee-paw-deh. . . . Zion will be redeemed through righteousness.

MANUFACTURER. Moskowitz, Moskowitz, with a head like yours, couldn't you be a better operator and not such a botcher?

(*Music: Bridge*)

BRANDEIS. There it is, gentlemen, this is the first collective agreement with enforcement machinery in it. I think it's a fine day's work. Gentlemen. I've learned something from you both. I'm fifty-four years old—all my life I've worked for something I call justice—social justice. I came here with curiosity. And I found that beneath all the bickering and the controversy and the passion, that there was something the preachers call brotherhood. And I found its expression —perhaps you may not accept this—but I found it expressed in terms of Judaism. For some one like myself who hardly considered himself a Jew—that means a good deal.

(*Music: Bridge to narrative theme and down*)

NARRATOR. This was a beginning for Louis Dembitz Brandeis. In the fifty-fourth year of his life . . . an idea burgeoning in a great man's mind. A man thinking, applying the scientific method, mixing, compounding, testing the idea, formulating a concept in the crucible of his conscience. Truly, is not this the spark of divinity that makes man only slightly less than the angels? And because he was not a closet speculator, because he was a man of action, he made his decision.

(*Music: Out*)

BRANDEIS. Filene.

FILENE. Yes?

BRANDEIS. I seem to have suddenly discovered a heritage.

FILENE. Yes?

BRANDEIS. I want to be worthy of the Jewish name. (*Pause— softly*) It isn't wealth, it isn't station, no, nor honor nor ambition. None of those things. It's like seeing a vision. Knowing that what is mean is not for us. Knowing that we must speak again for social justice and for righteousness.

Like Holmes, I would say that self-respect demands that we live not only honorably but worthily.

FILENE. But, Brandeis, this is what you've tried to be all your life.

BRANDEIS. Yes—as an American. All my life I have heard people speak of Americanism and Judaism as separate from each other. I know now it is not so. Place the pattern of Americanism over Judaism . . . Filene, they match. Filene, a Jew is an American . . . in the best, in the truest, in the deepest, richest sense of the word. And, Filene, it makes me very proud.

(*Music: Narrative theme and down*)

NARRATOR. What man alive has never held up a mirror to his own conscience and said to himself . . . this is what I truly believe; these are the things I will not compromise; these are the banners I must carry—without them I have no integrity. In the summer of 1910 these ideas came to Louis Dembitz Brandeis . . . the ideas came. He held them in the pan of his brain, he kneaded them like dough, he placed them in the oven of his heart to bake. And when months later a Rabbi came to him and spoke of Palestine, Brandeis answered.

(*Music: Out*)

BRANDEIS. I am an American, Rabbi.

RABBI. So am I. We are trying to found a refuge in Palestine for Jews who have no other land. The Jews of Middle Europe and Eastern Europe.

BRANDEIS. Can I support, can I as an American support, such a project?

RABBI. Because you are an American, Mr. Brandeis.

BRANDEIS. Rabbi, I have begun to feel that to be a better American I must become a better Jew.

RABBI. Carry it further, Mr. Brandeis . . . I hold that to be a good Jew you must help to fulfill the prophetic vision for the Holy Land.

BRANDEIS. Perhaps you are right, Rabbi, but I shall have to consider it carefully. If Palestine is to have any validity it cannot be just as another small state . . . as a small Duchy of Luxembourg, or another Montenegro. It must have a purpose . . . greater than nationalism.

RABBI. Yes, it can have that. With the help of men like yourself . . . I know it must.

(*Music: Narrative theme and down*)

NARRATOR. In the fifty-eighth year of his life . . . virtually in the hour when President Woodrow Wilson summoned him to the Supreme Court of the United States to take his place alongside Oliver Wendell Holmes, Louis Dembitz Brandeis, jurist, moralist, liberal, Jew, American, accepted the cause of Zionism and became its leader in America. And he spoke with the words of Ahad Ha'am.

(*Music: In the clear briefly . . . and hold under*)

BRANDEIS. I live for the sake of the perpetuation and happiness of the community of which I am a member; I die to make room for new individuals who will mould the community afresh. When the individual thus values the community as he values his own life, and strives after its happiness as though it were his individual well-being, he finds satisfaction (*Music fading*) and no longer feels so keenly the bitterness of his individual existence, because he sees the end for which he lives and suffers. (*Pause*) I am an American. And I have come to Zionism through Americanism. Let it be for what the prophets spoke. Let it be only that. Tzee-yohn b'mish-pawt tee-paw-deh. Zion will be redeemed through righteousness.

(*Music: Curtain*)

MY FATHER'S TALIS

MY FATHER'S TALIS

Toward the close of the war, Dr. Moshe Davis, program editor of The Eternal Light, *proposed a script which would explain the traditional place of the talis, or prayer shawl, in Jewish life. We agreed that we could achieve our purpose best by personalizing the talis. It happened that Dr. Davis's own son, who was less than two years old at the time, was engaged in a daily campaign for "a talis just like Daddy's." I found myself wondering if there were children like him still living in Germany. Little Zev Davis became Abraham Engel.*

The script having been written, the problem shifted to casting. What was called for was a boy who would sound not older than Abraham Engel's thirteen years and who would be able to pronounce the German words without trace of accent. Frank Papp searched his files, auditioned many hopefuls and found that while there were several young actors who could handle the English lines, none of them spoke German fluently. It was possible, of course, to spell out the German lines phonetically and drill a young actor until he was perfect. Screen and stage have the time for this. But radio deadlines are too close upon one another for such refinements. It seemed that we would either have to find a young actor speaking fluent German or that the Seminary would have to cancel the script. Characteristic of radio, neither thing happened.

My Father's Talis was produced and Abraham was played by a girl. Radio, being the illusion that it is, permitted such a solution. Susan Douglas, an ingenue whose voice can be very light and boyish, and whose German is impeccable, was letter-perfect as Abraham. The Father was played by Luis Van Rooten, Adelaide Klein was the Mother; others in the cast were Stefan Schnabel, Joseph Boland, Jack Lloyd, Julian Noa, and Bernard Lenrow. Cantor Robert H. Segal deserves special mention. My Father's Talis *was presented on October 14, 1945.*

MY FATHER'S TALIS

ABRAHAM. In my whole life I have wanted only three things. To see my mother again, not to live in a concentration camp, and to have a talis exactly like my father's. What is a talis? It is a prayer shawl. My father's talis was made of silk, pure white silk with blue stripes at the ends. He used to tell me how in the good days before I was born, when the synagogues were standing, a man could put on his prayer shawl on the Sabbaths and the holy days and not be molested. But I must tell my own story. How do you begin a story that has no beginning and has no end? (*Slight fade*) I shall begin on that morning when a strange voice spoke through the loud speaker.

ONE. (*P.A. filter*) You are no longer prisoners. Concentration Camp 48 is now under the protection of the United States Army. All able-bodied men are requested to line up for roll-call. All children report at once for medical inspection.

TWO. (*P.A. filter*) Ihr seit keine Gefangenen mehr. Von jetzt an steht das Konzentrationlager achtundvierzig unter dem Shutz der Amerikanischen Armee. Alle manner, die gehen konnen, sollen zum Appell antreten; alle kinder zur artzlichen Untersuchung kommen.

(*Music: Briefly*)

DOCTOR. Don't be afraid, boy. Sergeant, didn't you explain that I'm a doctor?

SERGEANT. Yes, sir.

DOCTOR. Then tell him to put his bundle down.

SERGEANT. He refuses, sir. He won't let that bundle out of his hand. Something about a talis in it. I don't know what he means.

DOCTOR. All right, Sergeant. Ask him his name.

SERGEANT. Yes, sir. Der Amerikanische Doktor mochte deinen Namen wissen.

ABRAHAM. Ich heisse Abraham Engel.

DOCTOR. I got that, Sergeant. How old is he?

SERGEANT. Wie alt bist du?

ABRAHAM. Dreizehn Jahre.

SERGEANT. He says he's thirteen, sir. But if he's a day past eleven, my name is Shirley Temple.

DOCTOR. Ask him to tell the truth. He doesn't have to fear us.

SERGEANT. Sag' die Wahrheit. Wie alt bist du?

ABRAHAM. Dreizehn Jahre.

SERGEANT. He sticks to thirteen, sir.

DOCTOR. Well, find out how long he's been in this place? That should get us somewhere.

SERGEANT. Wie lange warst du in diesem Konzentrationslager?

ABRAHAM. Zehn Jahre.

SERGEANT. Zehn Jahre?

ABRAHAM. Zehn Jahre.

DOCTOR. What does he say, Sergeant?

SERGEANT. He's been in this hell hole for ten years, sir. That's why he's so scrawny, I guess. Oh, Lord!

(*Pause*)

DOCTOR. Sergeant, see if you can find out why there are no other children here?

SERGEANT. Yes, sir. Der Doktor mochte wissen warum keine anderen Kinder hier sind?

ABRAHAM. Wenn viele sterben nur wenige werden geboren.

(*Pause*)

SERGEANT. (*Softly*) Thanks, kid. Doc . . . he says that when many are dying, only a few are born. Gee, kid, you look eleven, you say you're thirteen, but you speak like a middle-aged man.

DOCTOR. Yes, you're not wrong, Sergeant. Judging from his appearance he has no business being alive.

ABRAHAM. Jungens wie ich sind die biologischen Folgen dieses Krieges.

DOCTOR. What was that, Sergeant?

SERGEANT. He says that the young like him are the biological consequences of war.

DOCTOR. Oh . . . Abraham . . . try to understand me, please. We're friends, see . . . freunde . . . so take your shirt off, boy. I promise I won't hurt you. Put down your . . . your talis, whatever that is. No one's going to take it away. No one. I promise.

(*Music: Narrative theme and down*)

ABRAHAM. To them a talis is only a strip of silk with fringes at the corners. But isn't it also the badge of Israel? "And it shall be unto you for a fringe, that ye may look upon it, and remember all the commandments of the Lord, and do them . . . and be holy unto your God. I am the Lord your God, who brought you out of the land of Egypt." You must understand what this talis means. I shall tell you only a few things . . . first, we were brought to the concentration camp ten years ago . . . my mother, my father, and I. (*Music out*) It is my first memory of childhood . . . that first day in the camp.

JOSEPH. Hannah, why are you taking off your wedding ring?

HANNAH. The boy needs bread, Joseph.

JOSEPH. I don't understand.

HANNAH. There's a guard outside.

JOSEPH. He won't give you bread.

HANNAH. He might, Joseph. For this ring.

JOSEPH. All right, Hannah.

HANNAH. Abraham, you must not cry, my son. You stay with Father. Mother will be right back.

(*Music: Bridge*)

(*Door slams*) . .

JOSEPH. Well, Hannah?

HANNAH. I gave him my ring. He took it, Joseph.

JOSEPH. And the bread?
HANNAH. No bread. He took my ring, and said... "No bread."
JOSEPH. Don't grieve... we'll manage for the boy somehow.
HANNAH. If he had only laughed at me, Joseph. No, he just took the ring and looked at me with a face of stone.
JOSEPH. He didn't seem to be a bad fellow.
HANNAH. I thought so, too. I thought maybe he might even have a little boy of his own. So I showed him Abraham's picture.
JOSEPH. Why, Hannah, what good is that?
HANNAH. I'm sentimental, I suppose. I thought a little child's picture might create a bond between two human beings. (*Pause*) He looked at the picture... then said... "Move on, Jew."
(*Music: Bridge*)
(*Sound of board pried up*)
JOSEPH. Hannah, you don't hear the guard, do you?
HANNAH. (*Off mike*) No, it's all right, Joseph. But hurry.
JOSEPH. The board's almost up. (*Sound again*) There... it's up. We can hide it now. Abraham, quickly, bring me the bag. (*Pause*) Good boy. (*Projecting softly*) All right, Hannah?
HANNAH. (*Off*) Yes. But try to hurry.
JOSEPH. Abraham, try to remember what I'm saying. You are only a little boy. I don't expect you to understand; but try to remember. This little bag... my phylacteries are here and my talis. I'm going to hide them, Abraham. Do you understand? They must not take them away.
HANNAH. (*Off*) Please hurry, Joseph, I'm afraid.
JOSEPH. (*Quickly and intensely*) Listen, boy. These are symbols. I wish I had a simpler word. But they are symbols. Just as Mother's wedding ring was a symbol. They took her ring away, Abraham. They mustn't take this away also. For we are only people and people live and die by their symbols. When we lose them, we lose our dignity... and

that's even worse than dying. All right, Abraham. You put it here . . . that's right . . . under the board.

HANNAH. *(Coming on)* Let me help you replace the board.

JOSEPH. Yes, Hannah. You help, too, Abraham. Three human beings . . . burying their symbols. Step hard, Abraham. Step down hard.

(Sound of feet tramping on board)

(Music: Bridge to narrative theme and down)

ABRAHAM. A talis hidden beneath a wooden board. One symbol buried. And that night another symbol was taken away. We were fast asleep when the sudden footsteps came, a door opened and slammed shut. and my eyes saw black boots . . . many black boots. They had come to take my mother away. I felt the breath leave my father's body. I tasted her hot kiss on my mouth, but all I saw were the shiny boots, they were such clean boots, and so many, and so black with polish. And when the door slammed shut again and left us empty in the room, I reached my hand and touched the board where my father's talis lay buried. And it seemed then that the light that shone was like darkness . . .

(Music: Up and fade out quickly under following)

ABRAHAM. They told us she had been transferred to a camp for women. And for ten years, while we were beaten, and while we slowly starved, and saw the horror surround us that was more terrible than death, we kept each other alive, my father and I, praying that somewhere she was waiting for us. And for ten years my father gave me his words to listen to, the learning he remembered for my study, and always . . . the example of his own quiet way to follow.

(Music: Montage theme and down)

JOSEPH. Listen, Abraham. Why was man created on the sixth day? To teach that if he is ever swollen with pride, it can be said to him: A flea came ahead of thee in creation.

(Music: Up and down)

JOSEPH. Do you know why I teach you, Abraham? Because it is written in the Talmud that the world itself rests upon the breath of the little ones in the schoolhouse.

(*Music: Up and down*)

ABRAHAM. But, Father, how can anything be greater than the giving of the Law to Moses?

JOSEPH. The falling of rain is an event even greater.

ABRAHAM. But why?

JOSEPH. The giving of the Law was for Israel, but rain is for the entire world.

(*Music: Up and cut*)

JOSEPH. Are not all men knit together with bones and sinews and clothed with skin and flesh?

ABRAHAM. Then what is it, Father, that curdles the spirit and turns it sour against itself?

JOSEPH. Abraham, now I know you are no longer a boy?

(*Music: Finish*)

(*Voices briefly*)

ONE. Joseph, why do you spend all your time teaching the boy?

TWO. It's foolish. Here is where we stink like animals, here is where we rot, and here is where we're going to die. What good is the learning?

JOSEPH. Someday there will be a place in the world for learning.

ONE. You won't live to see it, Joseph.

JOSEPH. Perhaps not.

TWO. What are you smiling at?

JOSEPH. An old story my father told me.

ONE. Well, let's have it.

JOSEPH. Let Abraham tell it, he knows it.

TWO. Go ahead, boy.

ABRAHAM. A traveller once saw an old man planting a carob tree. "When will the tree bear fruit?" asked the traveller. "Oh, perhaps in seventy years," the old man answered. "Do

you expect to live to eat the fruit of that tree?" "No," said the old man, "but I didn't find the world desolate when I entered it, and as my fathers planted for me before I was born, so do I plant for those who come after me."
(*Pause*)

JOSEPH. Come along, Abraham, I think there are still trees to be planted.
(*Music: Narrative theme and down*)

ABRAHAM. There in the concentration camp my father and I planted such trees as must always blossom and yield fruit. And my father said that the trees would grow. For the ground was splintered with bone and clotted with blood and this, he told me, was the natural manure for man's learning. It was strange that he should speak so to me. For while we spoke of learning, the prison guards were shaking their fists at the sky against the planes. My father should have known the war was nearly over. Perhaps he would have showed me the talis sooner. But he didn't know.
(*Music: Out*)

JOSEPH. I've told you, Abraham. You must not speak of the talis.

ABRAHAM. Only pry the board up, Father. Just show it to me. Only let me hold it in my hand.

JOSEPH. No, Abraham, it isn't time.

ABRAHAM. Father, I even know the blessing for the talis.

JOSEPH. I pray you will know many blessings. May you know the blessings of the fruit of trees, the sustenance of land, and fragrant wood, and scented flowers, and faithful covenants in years of peace . . . and your mother's face. May you know all these blessings, Abraham . . . but it is not time for me to show you the talis.

ABRAHAM. When will it be time?

JOSEPH. I don't know. Perhaps when walls will not only shut out hate but also let in light. Perhaps when I am sure the

war is over. Now don't speak to me of the talis. We shall accept our bounty of lukewarm water and potato peelings and bless God they give us even that.
(*Music: Bridge*)
(*Sound of footsteps . . . heavily*)

ABRAHAM. (*Close*) Father, Father . . . it's the guard.
JOSEPH. (*Close*) Don't be afraid . . . he shan't do anything to you.
GUARD. You, there . . . you. I wish to speak with you.
JOSEPH. (*Close*) Stay close, Abraham. (*Pause*) What do you want with me?
GUARD. Here . . . take it . . . it's for the boy. (*Pause*) Well, what's the matter?
JOSEPH. I don't know.
GUARD. Take it, boy.
ABRAHAM. What is it, Father?
JOSEPH. Excuse me, he has never seen a whole potato before. Take it, Abraham. I just don't understand this.
GUARD. There's nothing to understand. The boy looks hungry, me . . . I'm not a mean man, so it's a present for the boy. (*Pause*) Well, aren't you going to thank me?
JOSEPH. (*Tensely*) Thank the prison guard, Abraham.
ABRAHAM. Thank you for the potato.
GUARD. (*Clears his throat—then, almost pleading*) I'm not such a bad sort, am I? When I beat you, before . . . well let bygones be bygones, I say. You'll tell them, won't you?
JOSEPH. Tell them?
GUARD. Oh, you know what I mean. There are good Germans and bad Germans. I'm not a bad fellow. You'll tell them, eh?
ABRAHAM. Father, he's speaking to you.
JOSEPH. Yes, I know. Yes, of course. It's a bit too much for me. You want me to . . . to protect you. (*Marvelling*) Me to protect you?
GUARD. Aah, you're a fine fellow. (*Moving off*) Eat the pota-

MY FATHER'S TALIS

to, boy. Maybe tomorrow I'll get you two potatoes. Sure.
(*Pause*)

ABRAHAM. Father . . . I think now you can pry up the board and show me the talis. The war must be nearly over.

(*Music: Bridge*)
(*Board pried up*)
(*Voices briefly then fade to background and drop out*)

ONE. Has it mildewed, Joseph?

JOSEPH. I hope not, Solomon. Open the little bag, Abraham, and take it out.

TWO. I think it's a risky business, Joseph. They'll kill you if they see it.

JOSEPH. No, it's not mildewed at all, is it. A little soiled . . . but it's the talis.

ABRAHAM. It's just like I remember it, Father.

(*Voices cut*)

ONE. Joseph, how many years is it since we were able to say a prayer together and put on a talis?

JOSEPH. You're quite right. I'm very selfish. I shall say the blessing and we will each put it around our shoulders in turn. You first, Abraham. Hold it a little while and then pass it. Baw-rooch ah-taw ah-doh-nawy ehloh-hay-noo meh-lehch haw-oh-lawm ah-shehr kid-shaw-noo b'mitz-voh-sawv v'tzee-vaw-noo l'his-ah-tayf bah-tzee-tzis. Jacob, once you could sing the melody. Won't you?

(*Cantor: Singing very softly . . . in the Haftorah Motif*)
Mah yaw-kawr chahs-deh-chaw eh-loh-heem, oo-v'nay aw-dawm b'tzayl . . .

(*He continues under narration*)

ABRAHAM. That's how he sang. He put on my father's talis and he shut his eyes and sang the words. "How precious is Thy loving kindness, O God, and the children of men take refuge under the shadow of Thy wings. They sate themselves with the fatness of Thy house; and Thou givest them to drink of the river of Thy pleasures. For with Thee is the fountain of life; in Thy light do we see light. O continue Thy loving kindness with them that know Thee, and Thy righteousness to the upright in heart." He sang the melody and the talis in which he was wrapped was no longer soiled. We heard no one, we saw no one. Oh, God above, we should have seen them. We shouldn't have shut our eyes. For they had come.

(*Sound of several pistol shots*)

(*Pause*)

(*Music: Deep with sorrow and under*)

ABRAHAM. (*Building with music*) They had come. The black boots. The shiny black boots. Boots all around us. Boots that were not dirty, boots that were clean, that glistened with polish. Strong boots, so many boots. And spilling over the boots . . . so slowly, oh, so slowly, drops of blood spilling, spilling over the shiny black boots. And my Father's talis, bright with red. (*Music cut sharply*) And my father's hand upon his talis.

(*Music: Agonized . . . briefly*)

ONE. Joseph, can you speak?

TWO. The boy wants to see him, Solomon?

ONE. No. Get some water for him first.

TWO. It's no use, Solomon. Let the boy see his father.

ONE. (*Angrily*) I tell you to get some water. Don't stand there and babble. He's still alive, isn't he? They'll give you some water at least even if they won't send a doctor. Man, in Heaven's name don't stand there.

TWO. Solomon, it isn't any use. Let the boy see his father before he dies.

(*Pause*)

ONE. I'm sorry. (*Pause*) Send the boy in.

ABRAHAM. I'm here.

ONE. Do you want us to leave you?

ABRAHAM. I'm frightened.

TWO. We'll stay with you, Abraham.

ABRAHAM. Father . . . (*Calling softly—he isn't wailing*) Father, can you hear me, Father? It's Abraham.
ONE. Joseph, it's your son. Joseph Engel, it's your son.
JOSEPH. Yes.
TWO. He's trying to say something.
JOSEPH. (*Very close*) Have you the talis?
ABRAHAM. I have it.
JOSEPH. A talis should be white . . . not red.
ABRAHAM. Yes, Father.
JOSEPH. A man should be buried in his talis.
ABRAHAM. We'll try, Father.
JOSEPH. They won't allow it. You have it, Abraham. You always wanted a talis exactly like this one.
ABRAHAM. No . . . I don't . . . no, Father, I . . .
JOSEPH. Keep it. This—and you Abraham—my symbols. You keep it. (*Pause*) Solomon.
ONE. Yes, Joseph?
JOSEPH. If his mother is alive . . . if you live . . . you'll help him find her?
ONE. I promise.
JOSEPH. Good. I'm satisfied.
(*Music: Bridge to narrative theme and down*)
ABRAHAM. There are many graves in Europe and there are no stones to mark them. "Are not all men knit together with bones and sinews and clothed with skin and flesh?" And bone becomes nothing, and sinews rot, and flesh sickens and becomes dust. And men plant trees and know that they will never harvest the fruit; yet the generations are not born into desolation.
(*Music: Out*)
ABRAHAM. All my life I have wanted three things . . . to see my mother again, not to live in a concentration camp, and to have a talis exactly like my father's. Now I have the talis. Some day I shall see my mother and on Sabbath she will say the Candle Blessing and I will sing the Sabbath

Kiddush. And perhaps that will be in Palestine. It is a good thing to stand beside the barbed wire and be able to see a dream. Yes, it is a good thing. And my generation will not be born into desolation, for I shall show them my father's talis.

(*Music: Curtain*)

THE RANSOM OF RABBI MEIR

THE RANSOM OF RABBI MEIR

The Ransom of Rabbi Meir *had a dramatic postscript. Rabbi Meir was portrayed by Juano Hernandez, one of radio's better actors. That night Mr. Hernandez attended an inter-racial meeting to which he had been invited as a spokesman for the Negroes of his community. A remark by a speaker and a reply by the moderator made Mr. Hernandez aware that Jews were excluded from attendance. His dismay became anger when a further remark contained a reference to good Jews and bad Jews.*

When it was Mr. Hernandez's turn to speak, he faced an audience beaming with self-approbation for their demonstrable brotherhood in inviting a Negro to address them. On the spur of the moment he decided not to deliver the address he had prepared. Instead he pulled from his pocket a copy of the script, briefly explained the nature of the program and the content of the first two scenes. Then he read the lines which Alexander spoke to Rabbi Meir in the third scene. "No one can say to me, 'Your existence on earth is justified because some of your people are good, or noble, or holy. Some of my people are not good, and not noble, and not holy. But we are people. People like other people. We are entitled to our ugly as well as to our good. If there are saints among us, they do not justify me. If there are sinners among us, they do not condemn me. I am a human being. I have a right to be judged for what I am.'" With that, Mr. Hernandez sat down. He has not been invited to speak again.

The Ransom of Rabbi Meir *was broadcast on March 3, 1946. Besides Mr. Hernandez, the cast included Alexander Scourby, Edgar Stehli, Delmar Nuetzman, Jack Lloyd, and Robert Harris.*

THE RANSOM OF RABBI MEIR

(*Music: Establish and hold under*)

MEIR. I have a story to tell you. It is yesterday's story and, therefore, it is tomorrow's story. For what is eternity but perpetual time? And what is every present moment if not preparation for the future? I tell you that the darkness of this day is no more and no less than your forgetfulness of the darkness that was. (*Pause*) The thing is passed; therefore, the thing is not passed. In the year 1286 in the German city of Rothenburg, I, Meir ben Baruch, was Rabbi, even as my father had been Rabbi and his fathers before him. It was a time when Emperor Rudolph, the first Hapsburg, reigned over the land; and terror was not yet a system; and cruelty was only haphazard; and murder was still occasional. In the German city of Rothenburg in the year 1286 life was not so bad. (*Music out*) Still, there were humiliations to be borne, and Alexander ben Elisha, who was one of the congregation, was young and impatient and easily vexed.

(*Door slams*)
(*Sound of scuffle*)
(*Voices ad lib quieting Alexander*)

ISRAEL. Rabbi Meir, help us with him.

ALEXANDER. Let me go back. I must go back.

ONE. Do you want to be murdered? Alexander, do you want us all to be murdered?

TWO. Rabbi Meir, tell him to stop.

MEIR. Israel, David, release him. Release him.

(*Pause*)

ISRAEL. Rabbi Meir, this young fool wishes to die. But I don't wish to die.
ALEXANDER. I'm going back.
ISRAEL. You'll stay here.
ALEXANDER. Look at me. Am I made of iron? Is my flesh steel? Was I born only to endure?
MEIR. Alexander, what happened?
ALEXANDER. I came to the city gate.
MEIR. Yes.
ALEXANDER. The watchman stopped me.
MEIR. There is nothing wrong in that.
ALEXANDER. A tax, he said. Jews and oxen pay five pennies tax.
ISRAEL. The fool, he struck the watchman.
ALEXANDER. I can't stand it. They scorn us, they taunt us. They cry, "Where now is the Rock of salvation? Why does He not stretch out His arm to uphold you?" (*Pause*) Rabbi Meir, I want to hide my face in the earth.
MEIR. Alexander, you still have a lesson to learn. It is easy enough to have compassion for the weak.
ALEXANDER. I don't know what you mean.
MEIR. I mean that your humanity must also extend to the strong.
ALEXANDER. They treat me as I wouldn't treat my dog.
MEIR. That is why the lesson is so hard. In the face of your humiliation you must remember that your enemy is your fellow. Alexander, that is the tax you pay for being what you are.
ALEXANDER. Then you say, endure.
MEIR. Yes, Alexander, this is not the first humiliation. This is not the last. I say, endure. (*Pause*)
ALEXANDER. Rabbi Meir, when my mother bore me, it was you who spoke a prayer over me. It was you, Rabbi Meir, who taught me to read. It was you who brought me my first prayer shawl and wept with me when my mother died.

And now I am ashamed of that. Ashamed for everything I owe you. Because, Rabbi Meir, you are a coward.

(*Music: Bridge to narrative theme and down*)

MEIR. Yes, he was foolish, and young and not a coward. And I was not foolish, and not young . . . and a reasonable man possessed of wisdom. There is such deception here. For how precious and good was my wisdom that was wise only to endure? Wisdom wise only to accept; wisdom wise only to retreat, to suffer, to protest, and to wait. Truly, in this wisdom there is fruit and no seed, but only a pale flower that deceives the senses and dies.

(*Music: Fading*)

Yes, in the year 1286, in the German city of Rothenburg, I was equipped only for endurance. Endurance to pay the taxes of the Emperor Rudolph.

RUDOLPH. Glad to see you, Rabbi.

MEIR. Yes, Your Majesty. Israel, you might place the money on the table.

RUDOLPH. Nothing of the sort. Nothing of the sort. Give it here.

MEIR. The silver is all there, Your Majesty. There is no need to count it.

RUDOLPH. Oh, of course. I trust you. It's my chamberlain. The man is a thief. (*Laughs*)

MEIR. Your Majesty, may I speak?

RUDOLPH. Speak away, my friend.

MEIR. We Jews are only a handful in the city of Rothenburg.

RUDOLPH. Yes?

MEIR. But we are taxed seven times the amount of the entire population.

RUDOLPH. You complain?

(*Pause*)

MEIR. Your Majesty, because of the tax, many in the congregation are without food.

RUDOLPH. That is hardly my concern. My friend, I shall tell

you something. In Munich, the Jews refused to pay the tax. I was no longer able to protect them.
(*Pause*)

MEIR. I understand.

RUDOLPH. That's what I like about you. I never have to put my finger in your mouth. You understand at once.

MEIR. Thank you, Your Majesty. (*Pause*) I assume there was a . . . a regrettable occurrence in the city of Munich.

RUDOLPH. Most regrettable. But, it will not happen in Rothenburg. You can be sure of that. Eh, you say the silver is all there?

MEIR. Every piece.

RUDOLPH. Fine. Fine. Very good. Unfortunate about Munich. Unfortunate. Come again, Rabbi. Be sure to come again.
(*Music: Bridge*)
(*Door shuts*)

MEIR. Is that you, Alexander?

ALEXANDER. (*Off*) Yes. You sent for me?
(*Pause*)

MEIR. Don't stay near the door. Please come closer.

ALEXANDER. (*On*) You sent for me, Rabbi Meir. I came.

MEIR. Not with hostility, Alexander ben Elisha.

ALEXANDER. Meir ben Baruch, I could never feel hostile toward you. I try, but I can't.

MEIR. I'm glad. (*Pause*) When Israel and I returned from seeing the Emperor, people said you were missing.

ALEXANDER. I went to Munich.

MEIR. Why Munich?

ALEXANDER. A man told me that in Munich there were Israelites who were capable of resisting.
(*Pause*)

MEIR. Yes, they resisted. I have already heard.

ALEXANDER. On October 11th one hundred and eighty men and women and children went to the synagogue to pray.

MEIR. Don't tell me any more.

ALEXANDER. Then the mob came. The doors were barricaded from the outside. First smoke, then fire. Burned down. The synagogue. One hundred and eighty men and women and children. Burned down.

MEIR. (*Softly*) Baw-rooch dah-yawn eh-mehs.

ALEXANDER. Rabbi Meir, it will not help them.

MEIR. (*Softly*) Blessed be the Righteous Judge.

ALEXANDER. I tell you that will not help them. They died. It is now; it is since; it is always; it is never; it is ended; it is newly begun.

MEIR. You must not lose yourself.

ALEXANDER. They said to me in Munich—Alexander ben Elisha, we will not do this to you. No. You are from Rothenburg. And Rabbi Meir is a good man. You are safe.

MEIR. Alexander, don't raise your voice.

ALEXANDER. I want to raise my voice. I am I, Alexander ben Elisha. I am a Jew. I am a man. How dare they say to me, we will not harm you because Rabbi Meir is good and pious? How do they dare?

MEIR. They meant to reassure you.

ALEXANDER. It was a curse. No one can say to me, Alexander, your existence on earth is justified because some of your people are good, or noble, or holy. Some of my people are not good, and not noble, and not holy. But we are people. People like other people. We are entitled to our ugly as well as to our good. If there are saints among us, they do not justify me. If there are sinners among us, they do not condemn me. Rabbi Meir, in the name of God, I am a human being. I am myself. I have a right to be judged for what I am.

(*Pause*)

MEIR. I deny nothing you say. But, Alexander, this is the year 1286, this is Germany.

ALEXANDER. I wish to leave Germany.

MEIR. It is not allowed.

ALEXANDER. My feet and my hands will allow it.

MEIR. Where will you go?

ALEXANDER. To the Holy Land.

(*Pause*)

MEIR. Alexander, the Holy Land is far away.

ALEXANDER. No, Rabbi Meir. The Holy Land is where it is. Only the Israelites are far away.

MEIR. Why do you wish to go? Because you want to escape?

ALEXANDER. No, I'm tired of escaping. I want to go there because my prayers lead me there. The prayer of each day's service, of the Sabbaths, of the festivals and the fast days and the blowing of the Ram's Horn. Because I face toward Jerusalem when I pray, and now I would go to Jerusalem.

(*Pause*)

MEIR. (*Slowly*) Yes. I know. Alexander, this Sabbath you were absent. We read from Holy Scriptures: "Then the Lord, thy God, will turn thy captivity, and have compassion upon thee, and will return and gather thee from all the peoples, whither the Lord, thy God, hath scattered thee. And the Lord, thy God, will bring thee into the land thy fathers possessed. (*Pause*) We read that.

ALEXANDER. Come with me, Rabbi Meir. Do not let me go alone.

MEIR. No, I cannot. Let it be enough that I pray for Zion.

ALEXANDER. God does not credit your intentions but only your deeds.

MEIR. No, Alexander. To be old is to be past the deed.

(*Pause*) May God watch over you.

(*Pause*)

ALEXANDER. Will you accept this, Rabbi Meir?

MEIR. This? This book?

ALEXANDER. It is all I own. A few poems of Yehuda Halevi— all I own. He was like me. At least I want to think so. Keep this book and look at it sometimes . . . and try to think of me.

(*Music: Bridge to narrative theme and down*)

MEIR. He left and only the book he gave me remained of Alexander, the son of Elisha. And I opened his book, and found a verse for him, and I prayed: "Lord, if Thou help me, who shall make me stumble? If Thou restrain me, who else can set me free? Lord, teach me. Let me tread along Thy truth and gently lead me on in judgment and condemn me not. Answer, O my God, and keep not silence; redeem me now, I pray, and say unto Thy servant, I am here!"

(*Music: Up and down*)

MEIR. He left us. Alexander, the son of Elisha. He left us and was hardly gone, when the mob rose again in the Valley of the Rhine, and seized our Holy Scrolls and burned them. In the year 1286 they burned the books. Even the books with the words of Ecclesiastes: "That which hath been is that which shall be; and that which hath been done is that which shall be done . . . and there is no new thing under the sun."

(*Music: Up and out*)
(*Sound of shovel into earth*)
(*Earth falling on wooden coffin*)
(*Cantor: "Ayl Maw-lay Rah-chah-meem" . . . Register very slowly, swell slightly, then fade to background*)

ISRAEL. Rabbi Meir, they tried to stop it. Why didn't I try?

MEIR. You tried, Israel, we all tried.

ISRAEL. But they died. And we didn't die. They are better than we. They are dead but they are better than we.

MEIR. The Book is gone . . . O, God of Israel, what is the people of the Book when the Book is gone?

ISRAEL. Rabbi, this coffin—this one—Alexander, the son of Elisha. (*Pause*) Yes, Rabbi Meir. He came back to resist. David saw him.

(*Pause*)

MEIR. Blessed be the Righteous Judge.

(*Pause*)
(*Cantor: In the clear as he continues . . . and down again*)
MEIR. Israel, why did he come back?
ISRAEL. I don't know. He was going to Jerusalem because of what is written in the Book . . . then he returned to save the Book. He had to. Didn't he, Rabbi Meir? Didn't he?
(*Music: Covers Cantor . . . hold for bridge*)
(*Voices . . . briefly*)
MEIR. Israel, open the Holy Ark. (*Pause*) I ask you, Israel, open the tabernacle of the Lord.
ISRAEL. But the Scrolls are gone. It is foolish.
MEIR. I ask you to open it.
(*Pause*)
(*Door creaks open . . . then second door*)
ISRAEL. I told you. Nothing.
MEIR. Was it for this—this emptiness that God chose Sinai? Moses, Aaron, is there another to replace this Law devoured by fire? Outside they say that it is day, but the day is astonished and ashamed that there is light. The heavenly fire revealed . . . the earthly fire consumed and extinguished and destroyed.
(*Pause*)
ISRAEL. What is the good, Rabbi Meir? What is the good of beholding emptiness and desolation? Come away.
(*Music: Bridge*)
(*Sound of hammer against wooden packing case slats . . . pegs driven in . . . no nails*)
MEIR. I leave you all the rest, Israel. I cannot take these things with me. Please accept them.
(*Pause*)
ISRAEL. Let me travel with you. I ask you again, Rabbi Meir.
MEIR. No. You must remain here in my place.
ISRAEL. You go to Jerusalem. Why can't I go?
MEIR. First, because I go as a stranger and a sojourner and to

seek a lodging place for my bones. (*Softly*) And also because another began a pilgrimage ... and did not live. I live. I go for Alexander, the son of Elisha. (*Pause*) Saddle the mules for me, Israel. I ask this last favor of you.

ISRAEL. It will be done.

MEIR. Israel, you will tend to Alexander's grave?

ISRAEL. To his grave and to the others.

MEIR. I believe you. One dieth in his full strength, being wholly at ease and quiet; his pails are full of milk and the marrow of his bones is moistened. And another dieth in between of soul, and hath never tasted of good. They lie down alike in the dust. And the worm covereth them.

(*Pause*)

ISRAEL. Rabbi Meir ... you are not an ordinary man. It is known that you are ready to depart. And if some men know it then the Emperor Rudolph will know it quickly. He will not allow it.

MEIR. I said that once to Alexander. And he answered ... my feet will allow and my hands will allow.

(*Pause*)

ISRAEL. I'm not sure. I'm not sure at all. Rabbi Meir, why don't you let me go with you? It would be safer that way. Much safer.

(*Music: Narrative theme and down*)

MEIR. In the year 1286, I, Rabbi Meir of Rothenburg, went out from the place of my birth toward the place of the Book. And as I rode past the hill where Alexander ben Elisha lay buried, I opened the book he gave me and I saw the words of the poet: "Jerusalem, thou art the throne of the Lord. I would fall with my face upon thine earth and take delight in thy stones and be tender to thy dust. The life of souls is in the air of thy land, of pure myrrh the grains of thy soil, and honey from the comb of thy rivers. I awake and I am yet with Thee, O God, and I give thanks, and it is sweet to thank Thee."

(*Music: Up and down*)

MEIR. I rode toward Zion and it was as though the living air spoke to me and said, "Thine is strength and thine is glory and thine a robe of honor. Thine is light like a sun that does not wane toward evening. Thine are the searchings out of counsel, thine is dignity, thine is the step to the fortress, built for a stronghold." So, the living air seemed to speak to me. But the minions of Emperor Rudolph spoke differently.

(*Music: Out*)

ONE. That's the one.

TWO. Good. Seize the Jew and carry him to the dungeon.

(*Music: Finish*)

(*Slight echo*)

(*Heavy door opens*)

ONE. (*Off*) Five minutes, no more. He's in there. Just five minutes.

(*Door swings shut*)

ISRAEL. (*Off*) Meir ben Baruch?

MEIR. Israel!

ISRAEL. (*Off*) I came as soon as I heard. (*Pause*) Rabbi Meir, where are you?

MEIR. Here.

ISRAEL. (*Closer*) I can't see. It's dark.

MEIR. I see you, Israel. You grow accustomed to the dark. Yes, Israel, you grow accustomed to the dark.

ISRAEL. Have they harmed you?

MEIR. Hardly. To Emperor Rudolph, I am worth half the royal treasury.

ISRAEL. I see you now. (*Pause*) Are you well?

MEIR. I am well.

(*Pause*)

ISRAEL. Rabbi Meir, what did you mean about the Emperor's treasury?

MEIR. He holds me for ransom.
(*Pause*)
ISRAEL. How much, Rabbi Meir? I might as well know.
MEIR. Twenty thousand pieces of gold.
ISRAEL. That isn't possible.
MEIR. Twenty thousand pieces of gold. That is the ransom.
ISRAEL. Then it will be done. Thank God, you are known to all the Jews of Germany. I shall go to every city. We will find the money.
MEIR. Israel, your eyes may be accustomed to the darkness . . . but not so much darkness. I forbid it.
ISRAEL. But your life.
MEIR. If you ransom me, what will prevent Emperor Rudolph from seizing me again—from seizing other Rabbis?
ISRAEL. It does not matter. I am no Rabbi but I know that it is written that the ransom of kidnapped Israelites must be collected and paid and delivered. Rabbi Meir, that is law.
MEIR. The law states also that nothing shall be done to make kidnapping a lucrative trade.
(*Pause*)
ISRAEL. I will come again. You will change your mind.
MEIR. Come again, Israel, but I will not change my mind.
(*Music: Bridge*)
RUDOLPH. We meet once more, Rabbi Meir.
MEIR. We meet once more, Your Majesty.
RUDOLPH. I wish twenty thousand pieces of gold.
MEIR. I do not have them.
RUDOLPH. A word from you and it will be obtained.
MEIR. Your Majesty, when the earth covers the blood, the final cry has a resting place.
RUDOLPH. Speak plainly, man. You mean you will make me kill you? Is that it?
MEIR. I pray to God for life. I do not wish to die.
RUDOLPH. You are either worth twenty thousand gold pieces to me . . . or else, Rabbi Meir, you are worth nothing. And

if you are worth nothing . . . well, then it will be nothing. And nothing and no one will help you.

MEIR. Your Majesty, in the Bible it is written, "They are in the land of their enemies, but I will not reject them."

RUDOLPH. All right, I quote the Bible, too, Rabbi . . . "Skin for skin, yea, all that a man hath will he give for his life."

MEIR. Your Majesty quotes accurately. Every word as it is written. Only who said it? Satan. First Satan, now the ruler of Germany.

(*Pause*)

EMPEROR. Rabbi Meir, I shall bury you alive in the dungeon.

MEIR. I am buried alive now, Your Majesty. Buried alive in the coffin of my skin. Between death and me there is but a single breath . . . the thickness of a fingernail . . . the whisper of a dream.

EMPEROR. I do not understand you. I think you do not understand yourself. I offer you your life for a ransom. Rabbi Meir, tell them to deliver the ransom.

MEIR. A young man named Alexander ben Elisha was right. You did not know him, and no one knew him, nor heard of him, nor even saw him. But he was right. Now, for those who do not die, there is only one ransom. There is a ransom in the land that is full of gates, the place of hope wherein we may trust, where there is a tongue of healing for bodies and life for flesh.

(*Pause*)

EMPEROR. (*Projecting*) Jailor, take him back to his dungeon and let him rot there.

(*Music: Closing narrative theme and down*)

MEIR. The story is told. The rest makes no difference. For seven years I sat in a dungeon. And then I died. And who will pay the ransom of Rabbi Meir? And what is eternity but perpetual time? And what is every present moment but preparation for the future? I tell you that the darkness

of this day is no more and no less than your forgetfulness of the darkness that was. (*Pause*) The words multiply. And it is foolish. The thing is passed; therefore, the thing is not passed. It is yesterday's story; will it be tomorrow's story? It is a question.
(*Music: Curtain*)

MY COUSIN AVIGDOR

MY COUSIN AVIGDOR

Romantic fiction used to describe the Bedouin as the child of the desert. It would have been more accurate to describe him as its father; for he created the desert. In Biblical times, and modern archeological evidence confirms this, the lands of the Middle East were a granary of the world and a place of standing forests. The Bedouin denuded the hills of timber and allowed the grasslands to erode. Palestine, described as a land flowing with milk and honey, became a desert, flinty, sterile, and hostile. After the issuance of the Balfour Declaration, Palestinian pioneers, chalutzim, began to fight the desert. To protect themselves against Bedouin marauders the pioneers carried a rifle in one hand and seed in the other. They burdened their backs like pack animals and carried water to the young trees they had planted. They revived old holidays like Lag Ba'Omer and the holiday of the Fifteenth Day of Sh'vaht, the New Year's Day of the trees. This became the great holiday of the children, and, as My Cousin Avigdor *explains, somehow the young trees and the young children merged in spirit and became inseparable. Therefore, when the Arabs struck against the Jewish settlements and attacked not houses but trees, it was as though they had struck against the children of Palestine.*

The script was broadcast on January 20, 1946 with Ben Cooper as the boy Narrator and Michael Artist as Avigdor. Roger De Koven was the Teacher, Arthur Kohl was the constable, Norman Rose was Jacob and the other speaking assignments were taken by William Wyatt and David Kurlan. In the last scene Cantor Robert H. Segal sang the 92nd Psalm, "The righteous shall flourish like the palm-tree; he shall grow like a cedar in Lebanon." My Cousin Avigdor *was suggested by the Palestinian short story by Ari Ibn Zahav, "A Brother's Grave."*

MY COUSIN AVIGDOR

BENJAMIN. (*About ten or eleven years old*) My cousin Avigdor is all right in his way, but he has peculiar ideas. He says a tree has a soul. And you can't argue with him. He is smaller than I am, but he is much louder. Also, his hands are not always very clean. My cousin Avigdor, he is always grubbing in the ground. He likes to plant trees. My cousin Avigdor is a fanatic.
(*Music: Establish narrative theme and down*)
BENJAMIN. We live in the settlement at the north end of the Valley of Yezriel. Every year on the fifteenth day of the month of Sh'vaht, which we call Chah-mishah Ah-sahr Bishvaht, there is a school holiday, and everybody and my cousin Avigdor leaves the classroom and goes out into the fields beyond the stockades and plants trees. That is because the fifteenth day of Sh'vaht of the Hebrew calendar, is the New Year's Day of the trees. We do that also because the fields and the hills are naked, like people who have lost their clothes. Everybody plants a tree. That is the ritual. Even Simcha Rosen, who is only going on five, and doesn't even belong in the classroom. But my cousin Avigdor, he wants to plant two trees. My cousin Avigdor is a fanatic.
(*Music out*) He always says to me, Benjamin, he says . . .
AVIGDOR. (*He is eight years old*) A tree has a soul.
BENJAMIN. Better blow your nose, Avigdor, it's running again.
AVIGDOR. I don't care. A tree has a soul. This tree that I am planting is my own brother.

BENJAMIN. Avigdor, you are crazy.
AVIGDOR. You stop that, Benjamin. King David won't like it.
BENJAMIN. Don't you think King David is a fancy name for a skinny little tree like that?
AVIGDOR. King David will rise up like a cedar of Lebanon.
BENJAMIN. Avigdor, you are very crazy. Orange trees don't grow that high.
AVIGDOR. Don't you say that about my brother.
BENJAMIN. You're nothing but a baby. How can a tree be your brother?
AVIGDOR. You're jealous. I've got King David, the prophet Ezekiel, Bar Kochba, and Yehuda Halevi. You're jealous of my brothers, Benjamin. I won't listen to you.
(*Music: Narrative theme and down*)
BENJAMIN. I like my cousin Avigdor, but he has peculiar ideas. Sometimes I think I would like to give him a good kick, but my cousin Avigdor is scrawny and I am always afraid I will break something. Sometimes I think that he has it in him to become the national dope of Palestine.
AVIGDOR. I'm not exactly stealing this fertilizer. But my brothers need it very much.
BENJAMIN. You see what I mean? Avigdor's brothers need fertilizer. (*Music fading*) It's all right to like a tree, but Avigdor carries it too far. He has no shame. Even in the classroom, Avigdor has no shame.
AVIGDOR. A tree has a soul.
TEACHER. You must not say that, Avigdor. Trees are not animate.
AVIGDOR. A tree has a soul. The Bible says so.
TEACHER. No, you're mistaken.
AVIGDOR. It says so. I memorized it. "When thou shalt besiege a city, in making war against it to take it, thou shalt not destroy the trees thereof by wielding an axe against them; for thou mayest eat of them, but thou shalt not cut them down, for the tree of the field is man's life."

TEACHER. And that proves that trees have a soul?
AVIGDOR. A tree is man's life. That's the same as his soul. Isn't it? Well, isn't it?
(*Music: Narrative theme and down*)
BENJAMIN. No one laughed and the Teacher didn't say anything, because my cousin Avigdor would have started to cry. And when my cousin Avigdor cries, his nose runs and he gets the hiccups. It was a mistake for Teacher to have kept quiet. After that, even Simcha Rosen, who is only going on five and who just hangs around the class, even Simcha began to give names to his trees. I wish the Teacher had explained to my cousin Avigdor that a tree doesn't really have a soul. Because when the trouble started, it made even more trouble. It started that day when two Arab constables drove up to the settlement. My cousin Avigdor sneaked up to listen. He had no business being there. (*Music out*) But somebody had to watch my cousin Avigdor; so I listened, too.
(*Voices behind—not loud*)
CONSTABLE. Jacob, where are all the men of the settlement?
JACOB. Some are in the dairy, some are plowing. Why do you ask, Constable?
CONSTABLE. Call them in, Jacob. Get them all here.
JACOB. Trouble?
CONSTABLE. Yes. I think you had better call them in.
JACOB. Aaron, you call the men from the dairy.
ONE. Yes, Jacob.
JACOB. Ben Tzion!
TWO. Right!
JACOB. Get Meyer, David, Abraham, one or two others.
TWO. I know where they are.
CONSTABLE. Do it quickly. I'll be waiting near the truck. We've brought some rifles.
JACOB. Constable, I didn't think it was that serious.
CONSTABLE. Yes, it's serious. I might as well tell you what we

know. Two days ago at Herzliah, fifteen hundred fruit trees were burned to the ground.

JACOB. Constable, a living tree is rather hard to ignite.

CONSTABLE. Very hard, Jacob. We took that into consideration. One of our men found some empty kerosene drums.

JACOB. That's bad.

CONSTABLE. That isn't all. Yesterday, three thousand trees were hacked down in the Balfour Forest. An Arab constable caught them at it. They shot him.

(*Pause*)

JACOB. Constable, have any of the settlements been attacked?

CONSTABLE. Not yet. But you can't tell.

JACOB. Thanks for telling us, Constable.

CONSTABLE. Jacob.

JACOB. Yes.

CONSTABLE. I want you to know . . . over in the Arab settlement . . . Ibn Musa, Ibrahim—they asked me to tell you that they're coming to help you.

JACOB. Thank you. That's good. You can tell Ibn Musa and Ibrahim that there are some people who want to make bad feeling between the settlements. We won't let it happen.

CONSTABLE. I'm glad you see it that way, Jacob. Whoever those vandals are, well . . . there are plenty of rifles in the truck. If you want more, ask the Constabulary.

JACOB. Thanks again, Constable. We'll know what to do.

CONSTABLE. Hold on. Jacob, when a man gets hold of a gun, sometimes his fingers begin to itch.

JACOB. Constable, we're farmers. We don't want any trouble.

CONSTABLE. That's good.

JACOB. But, Constable, those trees out there . . .

CONSTABLE. Yes?

JACOB. They're more than just trees. They are the promise of this land. (*Pause*) Constable, we shan't look for trouble. But we're not going to run away from it.

(*Music: Bridge*)

TEACHER. There will be no class today. Stay inside the walls of the settlement. No one is to go into the fields.

(*Pause*)

AVIGDOR. Teacher.

TEACHER. No one at all, Avigdor.

AVIGDOR. You're going out to guard the trees?

TEACHER. Yes, that's where I'm going.

AVIGDOR. I wish to go with you.

TEACHER. No, this isn't a job for children.

AVIGDOR. All the children can go with me. We shall put our arms around the trees . . . and then when they come with their axes, they will not strike us. No one will strike a child.

(*Pause*)

TEACHER. (*Softly*) Avigdor.

AVIGDOR. You will let us come?

TEACHER. No, Avigdor. Blow your nose. Just blow your nose.

(*Music: Narrative theme and down*)

BENJAMIN. Teacher went with the others to guard the trees. And Ibrahim and Ibn Musa came from the Arab Settlement to help. Some went at night, others went during the day. We could see the watch fires burning from our windows. My cousin Avigdor did not sleep very much. And during the day we could see that he had big black circles under his eyes. So the Teacher spoke to Jacob, and my cousin Avigdor was allowed to go out into the fields to see his brothers. (*Music out*) It was only because of Avigdor that Jacob allowed this.

AVIGDOR. They look all right, don't they, Teacher?

TEACHER. Just fine, Avigdor. They're the best trees in the Valley of Yezriel.

AVIGDOR. See, this is my Prophet Ezekiel. He is two years old.

TEACHER. He has very fine branches.

AVIGDOR. I think so myself. This is Bar Kochba, he is also

two years old. Yehuda Halevi is one year old. King David over here is the baby.

BENJAMIN. King David is growing nicely.

AVIGDOR. He will grow like a cedar of Lebanon, even though he is just an orange tree.

BENJAMIN. Yes, Avigdor, just like a cedar of Lebanon.

AVIGDOR. When I planted him, you said . . .

BENJAMIN. I was wrong.

(*Pause*)

TEACHER. The watchmen are signalling. It's time to go home.

AVIGDOR. No one will hurt them, Teacher? They will guard the trees?

TEACHER. Day and night.

AVIGDOR. No one must hurt them. Because a tree has a soul.

BENJAMIN. Yes, of course.

AVIGDOR. And because God said: "Let the earth put forth grass, herb yielding seed, and fruit trees bearing fruit after its kind. And it was so. And the earth brought forth grass, herb yielding seed after its kind, and tree bearing fruit . . . and God saw that it was good. And there was evening and there was morning, a third day."

(*Pause*)

TEACHER. Come home, Avigdor, it is getting late. And don't worry. Tonight, I shall watch your trees myself.

(*Music: Bridge*)
(*Sound of crickets*)

TEACHER. I said, who's there?

(*Sound of twigs snapped*)

TEACHER. Stop or I'll shoot. (*Pause*) Raise your hands and walk toward the fire. (*Pause*) Avigdor!

AVIGDOR. I came to help you guard the trees.

TEACHER. (*Angrily but softly*) You crazy little fool. We're not playing a game.

AVIGDOR. I know, Teacher. I brought a pitchfork.

TEACHER. Good Lord! Give it to me.

AVIGDOR. But I want to help.
TEACHER. Avigdor, you give me that pitchfork. (*Pause*) Come here. (*Pause*) Don't you know there was a raid on Mishmar last night?
AVIGDOR. That's why I came.
TEACHER. Ssh. No noise.
AVIGDOR. (*Whispering*) All right. I won't make a sound.
(*They whisper*)
TEACHER. Lie down across my knees.
AVIGDOR. What are you going to do?
TEACHER. What do you think I'm going to do?
AVIGDOR. What you're going to do.
TEACHER. And don't you dare make a sound. Absolute silence.
AVIGDOR. Maybe you'd better wait until tomorrow. I cry very easily.
TEACHER. No crying, Avigdor. I'm a teacher in a progressive school. I never struck a child in my life. But this is too much. Over my knees. And don't you dare make a sound.
(*Sound of spanking and hold under teacher*)
TEACHER. (*With exertion*) Not a word! (*Smack*) Not a single word! (*Smack*) Don't you dare cry! (*Smack*) That's for disobeying and coming out here! (*Smack*) That's for stealing a pitchfork! (*Smack*) That's for endangering every man on the night watch! (*Smack*) And that's because I'm angry! Now you can get up. (*Pause*) Does it hurt?
AVIGDOR. Of course it hurts.
TEACHER. Here, take this. But don't blow loud.
AVIGDOR. How can I blow, if I don't blow loud?
TEACHER. Not another word.
(*He blows softly*)
(*Music: Bridge to narrative theme and down*)
BENJAMIN. When the Teacher brought him back to the settlement, my cousin Avigdor's mother was so relieved she gave my cousin Avigdor another thrashing. This time he cried. For three nights there was no more trouble. Then on the

fourth night, Ben Tzion and Simcha Rosen's father were ambushed in the south field. (*Music out*) The nightwatch carried them back all bloody and wounded.

CONSTABLE. Jacob, where are those men going? Where are you going?

JACOB. Where do you think, Constable? We're going to protect our trees.

CONSTABLE. You've lost your mind!

JACOB. Have we?

CONSTABLE. That's just what those hoodlums want! They'll pick you off one by one, and they'll come for the settlement itself.

(*Pause*)

JACOB. Constable, they'll never get within shooting distance of these houses.

CONSTABLE. I'm responsible for lives and property in this district. Jacob, I say you stay here. Lives are more important.

JACOB. No, sir. They got the trees at Mishmar Ha-emek. They got the trees in Balfour Forest. Constable, they're not going to change this land back into a desert and a wilderness. Trees haven't got legs. They can't run away. They've got to be defended.

CONSTABLE. I tell you, man, they'll come for the settlement. This isn't the work of just a few hoodlums.

(*Sound of alarm—siren or old-fashioned auto horn through P.A.*)

ONE. (*Projecting from off mike*) Jacob, Constable . . . they're coming.

(*Burst of rifle fire*)

JACOB. (*Projecting*) Aaron, close that gate. Meyer, get the children and the women into the houses. Ibn Musa, turn those floodlights on. Get those lights working.

(*Increase rifle fire . . . add machine gun and take out with:*)

(*Music: Bridge to narrative theme and down . . . inter-*

sperse with shots)
BENJAMIN. We could see Jacob and the Constable shooting out into the blackness. Ben Tzion and Simcha Rosen's father were wounded, but we could see them firing with the other men. Then, from the south field first and then from the other fields, we could see the fires. Our trees were burning. "When thou shalt besiege a city, in making war against it to take it, thou shalt not destroy the trees thereof." There were no more shots . . . only smoke curling into the sky like a big feather on a woman's hat. The children came out of the houses and stood with the men. And no one said a word for a very long time.
(*Music: Out*)
JACOB. How many are wounded?
TWO. Six men.
JACOB. Anyone hit bad?
TWO. No, we were lucky.
JACOB. Yes, we were lucky.
TWO. Jacob, there's no use just standing here. We've got to go out and see what they've done.
JACOB. We'll go out. Assemble the men.
CONSTABLE. Not right now, Jacob. It might be dangerous.
JACOB. (*Slowly*) All right, Constable. We'll wait.
CONSTABLE. Cheer up, man, it could have been worse.
JACOB. (*Hotly*) If not for you, we could have saved those trees. Why didn't you let us alone? Why did you have to come here and . . . (*Slowly*) Yes, it could have been worse. I'm sorry, Constable.
CONSTABLE. It's all right, Jacob. (*Pause*) There's a little boy here who wants to speak with you.
JACOB. What? Oh. (*Pause*) Well, Benjamin, what is it?
BENJAMIN. It is my cousin, Avigdor.
JACOB. What about him?
BENJAMIN. He isn't here.
JACOB. You'll find him somewhere; just look again.

BENJAMIN. We looked all over.
JACOB. Look in the dairy; look in the henyard; you'll find him someplace.
BENJAMIN. The Teacher looked, Jacob. Avigdor isn't here.
(*Pause*)
JACOB. Get those men, Aaron. We're going out to find the boy.
CONSTABLE. No, Jacob. You can't do that.
JACOB. Stop telling us what we can do and what we can't do. If that boy is out there, we're going to find him and bring him back!
CONSTABLE. Easy, Jacob. Don't lose your head.
JACOB. I'll do anything I want to do.
CONSTABLE. Jacob!
JACOB. Come on, Aaron.
CONSTABLE. Stay where you are, Aaron.
JACOB. Constable, take your hand off his arm.
CONSTABLE. Easy, man, easy . . . you're tired.
JACOB. Yes, I'm tired. So what? So I'm tired. Constable, take your hand off his arm. We're going to find the boy.
CONSTABLE. Not now, Jacob.
JACOB. I say now.
CONSTABLE. Jacob, later. You'll find him later.
JACOB. Constable, this isn't your business. Keep your hands off.
(*Pause*)
CONSTABLE. (*Softly*) Jacob, Ibn Musa and Ibrahim came here to help. They came from the Arab Settlement. You might say it wasn't their business either. If you go out there, you . . . and those men . . . you may not come back. I think that is my business, Jacob.
(*Pause*)
TWO. The Constable is right, Jacob.
(*Pause*)
CONSTABLE. You know I'm right, Jacob. For all we know the

boy is somewhere in the settlement.

(*Pause*)

BENJAMIN. We can look again, Jacob.

JACOB. Yes, Aaron, you go with Benjamin. Try the dairy again. Try every house. Find the boy.

(*Music: Bridge*)

JACOB. Yes?

TEACHER. I've gone through the dairy again. I've looked in the schoolhouse. Avigdor isn't there.

ONE. Jacob, we've searched every cellar and every garret. He isn't here.

JACOB. Aaron?

TWO. Same thing. There's no sign of Avigdor.

(*Pause*)

CONSTABLE. At least we've made certain, Jacob.

JACOB. What do you suggest now, Constable?

CONSTABLE. First, we clean our rifles. Then we wait until the light is stronger. Then, we go out and look.

(*Music: Narrative theme and down*)

BENJAMIN. I went with them to look for my cousin Avigdor. We went through the fields which were black with smoke, and we counted the places where the trees had once stood. When we reached a rise of ground, we could look down and see the place where on the fifteenth day of the month of Sh'vaht, the children had come each year to plant their trees. And there, the young trees were uprooted and pulled out of the ground. It was the Teacher who saw my cousin Avigdor first. My cousin Avigdor didn't hear us, for he was busy making a grave. We stood on the rise of ground and we saw him put the young trees in the grave. And when we came close, we heard him.

AVIGDOR. Yis-gah-dahl v'yis-kah-dahsh shmay rah-baw b'awl-maw dee v'raw chir-oo-say, v'yam-leech mahl-choo-say . . .

(*Crying*) King David . . . good little King David . . . I've covered all your branches. They didn't even give you a chance to live. And you had no legs. You couldn't run away. You could have grown higher than the cedars of Lebanon. King David, you would have grown twice as high. And you . . . oh, King David. (*He cries*)

(*Music: Narrative theme and down*)

BENJAMIN. He was crying over the grave of his brothers. We took my cousin Avigdor home and my cousin Avigdor's mother washed his face and put his head in her lap and rocked him back and forth as though he were smaller than Simcha Rosen, who is only going on five. (*Music out*) And then my cousin Avigdor, and I, and the Teacher, and Simcha Rosen, and Simcha Rosen's father we all went back to the field. And Simcha Rosen's father sang.

(*Cantor: 92nd paslm . . . register unaccompanied and down*)

TEACHER. Don't cry any more, Avigdor. We shall replant the trees.

AVIGDOR. I'm not crying.

TEACHER. I promise. The trees will be replanted. For every tree cut down a hundred trees will stand.

AVIGDOR. The Prophet Ezekiel and Bar Kochba were two years old. They had very fine branches.

TEACHER. The finest branches in the world.

AVIGDOR. Yehuda Halevi was one year old.

TEACHER. Blow your nose, Avigdor.

AVIGDOR. And King David was only a baby, but he would have grown higher than the cedars of Lebanon. Oh, Teacher, King David was only a baby.

(*Music: Curtain*)

RABBI ISRAEL SALANTER

RABBI ISRAEL SALANTER

The fame achieved by Israel Salanter for the episode dramatized in this script has tended to obscure his less spectacular but more important contributions to Jewish life. In an age when Jewish learning was confined almost solely to the Talmud, Salanter applied the lesson of the fathers of the Talmud who were carpenters, blacksmiths, woodcutters and manual laborers, and urged that each student supplement his academic studies with some manual training.

Later, Salanter founded a school of thought which came to be known as the Mussar movement which stressed the ethical principles of religion, declaring that there was no dichotomy between a man's obligations to God and his obligations to his fellow-man; that a man who observed the ritual but was indifferent to his neighbors or was unscrupulous in business dealings was, in effect, guilty of blasphemy since the worship of God was one with the service to man.

The script was inspired by an essay on Rabbi Salanter in Professor Louis Ginzberg's Students, Scholars and Saints *and by informal conversations with the distinguished Talmudist at his home. It was broadcast on January 21, 1945, with Bartlett Robinson as Salanter and Alexander Scourby as the Narrator. Others in the cast were Bernard Lenrow, Jack Manning, Joseph Boland, Joseph Di Santis, Richard Keith, Toni Merrill, Alan P. Dreeben and John Sylvester White. Ira Avery was the director and the musical score was composed by Henry Brant.*

RABBI ISRAEL SALANTER

(*Cantor: "Eh-lee-yaw-hoo hah-naw-vee"*)
(*Music: Sneak in and hold under*)
NARRATOR. What are the three capital sins for the people of Israel? They are only three: idolatry, unchastity, and murder. And it is written in the Talmud, "There comes a time when it is considered a virtue to trespass a law of the Torah. There is even a time when a man may transgress all except the three capital injunctions . . . if thereby he saves a life for the world."
(*Cantor: Up briefly with music and down*)
NARRATOR. One hundred and five years ago there lived in the city of Vilna a man of piety and wisdom . . . the sage and scholar Rabbi Israel Salanter. And once, in the evening of his days . . . after a life of gentle and scrupulous devotion to the Law . . . he committed a great act of transgression.
(*Cantor and Music Fading*) On the solemn Day of Atonement, the Day of Yom Kippur, Rabbi Israel Salanter stood before the Holy Ark and said to the congregation of Vilna:
SALANTER. The Prophet Habakkuk has written that the righteous liveth by his faith. It is our faith to keep this day of Yom Kippur in prayer and fasting. I command you now to put away this fast. Take up bread in your hand, pronounce the benediction, and eat.
(*Crowd reaction*)
SALANTER. People of the congregation . . . I order you to break the fast . . . I order you to eat.
(*Music: Narrative theme and down*)

NARRATOR. They heard him and they were incredulous. And he commanded them again and they raised their voices against him. And then the look of the prophets came upon the face of Rabbi Israel and his voice was a thundering from the Holy Ark and the men and women of Vilna wept and refused to commit the transgression of the fast . . . and then Rabbi Israel Salanter wept also *(Music out)* . . . and he called to one by his side.

SALANTER. Bring me bread and salt and a glass of wine. I myself will be the first to eat and to make a blessing for bread on the day of Yom Kippur.

(Music: Theme and down)

NARRATOR. Who was this man who broke the sacred prohibition? He was a scholar of scholars and a man of gentleness. He measured his day with acts of righteousness even as the seconds measure the minutes and the minutes measure the hours. I recall once, when in a time of great urgency, Rabbi Israel encountered a man who was lamed in the foot. And the wife of Rabbi Israel, who was equally urgent, was greatly provoked.

(Music: Out)

WIFE. Now we are late, Rabbi Israel.

SALANTER. I am sorry, Leah . . . but the man was lame . . . I couldn't hurry.

WIFE. And why couldn't you?

SALANTER. Leah, you saw yourself . . . the man was lame.

WIFE. You're not lame. Now we're late. We're too late. See what you've done.

SALANTER. I cannot help it, Leah. He barely walks . . . would it be right for me to hurry?

WIFE. There is such a thing as carrying tact too far.

SALANTER. Tact, Leah?

WIFE. That's what I said.

SALANTER. Yes, Leah . . . tact, consideration, if you will . . . but something more. It is written in the Law that a man is forbidden to display unusual agility in the presence of the handicapped. It is a good law, Leah. If God wills, I will never violate it.

(*Cantor: "Eh-lee-yaw-hoo hah-naw-vee" . . . with orchestra for bridge and continue behind*)

NARRATOR. And yet this man, this humble man of God, Rabbi Israel Salanter, committed a breach of the Yom Kippur fast! Perhaps it was because of a momentary weakness, you may ask? Perhaps. But he was not a man of weakness. He was a man of moral strength . . . and considerable wisdom also. I mind the time when . . . (*Cantor and music fading*) . . . the time when Solomon Cohen died and left a will which was too troublesome for the Probate Court. And Meyer, the son of Solomon, came to Rabbi Israel in his perplexity.

MEYER. I thought my father loved me, Rabbi Israel?

SALANTER. He did, Meyer, he loved you very much.

MEYER. Then why this will?

SALANTER. He leaves you all his wealth . . . surely you have no complaint?

MEYER. Haven't I? Listen: "My son shall not receive his inheritance until he becomes foolish."

SALANTER. (*Chuckles*)

MEYER. It's no laughing matter, Rabbi Israel. (*Angrily*) What does he mean . . . "My son shall not receive his inheritance until he becomes foolish?"

SALANTER. Meyer . . . tell me, Meyer . . . are you married?

MEYER. How can a man marry without money?

SALANTER. I see . . . then there is someone?

MEYER. Naturally there is someone . . . Naomi, the grain-dealer's youngest daughter.

SALANTER. Marry her, Meyer. And then, when your firstborn arrives go to the Probate Court and you will be paid your inheritance.

MEYER. But, Rabbi Israel, I don't understand.

SALANTER. Meyer, your father was a very wise man . . . bless his memory.

MEYER. But . . . I . . .

SALANTER. Wait. Marry Naomi and have your firstborn. Don't you see, Meyer? When a man becomes a father, he romps on the floor with his child, he utters unseemly noises with his tongue, he bores his friends utterly with his simple stories. Have your child, Meyer. You will become properly human and properly foolish. You will justify your inheritance . . . Meyer, that is the meaning of your father's will.

(*Music: Bridge to narrative theme and down*)

NARRATOR. Rabbi Israel Salanter, a scholar and a sage, and withal a man of humor and understanding. Yet, this saintly person committed an act of transgression. And before I reveal to you the circumstance of his transgression, I must reveal once again the merits of Rabbi Israel. It happened on a certain day that the ghetto was disturbed by the voice of Moses, the wine-merchant.

(*Music: Out*)

MOSES. Don't let them get away. Hold those two men . . . they're thieves.

(*Crowd ad lib*)

ONE. What did they do, Moses?

MOSES. They robbed me. Hold them.

(*Crowd up and fade to background*)

TWO. Is this yours, Moses?

MOSES. This and this and this and this. Oh, the scoundrels.

TWO. What have you got to say for yourselves?

CRIPPLE. I didn't take it.

MOSES. He's a liar as well as a thief. It was on him.

CRIPPLE. I tell you. I couldn't have taken it.

TWO. No? I suppose the Angel Gabriel flew it under your coat?

CRIPPLE. How could I take it? Look down . . . look at my feet.

(*Pause*)

ONE. Moses, this man is a cripple.

MOSES. What . . . what did you say?

ONE. He's a cripple. Well, if he didn't take it the other man did. *(Pause)* Listen, you . . . it's very wicked to pass off your thievery on a poor helpless cripple.

BLIND MAN. I didn't pass anything off.

MOSES. Be still, you thief.

BLIND MAN. I'm telling you I passed nothing to him . . . and I'm not a thief. I couldn't . . . look here . . . look at my eyes.

TWO. In the name of God . . . the man is blind.

MOSES. Pay no attention to them. If one didn't take it the other did. I want them punished.

TWO. One second, Moses . . . this is too much for us to decide.

(Voices ad lib)

ONE. I know . . . take them to Rabbi Israel. He will decide.

(Music: Bridge and take out with:)

(Voices noisily)

SALANTER. Hush . . . ssh . . . everyone . . . silence, please.

(Crowd down)

MOSES. How was it done, Rabbi Israel?

SALANTER. I believe I know.

MOSES. Yes?

SALANTER. The cripple was carried by the blind man . . . that's how you were robbed, Moses.

TWO. Didn't I tell you Rabbi Israel would know?

(Voices ad lib)

SALANTER. Blind man, stand up.

(Pause)

BLIND MAN. Yes, Rabbi Israel.

SALANTER. A thief must be punished.

BLIND MAN. But I swear I haven't seen the light of day for twelve years.

SALANTER. Nevertheless a thief must be punished. Do you admit that?

BLIND MAN. All right, I admit it . . . but I'm not the thief . . . he took it.

CRIPPLE. How could I, Rabbi Israel . . . I haven't walked for fifteen years. I admit a thief must be punished, but if you punish me you punish an innocent man.

SALANTER. Attend me. Clearly only one man here is the thief . . . since one pair of eyes guided one pair of legs.

MOSES. Then who is to be punished?

SALANTER. Moses, the Talmud has decided. Place the crippled man on the blind man's back.

(*Sound of grunting, ad lib protests*)

SALANTER. Good. Observe . . . all of you. What do we behold?

MOSES. (*Panting*) A cripple on a blind man's back.

SALANTER. Yes, Moses . . . one pair of sound eyes . . . one pair of sound legs . . . people, this is the single thief. For the purposes of crime they were one; for the purposes of judgment let them also be one.

TWO. Then judge them, Rabbi Israel.

SALANTER. No, that is not proper. Take them to the Court.

TWO. No, you judge them yourself.

SALANTER. My son, Rabbi Ishmael said, "Judge not alone, for none may judge alone save the Holy One; neither say to thy colleague, 'Accept my opinion,' for he is free to choose but thou are not." Take them to the Court . . . and be quick . . . for the day is Friday . . . and dusk is at hand and we must hurry to the synagogue to welcome the Sabbath.

(*Cantor: "L'chaw Doh-dee" . . . with orchestra and down*)

NARRATOR. A song of the Sabbath, a song of welcome. L'chaw doh-dee lik-rahs kah-law . . . come, my friend, to meet the bride . . . for truly is not the Sabbath the bride of Israel? Thus they sang . . . and thus each Sabbath eve in the Synagogue of Vilna sang Rabbi Israel Salanter . . . it is an ancient poem to be sung with tenderness and with pride and not without a wetness of the eye. And in this manner, upon the song, Sabbath followed upon Sabbath. The night became long and was stricken with winter, and the houses of the Ghetto huddled together against the cold.

(*Cantor: In the clear briefly and fade out under with music*)

NARRATOR. The seasons changed and life in Vilna was uneventful and therefore the more to be cherished. And the people cherished their Rabbi, for he was a man of God, and good, and without blemish. And then, a month before the Day of Penitence . . . with neither pause nor warning . . . an affliction descended from the East. Some said it came from China, some said India . . . it did not matter . . . it was the cholera . . . and from it came death and the transgression of Israel Salanter . . . but first came death.

REBECCA. (*Toneless*) He didn't complain, Rabbi Israel. First the pain in the legs . . . then the cramping . . . he didn't complain. We buried him quickly as you said, Rabbi Israel.

SALANTER. Rouse yourself, Rebecca.

REBECCA. Why?

SALANTER. Rebecca, listen to me.

REBECCA. Why?

SALANTER. Rebecca!

REBECCA. Yes . . . all right . . . I'll listen.

SALANTER. Your brother is sick . . . your husband is sick. There is no one but you to care for them.

REBECCA. My baby is dead.

SALANTER. Rebecca, rouse yourself.

REBECCA. May he rest in peace.

SALANTER. Amen . . . Rebecca . . . you must tend to your husband and to your brother.

REBECCA. All right, Rabbi Israel . . . I'll tend to them.

SALANTER. They are taken bad . . . but you must tend them without fear.

REBECCA. I have already buried my child . . . how can I have fear?

SALANTER. Very well . . . hot stones wrapped in towels for the feet, Rebecca.

REBECCA. All right.

SALANTER. And they are to bring ice from the ice-house. The doctor says administer it by mouth . . . it may stop the vomiting.

REBECCA. Yes, of course.

SALANTER. And feed them, Rebecca . . . feed them frequently.

REBECCA. With what . . . I have nothing in the house. No one has anything now. Not a copeck, not a spoon of barley.

SALANTER. Then wait here. I'm going to see Moses the winemerchant. He will help.

(*Music: Bridge*)

MOSES. Oh, we have come on an evil time, Rabbi Israel.

SALANTER. Yes, yes, Moses, but . . .

MOSES. The Lord giveth and the Lord taketh away . . .

SALANTER. Of course, of course . . . but Moses, listen . . .

MOSES. Oh, Rabbi Israel, how great must be our sins that this punishment has been visited upon us?

SALANTER. In the name of Heaven, Moses, a little less verbal piety. These people need help.

MOSES. Ah, Rabbi Israel, we all need help. You must do your duty, Rabbi Israel. Tell them to trust in the Lord.

SALANTER. Moses, I have raised my hand against no man in all my life . . . but before God I believe it would be no sin if I struck you now.

MOSES. Rabbi Israel . . . someone might think I uttered a blasphemy. Is it such a terrible crime to trust in the Lord?

SALANTER. It *is* a crime for *you* to tell that to the needy.

MOSES. But I trust in God, why shouldn't they?

SALANTER. Moses, does that trust make you indifferent to the misfortune of others? They have no food, no money . . . you have . . . are you going to put your hand in your pocket, or are you going to let them starve?

MOSES. If they trust in God they will not starve.

SALANTER. Moses, sometimes there can be nothing more loathsome than a complacent man. Do you think you can perform your religious duties only in the seclusion of the House of Worship? Do you think it is enough to repeat a prayer, to observe the dietary laws, to make a false show of piety? Do you think a man of religion must only contemplate and never serve? Moses, put your hand in your pocket. We need food, we need medicines . . . and by all that's holy, never, Moses, never tell a needy man to trust in God before you yourself have helped him.

(*Music: Bridge*)

DOCTOR. Get into bed, Rebecca . . . you've fallen sick.

REBECCA. I can't, Doctor . . . there's no one left to help the others.

DOCTOR. Rabbi Israel, she must get into bed.

SALANTER. Do as the Doctor says, Rebecca.

REBECCA. I can't. I lost my child . . . I can't lose my husband and my brother.

SALANTER. I'll stay here . . . I'll tend you.

REBECCA. No, Rabbi . . . it's the Sabbath . . . your place is in the synagogue.

SALANTER. Rebecca . . . every house is a synagogue . . . every house where men are born and live and die. And remember, Rebecca, sah-kaw-nahs n'faw-shohs. In a time of danger for human life, observance of the Law may be set aside without sin. Is there a better place for me to pray than here . . . is there a better way for me to pray than by doing what I can for you and your family?

(*Pause*)

REBBECA. I'll go to bed. I'm very tired. I'll go, Rabbi Israel.

(*Pause*)

DOCTOR. (*Sotto*) I must talk to you, Rabbi Israel.

SALANTER. Yes, Doctor?

DOCTOR. Eight in every ten are dead and dying.

SALANTER. So bad, Doctor?

DOCTOR. Yes . . . so bad. And the others will surely die . . . and you will die with them . . . unless.

SALANTER. Unless what?

DOCTOR. If their resistance is broken. They need rest and care . . . and most of all they need food . . . they need food *every single day.*

SALANTER. Come to the point, Doctor.

DOCTOR. There must be no fasting on the Day of Atonement.

(*Pause*)

SALANTER. "On the tenth day of this seventh month is the day of atonement; there shall be a holy convocation unto you; and ye shall afflict your souls." Yes, Doctor, and ye shall afflict your souls, and take no manner of food and take no manner of drink.

DOCTOR. Don't quote Scripture, Rabbi Israel . . . there must be no fasting.

SALANTER. They would sooner die than break the solemn fast.

DOCTOR. If they don't break it they will surely die.

(*Pause*)

SALANTER. Tell me what to do, Doctor.

DOCTOR. I want you to break the Yom Kippur fast.

SALANTER. I cannot do that, Doctor. The righteous liveth by his faith. If it is God's will, I shall die. I am no longer young. Perhaps you cannot understand it, but if it is a choice of breaking the fast or dying, I have no alternative but to die.

DOCTOR. Suit yourself. I just can't understand it . . . but don't let them die . . . tell them they must live.

SALANTER. Yes, I can do that. Nothing is more sacred than life. All right, Doctor. I shall tell them to break the fast.

(*Music: Montage theme and down for:*)

(*Sound of hammer on nail*)

ONE. It's a notice from Rabbi Israel . . . There will be no fasting tomorrow . . . no fast on Yom Kippur.

(***Crowd reaction***)

(*Music: Up and down*)
TWO. Tear it down.
ONE. Wait . . . let's talk to him.
(*Music: Up and down*)
TWO. Rabbi Israel, will you break the solemn fast?
SALANTER. No.
TWO. Then neither do we.
(*Music: Up and down*)
DOCTOR. You must persuade them, Rabbi Israel.
SALANTER. I have done more, Doctor . . . I have commanded them . . . they won't listen.
(*Music: Up and down*)
DOCTOR. It's Yom Kippur, Rabbi Israel. If they fast today . . . not even a miracle will save them.
SALANTER. Very well, Doctor . . . I know what I must do.
(*Music: Up to "Kol Nidre"*)
(*Cantor: "Kol Nidre" and down with music under narration*)
NARRATOR. In the Synagogue of Vilna the cantor sang "Kol Nidre" on the solemn Day of Atonement. And outside the death-carts were piled high in the streets of the Ghetto. And the day was blacker than night, and no stars shone. And the cantor sang "Kol Nidre" and a remnant of Israel heard the melody and listened to the slow beat of its heart. The widows listened and the orphans and the bereaved men of the congregation . . . and they marveled that the cantor had strength to sing . . . for they barely had strength to listen. (*Cantor and music fading*) Then . . . Rabbi Israel Salanter . . . stepped slowly before the open Ark of the covenant, and touched his finger to the Holy Scroll, and turned to the congregation and spoke.
SALANTER. Wherefore have we feasted and Thou seest not? Wherefore have we afflicted our soul and Thou takest no knowledge? Is not this the fast that I have chosen? To loose the fetters of wickedness, to undo the bands of the yoke,

and to let the oppressed go free, and that ye break every yoke? Hear me, people of Vilna, wherefore do we fast? Is it not to deal our bread to the hungry and to bring the poor that are cast out to our house? And if the house is empty, whom shall we bring? *(Pause)* I, Rabbi Israel Salanter, charge you to break this fast. People of Vilna, in the name of God I command you to break bread, to pronounce the benediction, and to eat.

(Pause)

ONE. *(Off)* Rabbi Israel, as we have lived, so shall we die. We cannot break the fast.

SALANTER. I command you.

ONE. *(Off)* You shame us, Rabbi Israel, you shame us before the open Ark of the covenant.

SALANTER. Will you eat?

ONE. *(Off)* We will not.

SALANTER. Murder is a capital sin. You murder yourselves by not eating.

TWO. *(Closer)* Rabbi Israel, I am no scholar . . . I make no claim to learning . . . but there are some laws that may be transgressed . . . and some that may never be. And we will not break the law of the holiest of days.

SALANTER. My children, there comes a time when it is considered a virtue to trespass a law of the Torah. And this is such a time. There is even a time when a man may transgress every single one of the 613 precepts of the Torah . . . with the exception of the commandment against idolatry, the commandment against unchastity, and the commandment against murder. And this is also such a time. For by our transgression not a single life but many lives are saved for the world. And what is more holy than life?

TWO. *(Closer)* We commit no transgression today, Rabbi Israel. We are neither more nor less than you . . . and we will not do what you will not do.

(Pause)

SALANTER. Very well; (*Pause*) Blessed art Thou, O Lord our God, King of the Universe, who has kept us in life and hast preserved us and enabled us to reach this season. (*Pause*) Moses . . .

MOSES. (*On*) Yes, Rabbi Israel . . .

SALANTER. In my bag . . . take it from the bag.

MOSES. Take what?

SALANTER. A loaf of bread.

(*Pause*)

MOSES. (*Close*) Here is the loaf of bread, Rabbi Israel.

SALANTER. Say the benediction with me, Moses. Moses, say it with me!

(*Pause*)

TOGETHER. Blessed are Thou, O Lord our God, King of the Universe, who bringest forth bread from the ground.

(*Pause*)

SALANTER. Now, Moses . . . let us eat the Yom Kippur bread . . . and live.

(*Music: Narrative theme and down*)

NARRATOR. And the Rabbi Israel Salanter stood before the Ark of the Lord on the solemn Day of Atonement and ate bread. And the congregation of Vilna wept. Then Rabbi Israel closed the Ark and they returned to their houses and they ate and they lived. And when the city was cleansed, and the dead were buried, Rabbi Israel spoke to the congregation.

(*Music: Out*)

SALANTER. (*Softly*) O Lord, what is man that Thou shouldst magnify him? and that Thou shouldst set Thy heart upon him? and that Thou shouldst remember him every morning and try him every moment? Oh, Thou watcher of men, why hast Thou set me as a mark for Thee so that I am a burden to myself? I ask you Job's question, people of Israel, and I know the answer. Every man is the Lord's mark. Every life is one mortal atom of the Lord. Let us live each day as though it were the last of days. Let us do justly, let us honor all men, for all men are the handiwork of God. No, let us go to the synagogue, for the day is Friday, and the night is gathering. Let us rejoice and sing a welcome to the Sabbath.

(*Cantor: "L'chaw doh-dee" with orchestra . . . and finish*)

MY FAVORITE ASSASSIN

MY FAVORITE ASSASSIN

The French Foreign Legion, a brutal adjutant, men drilled unmercifully in the blazing Sahara sun, forced marches, a man's dreadful secret exposed! Hollywood melodrama? Perhaps. My Favorite Assassin *is in the best Beau Geste tradition of the movies but it is something more. For one thing, it is a true story. For another thing, it is an important story.*

In Europe or Asia or Africa or even America there lives a man who, conceivably, could have changed the destiny of the human race. Conceivably, he could have spared the one man who might have led Germany to a Pan-Europa of federated democracy instead of to the Festung Europa of the swastika, disgrace, and annihilation. This script is the hair-raising story of that man, and that man's individual effort to make restitution to society. There have been sensational stories to come out of the war but none like this.

My Favorite Assassin *appeared in* Harper's *in April, 1943, under the by-line of correspondent George W. Herald. Professor Abraham Heschel of the Jewish Theological Seminary either read it much later or remembered it from his earlier reading, but in any case early in 1946 he mildly suggested to Rabbi Davis that it might make a script. The Professor was right. The average script requires anywhere from ten hours to two days to write. This one wrote itself in about five excited hours. Its production on March 10, 1946, benefitted from a fine musical score by Morris Mamorsky and a performance by Stefan Schnabel as Tessier that was chilling. Roger De Koven as Gerson and Mr. Schnabel gave the short Hebrew lesson scene a quality of beauty mixed with terror. The three other members of a perfect cast were Guy Repp as Rathenau, Joseph Di Santis as Ullmann and Alexander Scourby as the Narrator. Frank Papp directed.*

MY FAVORITE ASSASSIN

(*Sound of men marching ... begin off and build under*)
(*Bugle call off mike*)

NARRATOR. I shall not tell you my name. I am important to this story only because I know the facts. The facts are not about me, but about Adjutant-Chief Ernest Tessier, officer of the French Foreign Legion. This is a true story. These are the facts in the order that I learned them.

(*Marching men and march into:*)
(*Music: Narrative theme and down*)

NARRATOR. In February, 1940, I joined the French Foreign Legion. At Fort Flatters in the desert near the Libyan border I met Adjutant Tessier. The commandant of the camp suffered from a speech disorder, and it was Adjutant Tessier who practically ran the whole show. He was about thirty-nine ... a tall man, rather slender ... with gray eyes ... hard gray eyes ... granite gray. But it was his jaw that you noticed most ... a big jaw ... brutal. You noticed that right away. And then when he spoke, you forgot about his jaw and his eyes. You remembered only his voice and the fact that it didn't belong to his face. There was something about the voice of Adjutant Tessier.

(*Music: Fading*)

TESSIER. (*Over fading music*) You are a war volunteer?
NARRATOR. Yes, sir.
TESSIER. You may stand at ease.
NARRATOR. Yes, sir.
TESSIER. You? Who are you?
GERSON. Legionnaire Gerson, mon adjutant.

Adapted from "My Favorite Assassin" by George W. Herald. By Permission of the Vanguard Press. Copyright, 1943, by George W. Herald.

TESSIER. Fix your cap.
GERSON. Yes, sir.
TESSIER. You?
ULLMANN. Legionnaire Ullmann, mon adjutant.
TESSIER. You are German?
ULLMANN. A refugee, mon adjutant.
TESSIER. You are Jewish?
ULLMANN. Yes, mon adjutant.
TESSIER. You, also?
GERSON. Yes, mon adjutant.
  (*Pause*)
TESSIER. You three, you came into this with your eyes open. I didn't ask you. Your companions are the refuse, the sediment, the offscourings, the filthy dregs, and the rotten scum of the world. Do you understand that?
NARRATOR. Yes, sir.
TESSIER. Vive La France!
NARRATOR. Vive La France.
TESSIER. No cynicism.
NARRATOR. Yes, sir.
TESSIER. You will leave cynicism to me.
NARRATOR. Yes, sir.
TESSIER. You three, you are soldiers. Your job is to kill. Your job is to be killed. You do your job. We'll all get along. It doesn't matter what you were before—a thief, or a murderer, or even a lawyer. Do your job. We'll get along. Now get out.
  (*Music: Theme and down*)
NARRATOR. We found out about him. Tessier did not speak for effect. He spoke with an ironical politeness. But he held the power of life and death over us. We knew it. We knew it in the look of his eyes, in the brutal line of his jaw, in the almost priestlike softness of his voice. (*Music out*) And we knew it most when he drilled us under the blazing, fatal sun of the Sahara Desert.

(*Bring in marching men above . . . hold under*)
TESSIER. Company, column right, march.
NARRATOR. Two hours in the sun.
TESSIER. Company, column left, march.
NARRATOR. The thermometer, 135 degrees.
TESSIER. Column right, march.
NARRATOR. The hot sand burning through our shoes.
TESSIER. To the rear, march.
NARRATOR. His voice unchanging, implacable.
TESSIER. To the rear, march.
NARRATOR. And there was something diabolical in his fine, judicious measurement of the limit of our endurance.
TESSIER. Company, halt.
(*Cut sound*)
TESSIER. At ease. (*Pause*) My compliments, gentlemen. Faultless execution. The precision of the ballet. (*Pause*) Legionnaire Gerson.
GERSON. (*Panting*) Yes. mon adjutant.
TESSIER. You march with three feet, don't you?
GERSON. Two feet, mon adjutant.
TESSIER. Thank you, I am reassured. (*Pause*) Legionnaire Ullmann.
ULLMANN. Yes, sir.
TESSIER. In the future do not fall upon your face as often. It is disturbing.
ULLMANN. Yes, sir.
TESSIER. We've rested enough. (*Pause*) Company, attention!
(*Clicking of heels*)
TESSIER. Company, march.
(*Sound of marching*)
TESSIER. To the rear, march. (*Pause*) Column left, march. (*Pause*) Column right, march. (*Pause*) Column left, march. (*Pause*) To the rear, march. (*Pause*) Column right, march. (*He continues into:*)
(*Music: Theme and down*)

NARRATOR. He was not a simple man, this Ernest Tessier, Adjutant of the French Foreign Legion. There was malice and perversity in him upon the surface. But Gerson and Ullmann and I, we sensed something beneath the surface. Something indefinite, indefinable, something we could not name. There was a flow of invective that could burst from his mouth . . . invective of a wonderful fluency and a terrible sincerity . . . and then . . . the curses would stop, and a look almost of regret would soften the granite eyes. No, Adjutant Tessier was not a simple man. (*Music out*) He made us wonder. He disturbed us.

ULLMANN. Adjutant Ernest Tessier. Where he spits no grass grows.

GERSON. Forget him, Ullmann.

ULLMANN. I think I shall go to the canteen and get drunk.

GERSON. It won't do any good.

ULLMANN. Who is he? Gerson, what is he?

GERSON. I don't know, Ullmann. Shut up, I'm tired.

ULLMANN. So you're tired. I'm tired, too. I was born tired. Who is he?

GERSON. Forget about Tessier.

ULLMANN. I don't like mysteries.

GERSON. Ullmann, listen: "Then they said unto him, 'Tell us, we pray thee, what is thine occupation, and whence comest thou? What is thy country? and of what people art thou?'"

ULLMANN. Well, what about it?

GERSON. There's no mystery about you and about me. "And he said unto them, 'I am a Hebrew; and I fear the Lord, the God of Heaven, which hath made the sea and the dry land.'" All right, Ullmann . . . you and me . . . we're defined. That's enough. Forget Tessier. I found a deck of cards. Let's play bridge.

(*Music: Narrative theme and down*)

NARRATOR. So I played bridge with two Jewish refugees. Perhaps this was more than a way of forgetting Tessier. The Legionnaires were rough and uncouth. We three, we were middle-class, bourgeois. A game of bridge . . . maybe that's what we were doing to protest our individuality, to proclaim in the desert the incomparable, indestructible self-satisfaction of the middle class. *(Music out)* We forgot the world; we found ourselves. We added our scores. But we were vulnerable.

TESSIER. Well, well, well. Keep seated, gentlemen. Why should you bother to salute me? After all I am only the adjutant-chief here.

(Sound of heels clicking)

GERSON. *(Stiffly)* Beg your pardon, sir.

TESSIER. Not at all, Gerson. This is a tropical pleasure resort.

GERSON. No, sir.

TESSIER. You and your friends—you are merely vacationists. *(Pause)* You three . . . you will report to my quarters at nine o'clock.

GERSON. Yes, sir.

TESSIER. *(Moving off)* I shall expect you there. Yes. You three. Promptly. Be sure you are not late.

(Pause)

ULLMANN. *(Close)* Gerson?

GERSON. *(Close)* Save the cards. I think we're going to need them in the guardhouse.

TESSIER. *(Off)* Legionnaire Ullmann!

ULLMANN. Yes, sir.

TESSIER. *(Coming back)* Legionnaire Ullmann. I believe you spoke. You were addressing me? I asked you a question, Legionnaire. You were addressing me?

ULLMANN. No, sir.

TESSIER. All right. You three . . . report at my quarters, nine o'clock.

(Music: Bridge)
(Door shuts)

TESSIER. Well?
GERSON. We are here, mon adjutant.
TESSIER. Sit down. (*Pause*) I said, sit down.
GERSON. Yes, sir.
(*Pause*)
TESSIER. Intimidated, yes, Gerson?
GERSON. No . . . I mean, yes, sir.
TESSIER. I've got a bottle here. The wine isn't good. But it's wine.
(*Cork out*)
(*He pours . . . four glasses*)
TESSIER. Legionnaires, a votre sante . . . To your good health. (*Pause*) I said to your good health. Drink.
(*Pause*)
(*Glasses set down*)
TESSIER. You three . . . you dislike me. don't you? Yes, Gerson?
(*Pause*)
GERSON. No, sir.
TESSIER. You are an honest man, Gerson. You don't dislike me. You hate me. You believe in the exact use of words, don't you?
GERSON. In Germany, mon adjutant, I was a philologist.
TESSIER. Yes, yes, I know. You three . . . you are the first civilized people I've seen in this Sahara hellhole for a long time.
(*Sound of deck riffled, cards shuffled*)
TESSIER. Drink the rest of your wine, gentlemen. And let us play bridge.
(*Music: Narrative theme and down*)
NARRATOR. We were bewildered now. Bewildered as well as intimidated. The important thing was to keep Tessier in good humor. We decided to let him win. But we found out that it took no effort to let him win. He played a resourceful game; he beat us easily. (*Music out*) We played a few rounds. Then Tessier put the cards down.

TESSIER. I wish to say something. (*Pause*) Gerson, Ullmann, you're Jews.
GERSON. Yes, mon adjutant.
TESSIER. Forget the title, Gerson. In here call me Tessier.
GERSON. All right.
TESSIER. You think I dislike you because most of the officers are like that. Well, Gerson, I'm not like that. No.
GERSON. Tessier, do you want to tell us . . . that . . .
TESSIER. What? Say it, Gerson.
GERSON. That some of your best friends are Jews?
TESSIER. Leave the cynicism to me. Gerson, don't make fun of me. (*Pause*) I will tell you something. I love all Jews. They belong to the finest and most gifted people in the world.
(*Pause*)
GERSON. Let's play cards, Tessier.
TESSIER. I know what you're thinking. There is anti-Semitism; there is inverted anti-Semitism.
GERSON. Tessier, let's play cards.
TESSIER. No. (*Pause*) Gerson . . . I quote . . . "How shall I repay my enemies if not by increasing my own good works."
GERSON. Ibn-Gabirol?
TESSIER. Correct. I quote Ibn-Gabirol. Solomon ben Judah Ibn-Gabirol, Hebrew poet. Born Malaga, circa 1021, died Valencia, circa 1058.
(*Pause*)
GERSON. Tessier, who are you?
TESSIER. Adjutant-Chief Ernest Tessier, French Foreign Legion.
GERSON. Tessier, who are you really?
TESSIER. A brute who has read the Talmud in translation.
(*Pause*)
GERSON. You know the Talmud?
TESSIER. Rabbi Akiba said, "Everything is foreseen, yet freedom of choice is given; and the world is judged by grace, yet all is according to the amount of the work."

(*Pause*)

GERSON. Tessier, who are you?

TESSIER. I am Ernest Tessier. Come, let us play cards.

(*Music: Narrative theme and down*)

NARRATOR. His eyes had turned hard again. There were no further questions. But we continued to play with him now every day after retreat. And to our amazement he revealed each day a knowledge and a grasp of Jewish history and literature that deepened the mystery of Ernest Tessier. How on earth had this adventurer who could swear like a gangster, how on earth had he become an erudite scholar of Judaism? (*Music fading*) A week later he asked Gerson to teach him Hebrew. And Gerson was stupefied; for Tessier already knew a good deal of the grammar. Now he wanted perfection.

TESSIER. My accent is not good. I understand the meanings, but I have learned the words from books. Now, Gerson, you teach me.

GERSON. All right, Tessier. "B'ray-shees baw-raw eh-loh-heem ehs hah-shaw-mah-yeem v'ehs haw-aw-retz." Do you understand?

TESSIER. Yes, "In the beginning God created the heaven and the earth. B'ray-shees baw-raw eh-loh-heem ehs hah-shaw-mah-yeem v'ehs haw-aw-retz."

GERSON. We'll turn here. "Vah-yiv-raw eh-loh-heem ehs haw-aw-dawm b'tzahl-moh."

TESSIER. "And God created man in his own image. Vah-yiv-raw eh-loh-heem ehs haw-aw-dawm b'tzahl-moh. And God blessed them and said unto them . . . be fruitful and multiply. Vah-yih-vaw-raych oh-sawm eh-loh-heem vah-yoh-mehr law-hehm eh-loh-heem, p'roo oo-r'voo oo-meel-oo ehs haw-aw-retz." (*Pause*) Gerson, the accent is quite bad, isn't it?

GERSON. Try to say it this way: "Vah-yih-vaw-raych oh-sawm eh-loh-heem vah-yoh-mehr law-hehm eh-loh-heem, p'roo oo-r'voo oo-meel-oo ehs haw-aw-retz."

TESSIER. I'll try, Gerson. I'm grateful.
(*Pause*)
GERSON. Tessier, I can't stand it. Who are you? What are you keeping back?
TESSIER. Teach me Hebrew, and keep your mouth shut. (*Pause*) I'm sorry. Let's go on with the lesson.
(*Music: Narrative theme and down*)
NARRATOR. Something had to happen, something had to break. And then it did. An old friend had just arrived at Fort Flatters. Gerson and Ullmann and I decided to bring him to one of our bridge parties at Tessier's quarters. (*Music out*) He introduced himself.
RATHENAU. Legionnaire Rathenau, mon adjutant.
TESSIER. What did you say?
RATHENAU. I am pleased to meet you, sir.
TESSIER. That isn't what you said. Say what you said.
RATHENAU. I said nothing.
TESSIER. Your name. Say it.
RATHENAU. Rathenau.
(*Pause*)
TESSIER. Rathenau. There was a statesman before Hitler, a German Jew, Walther Rathenau.
RATHENAU. Yes, sir. He was my uncle.
(*Pause*)
TESSIER. (*Tonelessly*) On June the 24th, 1922, in the Konigsallee in Berlin, three young men with guns and hand grenades killed Reich's Minister of Foreign Affairs, Walther Rathenau.
RATHENAU. Yes, sir. That's right . . . how do . . .
TESSIER. He believed that the restriction of the right of inheritance would put an end to the hereditary enslavement of the lower classes. With Lloyd George in 1922, he tried to organize a United States of Europe. If Walther Rathenau had lived, who knows?
RATHENAU. That's why Walther Rathenau was assassinated.

TESSIER. That's why and also because he was a Jew.
RATHENAU. Yes . . . three men. Two of them committed suicide when the police caught them. The third man, who was twenty-one, was surrendered to the police by his own relatives. His name was Ernst Werner Techow. He was sentenced to fifteen years in jail.
   (*Pause*)
TESSIER. Gerson, do you still want to ask questions?
GERSON. No.
TESSIER. Anyone else?
ULLMANN. No.
TESSIER. Legionnaire Rathenau.
RATHENAU. Yes, Tessier.
TESSIER. Not Tessier. Ernst Werner Techow. You stand in front of one of the murderers of your uncle.
   (*Music: Bridge to narrative theme and down*)
NARRATOR. Not a single muscle moved in Tessier's face. But his face was pale . . . the terrible pallor that should never blanch the face of a man alive . . . the pallor that comes from memory. Tessier began to speak . . .
   (*Music: In the clear very briefly and down*)
TESSIER. I was released from prison in 1927 . . . good behavior. I went to the French Foreign Legion . . . Morocco, Syria, Indo-China. In 1937 I was naturalized by the French Government. I began to study Jewish problems. In Syria I studied in my spare time. I discovered that the Nazis had falsified all the facts of Jewish history in order to get a pretext for committing excesses. I want to right a wrong. That's all.
NARRATOR. He stopped speaking. In the dim candle-light his features had lost their brutality. He suddenly looked old and tired. There wasn't much left to say. Rathenau squeezed the hand of his uncle's murderer. There was nothing to say. (*Music out*) Then Gerson asked the question.

GERSON. Why weren't you executed for the murder of Rathenau?

TESSIER. Open the drawer, Gerson.

GERSON. This one?

TESSIER. The one next to it.

(*Drawer opens*)

TESSIER. A sheet of paper, do you see it? It's turned slightly yellow.

GERSON. I have it.

TESSIER. Walther Rathenau's mother wrote the words written on it. Three days after the murder of her son, she wrote that to my mother. Read it, Gerson. Read what Frau Rathenau wrote to my mother.

(*Pause*)

GERSON. "In grief unspeakable, I give you my hand—you of all women the most pitiable. Say to your son that in the name and spirit of him he has murdered, I forgive, even as God may forgive, if before an earthly judge he make a full and frank confession of his guilt . . . and before a heavenly one repent. Had he known my son, the noblest man earth bore, he had rather turned the weapon on himself. May these words give peace to your soul. Mathilde Rathenau."

(*Pause*)

TESSIER. Gerson, I have learned some Hebrew. The word is Teshuva . . . repentance. You are a philologist, Gerson, tell me if I am wrong. The Hebrew verb "shoov" . . . to return.

GERSON. Tessier . . . in the Talmud it is written: "Repentance absolves from sins against God. But sins against man are absolved only when restitution has been made to man."

TESSIER. I should have been killed before. It would have been preferable. Now I must make payment. I must. I must be Techow. Not Tessier. Gerson, the Talmud is right. I must make restitution.

(*Music: Bridge to narrative theme and down*)

NARRATOR. In 1940, France was forced to yield to Hitler. There was an Armistice. All officers and men of German origin were now invited to break their contract with the Legion and return to the Reich. Seventy percent chose to do so, many of them who owed everything to France. Tessier shook his head and smiled. He had something to do.

(*Music: In the clear very briefly*)

NARRATOR. In February, 1941, I met Ernest Tessier again in Marseilles. The same hard gray, granite eyes. The same brutal jaw. (*Music out*) He was dressed like a dock worker. It was obviously a disguise. We met in a cheap harbor bistro.

TESSIER. Drink?

NARRATOR. Thanks.

(*Wine poured . . . two glasses*)

TESSIER. Tell me, do you know any Jews . . . Jews I could help to get out of here?

NARRATOR. Is that what you're doing?

TESSIER. Yes. It's Teshuva . . . you remember that word?

NARRATOR. I remember.

TESSIER. I've got exit visas, Casablanca permits. My specialty is to bring them across the border to Spain.

NARRATOR. I know a few people who would be interested. Tessier, I suppose it's a question of money.

TESSIER. Those who have some money—good. It doesn't bother me. If they haven't any money, they escape for nothing.

(*Pause*)

NARRATOR. Tessier, how many have you brought out?

TESSIER. So far?

NARRATOR. Yes.

TESSIER. Seven hundred. Seven hundred human beings. So far.

NARRATOR. Tessier . . .

TESSIER. The name is Techow. Ernst Werner Techow . . .

men cannot find repentance or salvation when they deny their name. My name is Techow, I am the assassin of the man who could have saved Germany.

NARRATOR. Yes. I know. If Frau Rathenau were still alive . . . I . . . I think I could go to her and say that you are making restitution.

TESSIER. I don't know. To every Jew alive I could get down on my knees and beg for pardon. But to the millions who are dead, because I helped to kill them, what shall I say?

(*Music: Closing narrative theme and down*)

NARRATOR. I did not see him again. But I read in the newspapers how a man called Ernest Tessier had captured twenty-four Nazis simply by shouting commands at them in German. It happened at Medjeb-el-Bab. I hope that when he took them prisoner Adjutant Ernest Tessier told them the story of Ernst Werner Techow.

(*Music: Curtain*)

FOR A SUIT OF NEW CLOTHES

FOR A SUIT OF NEW CLOTHES

..*There is more than a momentary resemblance between David Frishman's wistful short story which provides the basis of* For a Suit of New Clothes *and Sholom Aleichem's* A Pity for the Living. *Both are stories of childhood. Both are marked by tragedy. Both are saved from mere whimsy or sentimentality by the statement of a great ethical principle. And both, it should be said here, were originally suggested for adaptation by Rabbi Milton Steinberg.*

Frishman's story is available only in the original Hebrew under the title, Tis-chah-daysh. *It was translated by Howard Singer, a student in the Rabbinical school of the Seminary, who is presently serving as research assistant for the Eternal Light Program.*

The original story, like A Pity for the Living, *was very slight and the problem of adaptation became a problem of elaboration. It might be said that so long as the adaptor remains faithful to the spirit of the original work he may create new characters, new situations, transpose dialogue or invent it and do whatever his obligation to his medium and to his audience suggests.*

The script was broadcast on June 23, 1946. Alexander Scourby was the Narrator, Michael Artist was the boy, Juano Hernandez was the Tailor. Others in the cast were Joan Lazer, Mitzi Gould, Richard Keith, Gene Leonard, and Jack Lloyd. Cantor David Putterman sang the recurring Purim theme.

For a Suit of New Clothes *appears in this volume through the courtesy of Mrs. David Frishman, widow of the author.*

FOR A SUIT OF NEW CLOTHES

NARRATOR. Turn to the Book of Psalms, to the Ninth Chapter, to the Nineteenth Verse, and read: "For the needy shall not always be forgotten, nor the expectation of the poor perish forever." (*Pause*) I will tell you the story of a boy called Ephraim, who was the son of a poor tailor. Do not grieve over his story or allow your spirits to be saddened; for after all he was only the poor son of a poor tailor. And it doesn't matter, does it?
(*Music: "Shoh-shah-nahs Yah-ah-kohv" register plaintively and down*)
(*Cantor: Melancholy and sweetly . . . in the clear and down*)
NARRATOR. It was the time of the Purim festival and the song was "Shoh-shah-nahs Yah-ah-kohv" and the words were, "Israel rejoiced upon seeing Mordecai dressed in robes of purple." It should be a glad song, but the tailor was poor and his son was poor; and so in their house the melody was plaintive. The little boy, Ephraim, listened to his father, and his eyes were large as they were always large. (*Cantor and music fading*) The boy sat and listened and he shivered a bit because the song was so beautiful.
BOY. Papa, will you make a suit of new clothes for me?
TAILOR. I would like to, Ephraim.
BOY. Will you, Papa? I'll stand very quietly. You can measure me.
TAILOR. All right, Ephraim. I'll measure you. Right now. Come here. (*Pause*)
BOY. I've gotten bigger, haven't I, Papa?

TAILOR. Yes, yes. Much bigger.

BOY. Papa, you forgot to measure my arms.

TAILOR. How could I forget such a thing! The left one. (*Pause*) There. There. So. Now. Lower it. Now the right one. (*Pause*) See, I'm writing it down so that I won't forget.

BOY. When will my new suit be ready, Papa?

TAILOR. Just as soon as I buy the cloth.

BOY. And when will that be?

TAILOR. Oh, soon. Very soon, Ephraim.

(*Pause*)

BOY. I shall stand very straight in my new suit of clothes. And when we go to the synagogue all my friends will say, Ephraim, what a fine suit of clothes. Tis-chah-daysh, they will say. Tis-chah-daysh, Ephraim, wear it well.

(*Music: Narrative theme and down*)

NARRATOR. It was a little game the tailor played with his son. Before each festival they would plan a new suit of clothes for Ephraim. But somehow there were never any pennies to buy the cloth and so at night when Ephraim was sleeping his father would pick up the patched little trousers and mend a frayed knee or put another stitch in a small seam. And sometimes the boy would awaken, and he would see his father. (*Music out*) Then he would call to him.

BOY. Papa, you're very tired. Come to sleep.

TAILOR. I have a little work to do. Besides, I'm not sleepy.

BOY. I'm not sleepy either. Papa, tell me a story.

TAILOR. The same one?

BOY. The same one, Papa.

TAILOR. All right. Close your eyes, Ephraim. Very tight.

BOY. I'm squeezing.

TAILOR. Once upon a time there was a little boy. And very strange to say, he had never been taught how to read.

BOY. Papa, I try to imagine a boy who cannot read. But I never can.

TAILOR. Well, this little boy really couldn't read because no one had taught him. And so on the great festivals he would stand and watch the people praying in the synagogue; but he couldn't pray himself.
BOY. Because he didn't know how to read.
TAILOR. Yes. So he found a prayer book and he went up to the altar, and he raised his face, and he said: "Oh Lord, my God, I do not know how to read, and I cannot pray to you. But here in this book are the words of prayer. I open the book to you, O Lord. Choose whichever prayer you like best and let it be mine."
BOY. God liked that, didn't he, Papa?
TAILOR. Oh yes, Ephraim. It was the best prayer ever made.
(*Pause*)
BOY. Do you know something? I think that boy must be my size. When you make my suit of new clothes, I shall give it to him. And I will say, "Tis-chah-daysh, little boy, wear it well."
(*Music: Narrative theme and down*)
(*Cantor: Shoh-shah-nahs Yah-ah-kohv" . . . in the clear and down*)
NARRATOR. Purim came again, but Ephraim did not have a new suit of clothes. All day the tailor would sew fine clothes for other people, but never clothes for himself or his son. For he was poor and cloth was very dear. On the evenings of the festivals the tailor and his son would work almost until dusk and then hurriedly they would wash their faces and come to the synagogue where there was light and happiness and rest. But the tailor was tired and worn with toil and so sometimes he would doze and not hear the singing of the cantor, or the music made by new clothes as they rustled by. But Ephraim would hear the sound of new clothes rustling and the sound of the stiff lining underneath, and his face was very pale, and his eyes large, as they were always large.

(*Cantor and music out*)
Then Ephraim and his father would go home together and divide a slice of bread for the holiday meal.

BOY. Papa, all the boys in the synagogue said Tis-chah-daysh to one another.

TAILOR. Did they?

BOY. Yes.

BOY. Papa, why don't the boys ever say Tis-chah-daysh to me?

TAILOR. You do not say Tis-chah-daysh to someone who doesn't wear a new garment.

BOY. Then no one will ever say it to me.

TAILOR. That isn't true.

BOY. No one ever has. All my life no one has ever said Tis-chah-daysh to me.

TAILOR. Just wait and see. I've got my eye on a remnant of cloth. Why, it must be all of two and a half yards. You'll see, Ephraim. Just wait and see. Just wait.

(*Music: Narrative theme and down*)

NARRATOR. Ephraim waited as he had always waited. His eyes were large. And he began to dream, as he always dreamed.

(*Music: Up and segue to dream music and hold under*)

GIRL. Hello, Ephraim.

BOY. Who are you?

GIRL. I am a needle that sews.

BOY. Then why aren't you sewing?

GIRL. I am sewing. Can't you see?

BOY. No, I can't see. I can't see anything at all.

(*Music: Up and down*)

VOICE. Ephraim, touch me, I'm a bolt of cloth.

EPHRAIM. I can't see you. I can hear you, I can always hear you. But I never see you.

VOICE. I am very fine cloth. It's a pity. The cloth is for your new suit.

(*Music: Up and down*)

GIRL. Try it on, Ephraim. It's finished.
EPHRAIM. Where? Please show me where it is? I can't see it.
(*Music: Up and segue to narrative theme and down*)
NARRATOR. Ephraim stopped dreaming and he waited. There are people on the face of the earth who never have a new garment. There are people who always live on the side of the street where the sun does not shine. Ephraim did not know this. Awake and sleeping, he dreamed. And always the dream was the same. After school some days he sat beside his father and sewed other boy's clothes and the cloth in his hand, not the needle but the cloth . . . the cloth seemed to pierce his flesh. (*Music out*) One day a man came to his father's shop.
MAN. I want a suit made. I've brought the cloth.
TAILOR. This?
MAN. It's fine cloth, isn't it?
TAILOR. Yes, it's fine, but there's hardly enough for you.
MAN. It isn't for me. It's for my son. Next Friday is his birthday. I want the suit to be a surprise.
TAILOR. How tall is your son?
MAN. About up to . . . let's see. Ask your boy to stand up.
TAILOR. Put your needle down, Ephraim. Stand up.
(*Pause*)
MAN. Your boy is skinnier, but they're the same height all right. Can you do it, Tailor?
TAILOR. I think so.
MAN. And you'll have it for me before next Friday?
TAILOR. My son will deliver it himself.
MAN. That's wonderful. I can't wait to see the look on my boy's face when he puts his new clothes on.
BOY. And you'll say, Tis-chah-daysh?
MAN. Of course. Every one says, "Wear it well," for a new suit of clothes. Don't you?
(*Music: Bridge*)

MAN. *(Angrily)* I don't like to deal with people who don't keep their word to me.

TAILOR. But . . . but . . . I don't understand. I've kept my word.

MAN. You have not.

TAILOR. But I have. The suit was finished last night and delivered this morning.

MAN. That's a falsehood.

TAILOR. It isn't; it's the truth. Ephraim left with the suit more than an hour ago.

MAN. Tailor, I despise people who lie. Why don't you tell the truth?

TAILOR. It is the truth. Ephraim left with the suit more than an hour ago.

MAN. Then . . . Then he stole it.

TAILOR. You have called me a liar and now you call my son a thief.

MAN. Of course he's a thief.

(Sound of thump overhead)

MAN. What's that?

TAILOR. I don't know, I'm sure.

MAN. It sounded as though it came from the attic. Someone is there.

(Pause)

TAILOR. *(Projecting)* Ephraim. Is that you, Ephraim? *(Pause)* Ephraim?

BOY. *(Off mike)* Yes, Papa.

MAN. Do you see? Come down, you little thief.

TAILOR. Ephraim come down.

BOY. In one minute, Papa.

MAN. *(Bellowing)* You come down this moment.

(Footsteps going down . . . toward mike)
(Pause)

MAN. You little thief, take that suit off your back.

TAILOR. Don't call my son a thief.

MAN. What then is he? He stole those clothes.

TAILOR. He's only a boy. He wasn't stealing. (*Softly*) Ephraim, take the suit off.

MAN. I want you to beat him.

TAILOR. Take it off carefully, Ephraim.

MAN. I said I want you to beat him.

TAILOR. You paid for the suit. That's all.

MAN. I'll give you extra money. Beat him. Thieves must be punished.

TAILOR. God will judge him, not you.

MAN. You're a fool. (*Moved off*) If that suit is not delivered to my house in fifteen minutes, I shall beat him myself.
(*Door slams*)
(*Pause*)

TAILOR. Tell me, Ephraim, tell me why.

BOY. For just one minute, for just a tiny little minute . . . I wanted to see how it feels to wear a new suit.
(*Pause*)

TAILOR. Yes, I know. Take it off, now. Quickly.

BOY. All right. Here's the jacket, Papa. Papa, I won't have to bring it to his house, will I, Papa? Please say I won't have to.

TAILOR. No. I won't ask you to do that. I'll take it there myself.
(*Pause*)

BOY. Papa, you're good to me.

TAILOR. It's all right, boy. Careful of the trousers. Don't soil them.

BOY. Here, Papa. (*Slight pause*) They're not soiled. (*Crying*) Oh, Papa, you didn't even say Tis-chah-daysh. You didn't say it, Papa. You didn't.
(*Music: Bridge to narrative theme and down*)

NARRATOR. These next days the face of Ephraim, the tailor's son, grew paler. And he coughed at night and then during the day. And sometimes when he coughed there was a redness on the handkerchief he brought away from his mouth, and a burning in his eyes, a burning like the burning of live coals. And the soul that was within him burned also, and spilled itself out into yearning, a yearning for the word Tis-chah-daysh, wear it well, wear it well. It was as though a little mosquito dwelt in his brain.

(*Music: Up and buzzing and then down*)

NARRATOR. And the little mosquito kept drilling, and kept drilling into his brain

GIRL. (*Filter*) Tis-chah-daysh, Tis-chah-daysh, Tis-chah-daysh, Tis-chah-daysh.

NARRATOR. And the little mosquito drilled into his brain and made a great round hole and filled it with why-questions.

VOICE. Why haven't you a new suit?

GIRL. Tis-chah-daysh, Tis-chah-daysh.

VOICE. Why does everyone else have a new suit?

GIRL. Tis-chah-daysh, Tis-chah-daysh.

VOICE. Why is your father poor?

GIRL. Tis-chah-daysh, Tis-chah-daysh.

(*Music: Accenting*)

VOICE. Why?

GIRL. Why?

VOICE. Why?

(*Music: Cut*)

TAILOR. Ephraim, Ephraim . . . Ephraim, speak to me.

BOY. I'm all right, Papa.

TAILOR. Oh, no. No, you're not all right. You're sick.

BOY. I'm not sick. I'm tired. I'm just tired. Papa . . . Papa . . . did you do something wrong? Did you do a crime against someone? Papa, what was the crime?

TAILOR. Don't you know?

BOY. No, Papa.

TAILOR. I'm poor, Ephraim. That's a crime. In this world to be poor is such a terrible crime.

(*Music: Narrative theme and down*)
NARRATOR. Ephraim thought about this for a long time. It disturbed him but it also gave him a queer satisfaction. But his soul continued to shrivel and the strange light burned in the pupil of his eye.
(*Music: Out*)
(*Music: Narrative theme and down*)
NARRATOR. They washed their faces and they went to the synagogue, where there was light and happiness and rest. And once again, the tailor dozed and did not hear the cantor; but Ephraim heard. Even the sound of new clothes rustling. Then the Rabbi began to speak. (*Music out*) And then the Rabbi paused to ask a question.
VOICE. "When will justice reign, and when will mankind come unto truth?" It is a fateful question.
NARRATOR. (*Close*) And then a remarkable thing happened. For little Ephraim stood up and he said . . .
BOY. Rabbi, I know the answer.
NARRATOR. There was incredulous silence in the synagogue. Then some men murmured, but the Rabbi nodded his head for Ephraim to speak.
(*Slight pause*)
BOY. I know the answer. It is simple. Justice will reign and men will come unto truth when everyone will have a new suit of clothes. Everyone, even the children. They will all have new clothes. New clothes for everyone. Everyone. The day will come when everyone will go into the synagogue with a new suit of clothes and he will hear the word Tis-chah-daysh from his neighbor, and he will answer Tis-chah-daysh. It will be so good that all the angels in heaven will begin to sing.
NARRATOR. (*Softly*) And then Ephraim sat down and a terrible cough bruised his lips. The blood came forth from his mouth and gushed over his tattered clothes.

(*Music: Softly* ... "*Shoh-shah-nahs Yah-ah-kohv*" ...)
(*Cantor: Muted ... very close and almost humming ... hold under*)

NARRATOR. He weighed very little in his father's arms. His father carried him from the synagogue into the street where the birds were singing. But Ephraim could not hear them. He heard a song. A song that sang gently in his ear. A song of Mordecai dressed in robes of purple, a new suit for Mordecai. And Ephraim was Mordecai, and the people gathered round and raised their voices to the Lord: "Thou has ever been the salvation of the people of Israel, their hope from generation to generation." And the people praised Ephraim who was Mordecai, and Mordecai who was Ephraim.

(*Cantor: Up with music and down ... fading out*)

TAILOR. (*Fading slowly in*) Ephraim. It's your father, Ephraim. Can you hear me, Ephraim? Ephraim, the doctor is here. This is the doctor, Ephraim. Don't be frightened.

DOCTOR. Hello. (*Pause*) I'm not going to hurt you.

(*Pause*)

TAILOR. Ephraim, speak to the doctor. You remember him. He's an old friend of ours.

DOCTOR. You remember me, don't you? (*Pause*) He'll talk later. Don't worry. Once we get him to the hospital he'll be all right.

TAILOR. I wish he would speak. Ephraim, you remember the doctor? Why, he came to our shop only a few weeks ago. I made him a new suit of clothes. You remember.

DOCTOR. Of course, Ephraim. I'm wearing it now.

TAILOR. Speak to the doctor, Ephraim. Say something.

(*Pause*)

BOY. Tis-chah-daysh, Doctor. Wear it well.

(*Music: Bridge*)

NURSE. You're his father, aren't you?

TAILOR. Yes, Nurse. May I see him?

NURSE. Not now. It isn't wise.
TAILOR. You're sure?
NURSE. The doctor wishes him to be quiet.
TAILOR. Oh. (*Pause*) Does he . . . does he ask for me?
NURSE. Very often.
TAILOR. Nurse, when he asks for me again, please give this to him.
NURSE. This bundle?
TAILOR. I'll unwrap it. (*Sound of paper being undone*) It's a bolt of cloth.
NURSE. Are you sure you want me to give this to him?
TAILOR. It will make him well. It is the best medicine in the world for Ephraim. Say to him that this cloth is for his new suit. He will understand! You'll see, it will make him well. (*Pause*)
NURSE. All right. I'll give it to him.
TAILOR. And you'll tell him what I said?
NURSE. I'll tell him.
TAILOR. Then he will be well again. You'll see.
    (*Music: Narrative theme and down*)
NARRATOR. But Ephraim did not speak. There was only the dream left. The dream that had always come. But this time it was different.
    (*Music: Up into dream music and down*)
GIRL. Hello, Ephraim.
BOY. I know you. You are the needle that sews.
GIRL. Can you see me now?
BOY. Yes. You're very pretty.
GIRL. I'm glad you think so. Here is the bolt of cloth. He wants to talk to you.
VOICE. Can you see me, Ephraim?
BOY. Yes. I like you.
VOICE. That's good. Because I'm very fine cloth. There is no cloth like me short of heaven. See, they all say so.
NARRATOR. They all did. They all said so. For angels were de-

scending, so many angels that the world was full of them. And one carried a scissors, and another a spool of thread. And they went up and descended and descended and went up with a fluttering of wings while the bolt of cloth unwound and the needle sewed. In his ears, Ephraim heard a sweet song.

(*Music: Up and segue to "Shoh-shah-nahs Yah-ah-kohv"*)
(*Cantor: Registers and down*)

NARRATOR. And it was the festival again. And Ephraim had a new suit . . . a suit of white cloth. And the needle smiled at him and said:

(*Music: Cut*)

GIRL. Tis-chah-daysh, Ephraim. Wear it well.

NARRATOR. And suddenly there was a black angel.

(*Music: In and down*)

NARRATOR. On that day they buried him in new white garments, but his ears did not hear the word Tis-chah-daysh.

(*Cantor: In and under very softly . . . and build softly*)

NARRATOR. He was a boy, his name was Ephraim and he finally wore a new suit. Do not be saddened by his story or let your spirit grieve. He was only a rather foolish boy who believed that the world would come to justice and to truth when everyone could wear a new suit of clothes. Really, it was very foolish . . . and people have already forgotten what he said. For after all, he was poor and his father was poor. And to most of the world people like that hardly matter.

(*Cantor: Up and hold with orchestra to curtain*)

THE LANTERN IN THE INFERNO

The facsimile script which follows illustrates a format generally employed for NBC dramatic productions.

The format has been devised to enable the director, control-room engineer, actors, musical conductor, and sound effects technician to make an instant distinction between each of radio's elements of speech, music, and sound.

The reader interested in a detailed yet highly readable explanation of this important radio convention is recommended to Erik Barnouw's *Handbook of Radio Writing* (Little, Brown and Company).

When a director has read a script for the first time, his problem is casting it. Casting, as many directors will acknowledge, is the single most crucial operation in radio production. A good script will be spoiled by an incompetent cast, and a mediocre script can be made listenable by an excellent cast. The cast engaged is an infallible barometer of a director's taste—when the cast consists of the director's first choice. But, often, it will happen that a director will have to satisfy himself with a third or fourth or even fifth choice for an important part.

Fortunately, the cast of the second NBC broadcast of *The Lantern in the Inferno* consisted of Frank Papp's first choices. This is how he set it down on his cast sheet:

VOICE	Norman Rose
HARDY	Guy Spaull
PENINA	Alice Goodkin
TSVI	Leon Janney
ONE	Norman Rose
TWO	Bob Donley

THREE	Horace Braham
DOV	Alexander Scourby
OFFICER	Horace Braham
CHANA	Mitzi Gould
ONE	Bob Donley
PARTISAN	Joe Di Santis
HUNGARIAN	Joe Di Santis
VOICE	Guy Spaull

Some explanation is in order.
1. Casting is always done in the order of appearance of the characters.
2. "ONE," "TWO," and "THREE" are a writer's shorthand for VOICE 1, VOICE 2, or VOICE 3.
3. There are fourteen speaking parts in the script but only nine actors in the cast. Four actors are called upon to "double," or take more than one speaking part. Doubling makes for economical production but it demands versatile actors who can handle a multiplicity of speaking assignments without ever betraying to the listener that two characters are only one actor. An actor with unusual or distinctive voice quality is generally a poor double.

The Lantern in the Inferno leans heavily on a sound effect, always a dangerous thing in a radio production. For the first production of the script on December 9, 1945, Frank Papp decided against featuring the sound and asked Morris Mamorsky to write a score with a pizzicato effect to suggest the dripping of water. Mr. Mamorsky came up with a musical tour de force—a score that completely captured the stream-of-consciousness mood—rising, falling, beginning on a half-phrase, finishing unresolved, and over it all the sound of water dripping from the plucked strings of the violins.

For a second production Mr. Papp tested the ingenuity of sound effects technician Sam Monroe.

Mr. Monroe, disdaining a water-pipette, or such a mundane solution as the index and middle-finger tapped rhythmically against a wet palm, came up with a clever improvisation. A large tub of water was deposited on the studio floor. Bent closely over it was a gooseneck microphone. Mr. Monroe filled his hands with empty rifle cartridges and lovingly dropped each cartridge into the tub of water. The sound became eerily effective when it was relayed through an echo chamber.

Narrator Alexander Scourby played against the sound. His counting was in dull monotone by turns, in sharp protest by turns, and entreating by turns. Each numeral was a postscript to sound.

A word about the composition of the script. When *The Lantern in the Inferno* was written, virtually all that was known of Chana Senesh was contained in several articles which had appeared in the Hebrew language publication *Hadoar* and in the Yiddish publication, *Yiddishe Kempfer*. After the translations had been made by Gershon Cohen, a student in the Rabbinical School of the Jewish Theological Seminary, there were still enormous gaps missing in the story. And so Chana Senesh's training in Egypt, her adventures in Yugoslavia, and her itinerary in Hungary were necessarily fictionalized.

History and nature, however, as Oscar Wilde once suggested, imitate fiction. Because shortly after the first production of the script, an American representative of Haganah, complained about a "leak" of secret information. Chana Senesh and her group were members of Haganah working in co-operation with the Allied Armies. By a coincidence the fictionalized itinerary of the script corresponded in many important respects with her actual itinerary.

Chana Senesh belongs with the Maccabeeans. It is as such that modern Palestine regards her. The last entry in her diary was, "This week I left for Egypt. I am mobilized. I am a soldier. I like to believe that I have done the correct thing. Only time will tell."

She tried to write poetry in Hebrew, a language that she had acquired with difficulty. But nevertheless she wrote:
"Happy the match that struck and set ablaze,
Happy the blaze that burned in the depths of hearts,
Happy the hearts that knew how to stop beating with
   dignity. . . .
Happy the match that struck and set ablaze."

The title of the script was suggested by her first Hebrew poem. It is strange that this girl, who at the time of her execution was only twenty-two years old, should have left so great a legacy in a land that knew her for so short a space. And it is even stranger that a vessel bearing her name and carrying illegal immigrants was intercepted in 1946 by British destroyers. His Majesty's seamen seized the vessel and deported the immigrants, not conscious of the irony that they were laying a wreath of barbed wire on the grave of one of His Majesty's noblest heroines.

WNBC & NET   THE ETERNAL LIGHT   #111

( ) ( )   "THE LANTERN IN THE INFERNO"

12:30-1:00 PM, SUNDAY, DECEMBER 22, 1946

(MUSIC: CHORD...)

(CANTOR: SIGNATURE AND DOWN)

           (ECHO) And the Lord spake unto Moses, saying, Command the children of Israel that they bring unto thee pure oil olive, beaten for the light, to cause the lamps to burn continually in the tabernacle of the congregation, and it shall be a statute forever in your generations.

(CANTOR: UP WITH MUSIC AND OUT)

ANNCR: The Eternal Light!

(MUSIC: THEME AND DOWN)

ANNCR: The National Broadcasting Company and its affiliated independent stations present The Eternal Light, a program which comes to you under the auspices of the Jewish Theological Seminary of America. In celebration of the festival of Channukah, we present the second
                    (MORE)

ANNCR: CONT'D   radio performance of Morton Wishengrad's "The Lantern in the Inferno" -- A Story of a Modern Maccabee. Featured as the Narrator is _____ _____. Chana Senesh is played by _____.

(MUSIC: UP AND OUT)

VOICE: He who saves a human life is as one who saves the entire world. This is the story of a Palestinian girl named Chana Senesh who saved a world. And if she died in that act, let the Hebrew words Kiddush Ha'shem, be said of her, for she died for the "Sanctification of God's name."

(MUSIC: ESTABLISH NARRATIVE THEME AND DOWN)

VOICE: There is a gloomy dungeon beneath the ancient prison of the Hungarian city of Budapest. Toward the end of May, 1945, Leftenant Hardy of British Intelligence led a squad of men to the old dungeon. The heavy doors swung open and into the light stumbled the liberated scarecrows, animate lumps of protoplasm in the shape of human beings.

(MUSIC: FADING)

When they were assembled, Leftenant Hardy called the roll, and the protoplasm answered.

(HARDY PROJECTS SLIGHTLY ON ROLL CALL....THEY ANSWER WEAKLY FROM IN CLOSE)

HARDY: Penina Yardaynee.

PENINA: Here.

HARDY: Tsvi Marcus. (PRONOUNCED SVI)

TSVI: Yes.

HARDY: Shlomo Dichter.

ONE: Here.

HARDY: David Gen Giora.

TWO: Here.

HARDY: Chana Senesh. (PAUSE) Chana Senesh. (PAUSE) Make a note of it, Quimby.

THREE: Yes, Sir.

HARDY: Dov Nathanson. (PAUSE) Dov Nathanson.

PENINA: Dov, the Leftenant called your name.

HARDY: Dov Nathanson.

DOV: Two hundred and sixty-four. Two hundred and sixty-five...

PENINA: Dov!

DOV: Two hundred and sixty-six. (CONTINUES TO COUNT)

PENINA: Please, Dov.

DOV: Two hundred and sixty-seven.

HARDY: Quimby, get a doctor for this man.

THREE: Right away, Leftenant.

DOV: (COUNTING)

PENINA: Dov, listen to me, it's Penina. Please stop counting. You're among friends now. Dov, you're no longer in the dungeon. Please, Dov.

HARDY: What is he counting? Why does he do that?

PENINA: Drops of water, Leftenant. He's counting the drops of water falling from the ceiling of the dungeon.

DOV: CONTINUES COUNTING AS:
    (SOUND OF WATER DRIPPING FADES IN....FULL ECHO AT FIRST THEN DIMINISH UNDER)

(MUSIC: STREAM-OF-CONSCIOUSNESS)

DOV: I mustn't lose count...ninety-three...ninety-four...I mustn't lose count...Dov, you're going mad ...Dov, you mustn't lose count...
                    (MORE)

DOV: CONT'D   dripping...dripping...Chana...
              Chana Senesh...can you hear it?...
              from where you are...Can you hear
              it, Chana?...Chana, this is Buda-
              pest....Palestine is so far away
              ...very far...I wonder...in our
              cooperative colony at S'dot Yam, do
              they remember you?...Three hundred
              and four...five...six... Only a
              year ago, Chana...from the co-
              operative of S'dot Yam we could see
              the Mediterranean...it was your
              twentieth birthday...(SOUND OUT)
              ...and instead of celebrating, you
              and I and Penina and Tsvi and the
              others of Haganah...

(MUSIC: FADING)

              we sat and listened to the British
              officer who had come that morning.

                   (VOICES BRIEFLY)

OFFICER: Please follow me on the map.
              (VOICES OUT)   This is Yugoslavia.
              In this area here, behind the enemy
              lines, groups of Partisan fighters
              are organized. They need immediate
              reinforcements.

                   (PAUSE)

CHANA: (SLIGHTLY OFF)   I am Chana Senesh.
              The others have asked me to speak
              for them.

TSVI: (FURTHER OFF)   That's right, sir.

CHANA: Suppose we volunteer? How do we reach Yugoslavia?

OFFICER: By parachute. (PAUSE) Make no mistake about it, this is a dangerous mission. You will be parachuted down in the dead of night.

CHANA: We understand, sir. (PAUSE) Is our mission limited to specific objectives?

OFFICER: Yes and no. The specific purpose is to dynamite and destroy these three centers of enemy communications. Here -- here -- here. You will also be expected to do everything possible to disrupt the enemy's transport.

(PAUSE)

CHANA: One more question, sir.

OFFICER: Yes?

CHANA: Some of us here are anxious to rescue Jewish children who are trapped in Yugoslavia and Hungary.

OFFICER: This mission is confined to Yugoslavia.

CHANA: I understand, sir. But Hungary borders on Yugoslavia.

OFFICER: Go on, please.

CHANA:	We think that while we are in Yugoslavia it may be possible to organize rescue stations for children right up to the Hungarian border.
OFFICER:	If your work does not interfere with the primary purpose of this mission, by all means. It seems to me that we're all trying to save lives. (PAUSE) Will you undertake the mission?
	(PAUSE)
CHANA:	Tsvi?
TSVI:	All right, Chana.
CHANA:	Dov?
DOV:	(SAME PERSPECTIVE) I'll go along.
CHANA:	Penina?
PENINA:	(CLOSER) I think we all agree.
CAST:	(OFF) Yes, sure, Chana, etc.
	(PAUSE)
CHANA:	Seventeen men, sir, and three women.
OFFICER:	Very good. Tomorrow after sunrise, two lorries will be waiting here. Take no clothing, only what you wear. (PAUSE) I shall expect you in Cairo Tuesday morning.

(MUSIC: BRIDGE TO THEME AND DOWN)

      (WATER DRIPPING...ECHO AND DIMINISH UNDER)

DOV: Three hundred and eight...nine...ten....Chana Senesh...listen, do you hear water dripping...drip...drip...drip...like a clock ticking...like a heart beating...three hundred and sixteen...Chana, this Budapest...we went to join the Partisans and to save the children ...but this is Budapest....(SOUND OUT) (MUSIC FADING)...And before Budapest...so long before...we were in Egypt...and to be trained.

(MUSIC: MONTAGE THEME AND DOWN)

      (SOUND OF PISTOL SHOTS IN SLOW SUCCESSION)

OFFICER: Better, Chana, much better. But squeeze the trigger. Squeeze... don't pull.

(MUSIC: UP AND DOWN)

PENINA: Nose fuse.

OFFICER: Right.

DOV: Primer Detonator.

OFFICER: Right.

CHANA: Booster charge.

OFFICER:	Right.
TSVI:	Arming wire, suspension lug.
OFFICER:	Good enough.
(MUSIC:	UP AND DOWN)
CHANA:	All clear, this end.
DOV:	(OFF) All clear from here.
OFFICER:	(PROJECTING) Heads down...heads down, everyone.

(EXPLOSION)

(MUSIC:	UP AND DOWN)

(PLANE ENGINES)

OFFICER:	You've jumped in daylight. Now you jump in the darkness. Ready, Chana?
CHANA:	Ready, sir.
OFFICER:	Don't freeze to the ripcord. (PAUSE) Jump.
(MUSIC:	UP AND FINISH)
CHANA:	Dov, you're not looking at the map.
DOV:	I'd rather look at you, Chana.

(PAUSE)

CHANA: Tomorrow we may be in Yugoslavia.

DOV: Uh huh. Your nose is twitching again. The tip of your nose.

CHANA: I wonder how many children we can bring out.

DOV: You know, Chana, if your eyes were just the merest bit larger...

CHANA: Dov, we've got to find the children.

DOV: Chana, you're not pretty, you know. Not really, that is.

CHANA: Please, Dov. I can't get the children out of my mind.

DOV: I'm sorry.

CHANA: Maybe we can bring them back to S'dot Yam.

DOV: Maybe.

CHANA: Put them on the land, teach them to farm. Watch them grow, see them become normal men and women.

DOV: That's all you want, Chana?

CHANA: Right now? Yes...right now it's all I want.

DOV: All right.

(PAUSE)

CHANA: I'm sorry, Dov. When we come back from Yugoslavia, there'll be time to talk of other things.

DOV: Sure, all right.

CHANA: Don't be moody, Dov...there's time. Besides, tomorrow we'll be in Yugoslavia.

(MUSIC: <u>BRIDGE TO NARRATIVE THEME AND DOWN</u>)

(WATER DRIPPING...ECHO AND DIMINISH UNDER)

DOV: Always time, Chana...always time for...three hundred and thirty-seven...thirty-eight...that night the planes took off from Egypt... our clothes were black, parachutes black...black night...darkness... "And the Lord said, Stretch out thy hand toward heaven, that there may be darkness over the land of Egypt, even darkness which may be felt! And Moses stretched forth his hand, and there was..." Three hundred and thirty-nine...

(SOUND OUT)

(MUSIC: <u>FADING</u>)

DOV: Drops of water...falling...falling...seventeen men...three women...falling...falling...falling through the darkness...into the night of Yugoslavia...

               (SOUND OF CRICKETS)

               (BIRD CALL...WELL OF MIKE...REPEAT)

CHANA: (CLOSE) There it is.

TSVI: Wait. We must be sure.

               (BIRD CALL...OFF)

CHANA: All right, Tsvi. Answer him.

               (BIRD CALL...ON MIKE...REPEAT...)

DOV: (PROJECTING SOFTLY) Shlomo, David, Penina...guns ready!

ONE: (OFF) Right.

               (GUNS COCKING...MANY GUNS)

               (CRICKETS OUT)

CHANA: See anyone?

               (PAUSE)

DOV: No. Why doesn't he come?

               (BIRD CALL...CLOSER TO MIKE)

ONE: There he is.

CHANA: Answer him, Tsvi.

(BIRD CALL ON)

(PAUSE)

PARTISAN: Hello.

CHANA: Hello. We're glad to see you.

PARTISAN: How many?

CHANA: Seventeen men. Three women.

PARTISAN: That's good. We've got mules waiting below.

CHANA: Friend, are there any Jewish children here?

PARTISAN: No children. Only Nazis. Come on. We have work. First there's a German troop train to take care of.

(MUSIC: BRIDGE)

(SOUND OF TRAIN APPROACHING... TRAIN BUILDS)

CHANA: Not yet, Tsvi...not yet.

(TRAIN COMING CLOSER)

CHANA: Not too soon. Wait...wait...

(TRAIN ON MIKE)

CHANA: (PROJECTING) Tsvi...now...

(EXPLOSION) (PAUSE)

(MUSIC: BRIDGE)

(SOUND OF MULES PLODDING...
MULE BRAYING OFF)

CHANA: You look foolish on the mule.
You're bigger than he is, Dov.

DOV: A mule is not a he. He's an it.

CHANA: You still look foolish.

DOV: You ought to be used to it. Chana, how many weeks have we been riding these Yugoslav taxicabs?

CHANA: I'm not sure. (PAUSE) I'm not sure of anything any more. We come to destroy and...to save....It's confusing.

DOV: We've done all right.

CHANA: I hope so, Dov. It's a queer world. We're like people carrying a lantern into an inferno. And we're helping to build the inferno. Dov, we've got to see the children, and how can we see them when we create the fire that blinds our eyes?

(MUSIC: BRIDGE TO NARRATIVE THEME AND DOWN)

(SOUND OF WATER DRIPPING...
ECHO AND DIMINISH)

DOV: Chana Senesh...a lantern in the inferno...three hundred and sixty-two...sixty-three...three primary objectives...that's what the British officer said, Chana, didn't he?...Three explosions...primary mission completed...only where were the children?...Where were the...three hundred seventy-nine ...eighty...eighty-one...

(SOUND OUT...)

(MUSIC: FADING)

So we went north...north toward the Hungarian border...Penina and Tsvi and Chana and I...north...looking for the children.

CHANA: Tsvi, what did you find out?

TSVI: Something. Across the Hungarian border...the city of Szeged. Thirty Jewish children are hidden there.

CHANA: What else, Tsvi?

TSVI: Spread your map, Penina.

(CRACKLE OF PAPER)

Look, this is where we are, north
(MORE)

399

TSVI: CONT'D	of Subotica. If we can get the children to Subotica, we can make contact with the Partisans. There are relay stations here at Topola, Sombor, Srbobran, and then due west right to the Coast. Once we get the children to the Coast, fishing boats will take them out. But the big job is in Szeged.
CHANA:	What do you think, Dov?
DOV:	How do we work past the border guard?
TSVI:	That's the rub. Nazi patrols there are thicker than bedbugs. We'll have to split up.
DOV:	I don't like that, Chana.
CHANA:	I don't either. But it's better that way. (PAUSE) If one of us is stopped...at least the others will get through.
TSVI:	It's the only sensible thing.
CHANA:	If we get through to Szeged, where do we meet?
TSVI:	There's a big church off the main square. We meet at the church.
(MUSIC:	BRIDGE)

(CHURCHBELLS TOLLING)

DOV: We're being watched.

CHANA: Just lean against the wall. Talk casually.

(PAUSE)

DOV: You all right, Chana?

CHANA: Good enough. Where are Tsvi and Penina?

DOV: Inside the church. The priest is our contact.

CHANA: Fine. And the children?

DOV: Only fifteen.

CHANA: Tsvi said there were thirty.

DOV: Only fifteen left, Chana. The priest thinks the Nazis have spotted the others. We have to work fast.

(PAUSE)

CHANA: When?

DOV: Tonight.

CHANA: Where?

DOV: There's a river or a lake...I don't know which. There'll be four rowboats. Four pairs of oars. We divide the children in the boats. (PAUSE) Chana, it means we're still separated.

CHANA: Dov, they're watching us. Keep your head turned away.

           (PAUSE)

DOV: Sure.

           (PAUSE)

CHANA: Will Tsvi bring the children?

DOV: Tsvi and the priest. Penina will wait with us.

CHANA: That's fine.

DOV: Chana.

CHANA: Yes, Dov.

DOV: You're not pretty, not really, that is.

           (PAUSE)

CHANA: Dov.

DOV: Yes?

CHANA: Thank you.

(MUSIC: BRIDGE)

           (FEATURE OARLOCKS CREAKING, OARS SPLASHING)

                    (THEN...GRATING SOUND OF BOAT
                    BEACHING)

CHANA: (URGENTLY) Tsvi, why did you take
                    so long? We were worried.

TSVI: (PANTING) Your load safe?

CHANA: In the woods...Children, this way.
                    No talking.

                    (FEET BUMPING SIDE OF BOAT...
                    SPLASHING)

CHANA: Go toward the flashlight in the
                    woods.

                    (FEET ON GRAVEL, MOVING OFF)

TSVI: (PANTING) Penina, all right?

CHANA: Yes, and so is Dov. The children
                    are with them. Tsvi, what's wrong?

TSVI: Chana...there are two little girls
                    ...on the other side.

CHANA: In God's name, Tsvi, why didn't you
                    wait for them?

TSVI: (PANTING) My arm...I fell...I
                    couldn't go back. (PAUSE) Chana,
                    don't do it.

                    (THUD IN BOAT)

                    (OARLOCKS CREAKING, OARS
                    SPLASHING, FADE AS SHE FADES)

TSVI: (PROJECTING) Come back, Chana.

CHANA: (OFF) If I'm not back in a half hour, tell Dov to go on.

TSVI: (PROJECTING) Chana, come back.

CHANA: (FURTHER OFF) A half hour, Tsvi... don't forget.

(MUSIC: BRIDGE TO NARRATIVE THEME AND DOWN)

(SOUND OF WATER DRIPPING... ECHO AND DIMINISH)

DOV: Like a clock ticking....Like a heart beating...four hundred and twelve...four hundred and thirteen ...you knew they would catch you, Chana...we saw the lights...we heard the shots...we knew...Chana, I think the children are safe...but why did you go back?...Didn't you know that once the children were safe, we'd come after you?...Yes ...we weren't very lucky either... we were...four hundred and twenty-four.

(MUSIC: FADING)

(SOUND OUT)

We were told they had taken you to Budapest...we had to follow. They caught us outside the town of Cegled.

404

(TRUCK ENGINE STARTED)

HUNGARIAN: You three, inside the truck.

TSVI: Guard, did you hear anything of another Palestinian?

PENINA: A girl...about my height.

HUNGARIAN: I heard. Inside the truck.

(ENGINE IDLING)

DOV: Is she all right?

HUNGARIAN: For now, yes. She shot a soldier. For now, she's all right.

DOV: What are they going to do to her?

HUNGARIAN: What do you think? Inside the truck. You'll see her soon enough. (PROJECTING) All right, driver. They're in.

(TRUCK STARTING...SUSTAIN AND COVER WITH:)

MUSIC: BRIDGE)

(CELL DOOR SWUNG OPEN)

(SLIGHT ECHO)

TSVI: Dov.

DOV: Yes.

TSVI: What did they do to you.

DOV: Nothing. (PAUSE) They let me see her.

TSVI: Chana?

DOV: Yes.

TSVI: Is she...

DOV: Tomorrow.

TSVI: It's my fault.

DOV: No, Tsvi, it's not your fault. (PAUSE) It was hard to talk to her. Every tooth in her mouth was gone. Her teeth were nice, weren't they, Tsvi?

(PAUSE)

TSVI: The guard said they would accept a plea for clemency.

DOV: She told me. She told them clemency was for criminals.

(PAUSE)

TSVI: Yes, sure. Sure.

DOV: She says they haven't treated her too badly.

TSVI: She say anything else?

DOV: Not much. Just that she's glad the children were rescued.

TSVI: Yes, sure, the children were rescued. Sure.

MUSIC: <u>BRIDGE TO NARRATIVE THEME AND DOWN)</u>

            (SOUND OF WATER DRIPPING... ECHO AND DIMINISH)

DOV: Chana, we could hear it...three shots...just three shots...then nothing...like a clock ticking...like a heart beating...four hundred and thirty-eight...thirty-nine...counting the drops...nothing to do but count the drops...

            (BUILD SOUND AND ECHO...AND THEN)

            (HE FADES WITH SOUND) forty-three ...forty-four...forty-five...forty-six...forty-seven...forty-eight...forty-nine...

MUSIC: <u>COVERING...SWIRLING...UP FOR BRIDGE)</u>

VOICE: He's coming out of it, Leftenant.

HARDY: Thank you, Doctor.

VOICE: I wouldn't make him talk too much...

HARDY: Yes, of course. (PAUSE) Dov... Dov Nathanson, it's Leftenant Hardy ...you're all right now.

DOV: Tsvi...Penina?

HARDY: They're fine.

DOV: I'm glad.

HARDY: You mustn't talk too much now. In a short time there will be a plane to take you home to Palestine.

DOV: That's good. (PAUSE) Leftenant. I want to go home soon.

HARDY: Yes?

DOV: Make it soon. (PAUSE) Perhaps in time for Channukah.

HARDY: Dov, you're not to talk.

DOV: I want to tell them of Chana Senesh.

HARDY: I'll try, Dov.

(PAUSE)

DOV: Leftenant, she was a lantern in the inferno.

HARDY: Yes, yes, of course. A lantern.

(MUSIC: SNEAK IN...AND DOWN)

DOV: In many places these last eight days the Channukah candles of the Feast of Lights have burned very brightly. Here in Palestine the lamps were kindled from upper Galilee down through Beersheba in Gaza and south to the Egyptian border. But I think that nowhere have the lamps burned so brightly as in our own cooperative colony of S'dot Yam. For while in the rest of Palestine the candles were lighted to commemorate the ancient exploits of the Maccabees, here in the colony of S'dot Yam our candles burned also for another Maccabee, a girl called Chana Senesh, who was one of us, and who died that others might live.

(MUSIC: CODA)

ANNCR: If you would like a free copy of the script just heard, write to The Eternal Light, 3080 Broadway, New York 27, New York. And now we present _____

SPEAKER: (THREE-MINUTE TALK)

ANNCR: Thank you, _____.

(MUSIC: CLOSING THEME AND DOWN)

ANNCR: Today's Eternal Light program, "The Lantern in the Inferno," was written by Morton Wishengrad. The

(MORE)

ANNCR: music was composed by Morris Mamor-
CONT'D   sky and conducted by Milton Katims.
Cantor David Putterman sang the liturgical music. Featured as Chana Senesh was _____ and _____ was the Narrator.

(MUSIC: UP AND DOWN)

ANNCR: This program is a presentation of the National Broadcasting Company and its affiliated independent stations and comes to you each week at this same time under the auspices of the Jewish Theological Seminary of America. If you would like a free copy of today's script, write to The Eternal Light, 3080 Broadway, New York 27, New York.
THIS IS NBC, THE NATIONAL BROADCASTING COMPANY.

GLOSSARY OF RADIO TERMS

Bridge — The radio medium's sound or music substitute for the camera dissolve and the stage curtain—a method of transition from scene to scene.

Close — A direction which brings the actor nearer to the microphone and with less voice.

Crossfade — The fading out of one sound simultaneous with the fading in of another. This is a device of transition.

Cut — To end abruptly.

Echo — An effect produced by sending a word or sound through a special resonating chamber to suggest the hollowness of a cave or half-filled auditorium. The echo effect is also one of grandeur.

Fade — An increase or decrease in volume (a voice can fade up as well as down) which may be accomplished in two ways. The first way is for an actor to move away from or toward the microphone. The second way is for the engineer at the control board to increase or diminish the volume.

Filter — A mechanical device used to change the quality of a voice by eliminating high or low (or both) frequencies—"filtering."

Montage — A rapid succession of extremely brief vignettes framed by music. The purpose of montage is compression.

Off — Away from the microphone, and therefore lower in volume.

On	The level or volume of sound which is the norm.
P.A.	Public Address system.
Project	To use more voice.
Register	To establish or hold in the clear—radio parlance for *featuring* a sound or music, or a vocal effect such as the sound of a crowd.
Segue	(Pronounced *seg-way*) To blend into without a break.
Top	To cover or drown out.
Under	*Underneath.* Sound or music that is under or behind dialogue or narration is said to be in the background.